POCKET
BOOKS

ALSO BY BOB WOODWARD

BUSH
AT WAR

BOB
WOODWARD

POCKET
BOOKS

LONDON • SYDNEY • NEW YORK • TORONTO

This edition first published by Pocket Books, 2003
An imprint of Simon & Schuster UK Ltd
A Viacom Company

5 7 9 10 8 6

Simon & Schuster UK Ltd
Africa House
64-78 Kingsway
London WC2B 6AH

www.simonsays.co.uk

Simon & Schuster Australia
Sydney

A CIP catalogue record for this book is
available from the British Library

ISBN 0-7434-6107-X

Printed and bound in Great Britain by
Cox & Wyman Ltd, Reading, Berks

AUTHOR'S NOTE

Mark Malseed, a 1997 Phi Beta Kappa architecture graduate of Lehigh University, assisted me full-time in the reporting, writing, editing, research—and thinking—for this book. He is one of the brightest, calmest, most remarkable young men I have ever encountered or worked with. He began as my assistant in May 2002, and in just six months mastered the subjects of Bush, his war cabinet, their debates and strategies. Well-read and meticulous, Mark always had superb ideas for improving the structure, substance and language of this story. He has a natural sense of order and was able to juggle a half-dozen tasks and persevere through 12-hour days with grace. He is tough-minded but scrupulously fair. I found I could trust him without question. Every day working with Mark was a joy, and I treasure our friendship. This book is a collaboration—his as much as mine.

To Donald E. Graham, who so brilliantly carries on the legacy of his mother, Katharine Graham: hands off, mind on—a spirit of unfettered, independent inquiry and a willingness to listen

A NOTE TO READERS

This is an account of President George W. Bush at war during the first 100 days after the September 11, 2001, terrorist attacks.

The information I obtained for this book includes contemporaneous notes taken during more than 50 National Security Council and other meetings where the most important decisions were discussed and made. Many direct quotations of the president and the war cabinet members come from these notes. Other personal notes, memos, calendars, written internal chronologies, transcripts and other documents also were the basis for direct quotations and other parts of this story.

In addition, I interviewed more than 100 people involved in the decision making and execution of the war, including President Bush, key war cabinet members, the White House staff, and officials currently serving at various levels of the Defense and State Departments and the CIA. Most sources were interviewed multiple times, several a half-dozen or more times. Most of the interviews were conducted on background—meaning that I could use the information but the sources would not be identified by name in this book. Nearly all allowed me to tape-record our interviews, so the story could be told more fully and with the exact language they used.

I have attributed thoughts, conclusions and feelings to the participants. These come either from the person himself, a colleague

with direct knowledge of them, or the written record—both classified and unclassified.

President Bush was interviewed on the record twice—once for
90 minutes by myself and Dan Balz, a colleague at *The Washington
Post*, for a lengthy eight-part series, "Ten Days in September," which
was published in the *Post* in early 2002. I have drawn on that interview and the series for a portion of this book. I interviewed President Bush a second time on August 20, 2002, at his ranch in
Crawford, Texas, for two hours and 25 minutes. The transcript
shows that I asked questions or made short comments 300 times.
The president gave specific answers, often very detailed, about his
reactions and reasoning behind the main decisions and turning
points in the war.

War planning and war making involve secret information. I
have used a good deal of it, trying to provide new specific details
without harming sensitive operations or relationships with foreign
governments. This is not a sanitized version, and the censors, if we
had them in the United States—thank God we don't—would no
doubt draw the line at a different, more restrictive place than I
have.

This book contains a voluminous amount of new, documented
information which I was able to obtain while memories were freshest and notes could be deciphered. It is an inside account, largely the
story as the insiders saw it, heard it and lived it. Since it covers
events and secret deliberations that began just over a year ago, it is
an early version. But I was able to test the information I had for ac-
curacy and context with trusted sources I have known for years and
in some cases decades. Criticism, the judgments of history and other
information may, over the coming months and years, alter the historical understanding of this era. This is my effort to get the best ob-
tainable version of the truth.

In 1991, I published a book called *The Commanders* which was
about the 1989 invasion of Panama and the lead-up to the Gulf War
during the presidency of Bush's father, President George H.W. Bush.

"The decision to go to war is one that defines a nation, both to the world and, perhaps more importantly, to itself," I wrote at the beginning of that book. "There is no more serious business for a national government, no more accurate measure of national leadership."

That is truer today than perhaps ever.

Bob Woodward
October 11, 2002
Washington, D.C.

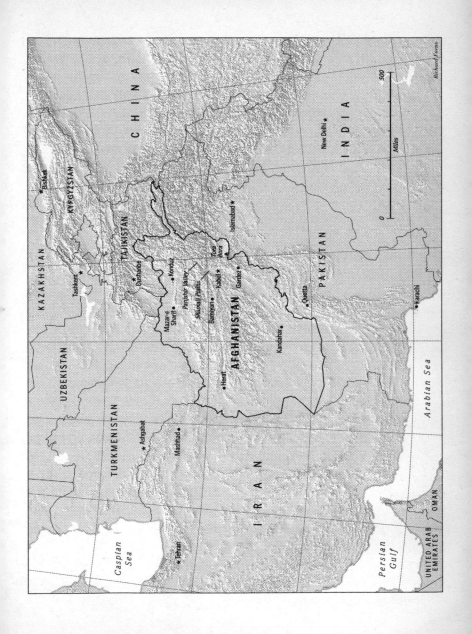

CAST OF CHARACTERS

THE PRESIDENT OF THE UNITED STATES
George W. Bush

THE PRINCIPALS
Vice President of the United States
Dick Cheney

Secretary of State
Colin L. Powell

Secretary of Defense
Donald H. Rumsfeld

Assistant to the President for National Security Affairs
Condoleezza Rice

Director of the Central Intelligence Agency
George J. Tenet

Chairman of the Joint Chiefs of Staff
General Richard B. Myers, United States Air Force

White House Chief of Staff
Andrew H. Card Jr.

THE DEPUTIES

Chief of Staff to the Vice President
I. Lewis "Scooter" Libby

Deputy Secretary of State
Richard L. Armitage

Deputy Secretary of Defense
Paul D. Wolfowitz

Deputy Assistant to the President for National Security Affairs
Stephen J. Hadley

Deputy Director of the Central Intelligence Agency
John E. McLaughlin

Vice Chairman of the Joint Chiefs of Staff
General Peter Pace, United States Marine Corps

OTHER KEY ADVISERS

Commander in Chief, U.S. Central Command
General Tommy Franks, United States Army

Attorney General of the United States
John D. Ashcroft

Director of the Federal Bureau of Investigation
Robert S. Mueller III

Counselor to the President
Karen P. Hughes

Senior Adviser to the President
Karl Rove

White House Press Secretary
Ari Fleischer

THE CENTRAL INTELLIGENCE AGENCY

Deputy Director for Operations
James L. Pavitt

Director of the Counterterrorism Center
Cofer Black

Chief of Counterterrorist Special Operations
Hank

Jawbreaker Team Leader
Gary

THE NORTHERN ALLIANCE

Lead Commander
Mohammed Fahim

Commander of Forces in Northern Afghanistan
Abdurrashid Dostum

Commander of Forces in Northern Afghanistan
Attah Mohammad

Commander of Forces in Central Afghanistan
Karim Khalili

Commander of Forces in Western Afghanistan
Ismail Khan

Foreign Minister
Abdullah Abdullah

Chief of Security
Engineer Muhammed Arif Sawari

INTERIM LEADER OF AFGHANISTAN

Hamid Karzai

BUSH AT WAR

1

TUESDAY, SEPTEMBER 11, 2001, began as one of those spectacular pre-fall days on the East Coast, sunny, temperatures in the 70s, light winds, the sky a vivid light blue. With President George W. Bush traveling in Florida that morning promoting his education agenda, his intelligence chief, CIA Director George J. Tenet, didn't have to observe the 8 A.M. ritual of personally briefing the president at the White House on the latest and most important top secret information flowing into America's vast spy empire.

Instead Tenet, 48, a hefty, outgoing son of Greek immigrants, was having a leisurely breakfast at the St. Regis Hotel, three blocks north of the White House, with the man who was most responsible for his rise in the world of secret intelligence—former Oklahoma Democratic Senator David L. Boren. The two had struck up an unusually close friendship going back 13 years when Tenet was a mid-level staffer on the Senate Intelligence Committee, which Boren chaired. Boren had found Tenet to be a gifted briefer and had jumped him over others with more seniority to make him staff director, a post which granted him access to virtually all the nation's intelligence secrets.

Boren then recommended Tenet to President-elect Bill Clinton in 1992, urging that he be appointed to head the administration's transition team on intelligence. The following year, Tenet was named National Security Council staff director for intelligence, responsible for coordinating all intelligence matters for the White House, including covert action. In 1995, Clinton named him deputy CIA director, and two years after that, he appointed him director of central intelligence (DCI), charged with heading the CIA and the vast U.S. intelligence community.

High-strung and a workaholic, Tenet had a heart attack while he was NSC intelligence staff director. He could be volatile. During President Clinton's second term, when he was CIA director, he stormed out of a principals' committee meeting that included the secretaries of state and defense but not the president. He thought the meeting, which was keeping him from attending his son's school Christmas play, was droning on too long. "Fuck you, I'm leaving" had been his parting comment. But Tenet had since learned how to control his temper.

In early 2001, Boren called President-elect Bush, praising Tenet as nonpartisan and urging him to keep him on as CIA director. Ask your father, he suggested. When the younger Bush did, the former President George H.W. Bush said, "From what I hear, he's a good fellow," one of the highest accolades in the Bush family lexicon. Tenet, who has a keen nose for cultivating political alliances, had helped the senior Bush push through the controversial nomination of Robert Gates as CIA director in 1991, and later led the effort to rename CIA headquarters for Bush, himself a former DCI.

The former president also told his son, the most important thing you'll do as president every day is get your intelligence briefing.

BEGINNING WITH HIS time heading the Senate Intelligence Committee staff, Tenet had developed an understanding of the importance of human intelligence, HUMINT in spycraft. In an era of dazzling breakthroughs in signals intelligence, SIGINT—phone, teletype and communications intercepts and code breaking—and overhead satellite photography and radar imagery, the CIA had downgraded the role of HUMINT. But Tenet earmarked more money for human intelligence and the training of case officers, the clandestine service operatives who work undercover recruiting and paying spies and agents in foreign governments—called "sources" or "assets."

Without case officers, Tenet knew, there would be no human sources to provide intelligence, no access to governments, opposition groups or other organizations abroad, little inside information, little opportunity for covert action. And covert action to effect change in foreign countries was part of the agency's charter, however controversial, misguided or bungled it may have been over the years.

The case officers were the critical first step. At one point in the 1990s, only 12 were being trained for the future in the year-long intensive program at the CIA facility called "the Farm" in the Virginia countryside. In 2001, Tenet had 10 times as many in training, an incredible jump. It was designed to increase HUMINT and make covert action, if authorized by the president, possible. All this had been done during the Clinton years.

"WHAT ARE YOU worried about these days?" Boren asked Tenet that morning.

"Bin Laden," Tenet replied, referring to terrorist leader Osama bin Laden, an exiled Saudi who was living in Afghanistan and had developed the worldwide network al Qaeda, Arabic for "the Base." He was convinced that bin Laden was going to do something big, he said.

"Oh, George!" Boren said. For the last two years he had been listening to his friend's concerns about bin Laden. How could one private person without the resources of a foreign government be such a threat? he asked.

"You don't understand the capabilities and the reach of what they're putting together," Tenet said.

Boren was worried that his friend had developed an unhealthy obsession about bin Laden. Nearly two years earlier, just before the 2000 millennium celebration, Tenet had taken the highly unusual and risky step of personally warning Boren not to travel or appear at big public events over New Year's Eve or New Year's Day because he anticipated major attacks.

More recently, Tenet had worried that there would be attacks during the July 4, 2001, celebration. Though he didn't disclose it to Boren, there had been 34 specific communications intercepts among various bin Laden associates that summer making declarations such as "Zero hour is tomorrow" or "Something spectacular is coming." There had been so many of these intercepts—often called chatter—picked up in the intelligence system and so many reports of threats that Tenet had gone to maximum alert. It seemed like an attack of some sort was imminent against U.S. embassies abroad or concentrations of American tourists, but the intelligence never pinpointed when or where or by what method.

Nothing had happened, but Tenet said it was the issue he was losing sleep over.

Suddenly, several of Tenet's security guards approached. They were not strolling. They were bolting toward the table.

Uh-oh, Boren thought.

"Mr. Director," one of them said, "there's a serious problem."

"What is it?" Tenet asked, indicating that it was okay to speak freely.

"The World Trade tower has been attacked."

One of them handed Tenet a cell phone and he called headquarters.

"So they put the plane into the building itself?" Tenet asked incredulously.

He ordered his key people to gather in his conference room at CIA headquarters. He would be there in about 15–20 minutes.

"This has bin Laden all over it," Tenet told Boren. "I've got to go." He also had another reaction, one that raised the real possibility that the CIA and the FBI had not done all that could have been done to prevent the terrorist attack. "I wonder," Tenet said, "if it has anything to do with this guy taking pilot training." He was referring to Zacarias Moussaoui, a French citizen of Moroccan descent whom the FBI had detained in Minnesota the previous month after he had acted suspiciously at a local flight training school.

Moussaoui's case was very much on his mind. In August, the FBI had asked the CIA and the National Security Agency to run phone traces on any calls Moussaoui had made abroad. He was already the subject of a five-inch-thick file in the bureau. As Tenet hopped in his car to go to the 258-acre CIA headquarters in Langley, Virginia, the past, present and future of his counterterrorism efforts were swirling in his head.

The CIA had been after bin Laden for more than five years, and increasingly so after the devastating 1998 bin Laden–sponsored terrorist bombings of the U.S. embassies in Kenya and Tanzania that had left more than 200 people dead. At that time, President Clinton directed the U.S. military to launch 66 cruise missiles into terrorist training camps in Afghanistan where bin Laden was believed to be in a high-level meeting. But he had apparently left a few hours before the missiles arrived.

In 1999, the CIA commenced a covert operation to train 60 commandos from the Pakistani intelligence agency to enter Afghanistan to capture bin Laden. But the operation was aborted because of a military coup in Pakistan. More ambitious and riskier options had been weighed in seemingly endless meetings with the top Clinton national security officials.

One option that had been considered was a clandestine helicopter-borne night assault on bin Laden with a small, elite U.S. military Special Forces unit of roughly 40 men. It would require aerial refueling, as the helicopters would have to fly some 900 miles. But they were spooked by the 1980 Desert One operation President Carter had ordered to rescue the American hostages held in Iran when several aircraft had crashed in the desert, and the downing of two Blackhawk helicopters in Somalia during a 1993 mission, which had led to 18 American deaths. The military said a raid on bin Laden might fail and could involve substantial U.S. casualties. Intelligence reports also showed that bin Laden had his key lieutenants keep their families with the entourage, and Clinton was opposed to any operation that might kill women and children.

A U.S. Special Forces unit and U.S. submarines capable of firing cruise missiles were put on alert, but they required six to ten hours advance warning about bin Laden's future location.

One of the most guarded secrets in the CIA was the existence of 30 recruited Afghan agents, operating under the codeword GE/SENIORS, who had been paid to track bin Laden around Afghanistan for the last three years. The group, which was paid $10,000 a month, could move together or break into smaller tracking teams of five men.

The CIA had daily secure communications with the "Seniors" as they were called, and had bought them vehicles and motorcycles. But tracking bin Laden grew increasingly difficult. He moved at irregular times, often departing suddenly at night.

Incredibly, the Seniors seemed to have him located most of the time, but they were never able to provide "actionable" intelligence—to say with any confidence that he would remain there for the time needed to shoot cruise missiles at the location. And the CIA failed to recruit a reliable human spy in bin Laden's circle who could tip them to his plans.

There were those in the Clinton White House and national security apparatus who were skeptical of the Seniors, because at times there was contradictory intelligence about bin Laden's location. And in Afghanistan people, especially intelligence assets, were regularly bought off.

Neither Clinton, nor Bush to this moment, had given the CIA lethal authority to send the Seniors or other paid CIA assets to kill or assassinate bin Laden. The presidential ban on assassination, first signed by President Gerald Ford, had the force of law.

During one period, the leader of the Afghan Seniors had met several times with the CIA station chief from Islamabad, Pakistan, who controlled and paid them. The Senior leader maintained that they had shot at bin Laden's convoy on two occasions in self-defense, which was permissible, but he wanted to go after the convoy in a concerted way, proposing an ambush—shoot everything up, kill everyone and then run.

The CIA station chief kept saying, "No, you can't, you can't do that." It would violate U.S. law.

Given the money that was available, the covert action resources and the atmosphere, Tenet figured the CIA had done everything they knew how to do. But he had never requested a change in the rules, had never asked Clinton for an intelligence order that would have permitted the Seniors to ambush bin Laden.

The lawyers at the Justice Department or the White House, he believed, would have said no, that it would have violated the assassination ban. He felt bound by the dovish attitude of Clinton and his advisers. Everything was "lawyered to death," he would say. But he too had contributed to that atmosphere during his five and a half years as Clinton's DCI and deputy DCI.

What the rules did permit was for the CIA to seize bin Laden and turn him over to law enforcement, an operation legally known as a "rendering." A big operation to do this was put on the covert action drawing boards. Tenet was convinced that bin Laden would never allow himself to be taken alive, so such an operation, if successful, would lead to his demise.

But all the CIA experts in the Directorate of Operations thought it would not work—that it would lead to a lot of people getting killed, and not necessarily bin Laden. And Tenet agreed. The plan never went further. A proposal by the Saudis that the CIA place a homing device in the luggage of bin Laden's mother, who was traveling from Saudi Arabia to visit her son in Afghanistan, was also rejected as risky and unlikely to work.

BY 9:50 A.M., Tenet was in his seventh floor office. Two commercial passenger airliners had already struck both World Trade Center

towers and a third had hit the Pentagon. A fourth hijacked plane
was over Pennsylvania apparently heading for the Washington area.

Reports were swamping the system saying that future targets
included the White House, the Capitol and the State Department.
CIA headquarters, a highly visible and recognizable landmark near
the Potomac River, was a possible target. Investigators knew that
Ramzi Yousef, an al Qaeda terrorist who was responsible for the
first World Trade Center attack in 1993, had had plans to fly a plane
packed with explosives into the CIA buildings.

"We have to save our people," Tenet told his senior leadership.
"We have to evacuate the building." He wanted everyone out, even
the core staff of hundreds from the Counterterrorism Center (CTC)
down in the windowless bowels of the building.

Cofer Black, the head of the CTC, looked on this order with
skepticism, almost shaking his head. At 52, Black was a veteran
covert operator and one of the agency's legends. He had helped in
the 1994 capture of Carlos the Jackal, perhaps the most notorious
pre–bin Laden international terrorist. Black had thinning hair and
wore prominent eyeglasses, and bore a striking resemblance to Karl
Rove, President Bush's chief political strategist. He was a throw-
back to the era when the agency was filled with colorful and eccen-
tric figures. While most everyone in the CIA called Tenet by his first
name, Black observed old-school protocol, calling him "Mr. Director" or simply "Sir."

"Sir," Black said, "we're going to have to exempt CTC from
this because we need to have our people working the computers."

"Well," Tenet said, "the Global Response Center . . ." He was
referring to the eight people on watch on the sixth floor, near the
top of the building, who monitored the latest intelligence on terrorism throughout the world. "They're going to be at risk."

"This is an element—we're going to have to keep them in
place."

"Well, we have to get those people out," Tenet insisted.

"No, sir, we're going to have to leave them there because they have a key function to play in a crisis like this. This is exactly why we have the Global Response Center."

"Well, they could die."

"Sir, then they're just going to have to die."

Tenet paused.

The CIA director was a sort of father protector to the thousands who worked there. In the popular culture and to many in Washington, the CIA was a broken, even unnecessary institution; at best, it was an endangered species of sorts. A director protected.

"You're absolutely right," Tenet finally told Black. The rules, maybe all of them, had changed that morning. Thousands were already dead in New York City and at the Pentagon.

Black sensed an important shift. People, including the director, were maturing before his eyes in a very short period of time, moving from the bureaucratic mode to acceptance of risk, even death. Black was not at all surprised by the attack, but even he was shocked at the level of carnage.

In his three years as counterterrorism chief, he had concluded that if the CTC chief was not more aggressive than his superiors, then they had the wrong person in the job. He had operated against al Qaeda when he was station chief in Khartoum, Sudan, and had been the target of a failed ambush and assassination attempt in 1994. He had made some aggressive, lethal covert action proposals to get bin Laden, but they had been rejected. He figured given the climate, it was probably inevitable.

Now all that had changed.

Tenet ordered the building evacuated, except for those in the Global Response Center.

IN LIMA, PERU, that morning, Secretary of State Colin L. Powell had just sat down to breakfast with the new president, Alejandro Toledo. Powell was attending an Organization of American States meeting. He anticipated a pleasant series of events with the foreign ministers or leaders of 34 of the 35 countries in the region. Cuba had not been invited.

Toledo was going on and on about U.S. textile quotas. He wanted an exemption for high-quality cotton which he maintained would not compete with lower-quality cotton produced in certain Southern states of the U.S. which of course insisted on the quotas.

Suddenly, the door opened and Craig Kelly, Powell's executive assistant, rushed in with a note written on a piece of paper that had been ripped out of a spiral wire notepad: Two airplanes had crashed into the World Trade Center.

Two is not an accident, Powell realized. The next note said it was two jets. Powell thought, I've got to go home. No matter what it was, it was too big for him to be sitting around at a conference of foreign ministers in Peru. The plane, get the plane, he told Kelly. Go tell them we're leaving.

It would take about an hour to get the plane ready, so Powell stopped by the conference. Other foreign ministers made speeches of sympathy. Powell spoke briefly, thanking the assembly members for their condolences and vowing that the U.S. would respond and ultimately prevail. "A terrible, terrible tragedy has befallen my nation," he said, "but . . . you can be sure that America will deal with this tragedy in a way that brings those responsible to justice. You can be sure that as terrible a day as this is for us, we will get through it because we are a strong nation, a nation that believes in itself."

The others stood and applauded. Powell then raced to the airport for the seven-hour flight. Once the plane took off, Powell found that he couldn't talk to anybody because his communications were connected to the system in the U.S., which was swamped. Without a phone or his e-mail, he was like a man without a country.

After a few minutes, he went to the front of the plane to call over the radio. That meant over-and-out, nonsecure communications. He reached Richard L. Armitage, the deputy secretary of state and his best friend. They spoke several times, but real talk was hopeless. Armitage, a 1967 Naval Academy graduate, had served four tours in Vietnam, and later as an assistant secretary of defense in the Reagan administration. He was an outspoken, muscular, barrel-chested man who deplored fancy-pants, pin-striped diplomatic talk. Even before they took over the State Department, Powell and Armitage talked several times each day. "I would trust him with my life, my children, my reputation, everything I have," Powell said of Armitage.

Of all the things Powell hated, being out of the action was at the top of the list. A central part of national security policymaking was crisis management. No matter what structure a president, a White House or a national security team might try to impose on the process of policymaking, there was a random quality to some of the big moments. Crisis provided the greatest danger and the greatest opportunity.

At 64, Powell had already sat in three of the seats in the White House Situation Room—national security adviser to President Reagan for a year, then chairman of the Joint Chiefs of Staff to the first President Bush during the Gulf War and now secretary of state to the new Bush for the last nine months.

A report came that another airliner had hit the Pentagon, and there were vague reports and rumors flying around about all kinds of other planes all over the place.

Powell started to scribble notes to himself. Ever the soldier, he wrote, What are my people going to be responsible for? How is the world, the United States going to respond to this? What about the United Nations? What about NATO? How do I start calling people together?

The seven hours of isolation seemed an eternity for the man who could have been commander in chief.

In 1995, Powell, two years retired from the Army, had considered running for president. He wrote an autobiography, *My American Journey,* which became a No. 1 national best-seller. He was poised at the epicenter of American politics, with stratospheric poll ratings, the Republican nomination nearly his for the asking, and the presidency within reach.

Armitage had been passionately against it. "It's not worth it. Don't do it," he advised, finally telling his friend, "I don't think you're ready for this." The process of campaigning would be everything Powell hated, "every bad thing you could imagine." Powell liked well-laid plans, order, predictability, a level of certainty that was not part of the hurly-burly of American politics.

It was well known his wife, Alma, was opposed to his running. What was secret was that Alma had flatly told him that if he ran for president she would leave him. "If you run, I'm gone," she said. She feared he would be attacked or shot. Running for president, becoming president, making her first lady was not what she wanted for her life. "You will have to do it alone," she said.

After Bush won the 2000 Republican presidential nomination, Powell signed on to help, but Karl Rove found that the campaign had to move heaven and earth to get him to appear at an event with Bush. Nearly every other important Republican fell in line, not Powell. His people always wanted to know who else would be at an event, what would be said, who the audience was, what was the political purpose. All this seemed designed to determine the political fallout—on Powell, not Bush. Rove detected a subtle, subversive tendency, as if Powell were protecting his centrist credentials and his own political future at Bush's expense.

Nevertheless, he was an available vehicle to move Bush toward the center, and he became the almost certain choice for secretary of state if Bush were elected. Powell let it be known this was a post he would accept. Within his inner circle, there was a strong sense that voters knew they were choosing a team—not just Bush and his vice presidential running mate, former Secretary of Defense Dick Cheney, but also Powell.

When the Supreme Court declared Bush the winner by 537 votes in the Florida saga, Powell's advisers were convinced that their boss had clearly provided the margin of victory many, many times over.

• • •

IN HIS FIRST months as secretary of state, Powell had never really closed the personal loop with Bush, never established a comfort level—the natural, at-ease state of closeness that both had with others. There existed a distance between these two affable men—a wariness—as if they were stalking each other from afar, never sitting down and having it out, whatever the "it" was. Both Bush and Powell used barracks-room humor freely with others, but rarely with each other.

Rove was disturbed and felt Powell was beyond political control and operating out of a sense of entitlement. "It's constantly, you know, 'I'm in charge, and this is all politics and I'm going to win the internecine political game,' " Rove said privately.

Whenever Powell was too out in front on an issue and became the public face of the administration, the political and communications operations at the White House reined him in, kept him out of the limelight. Rove and Karen P. Hughes, Bush's longtime communications director, now White House counselor, decided who from the administration would appear on the Sunday talk shows, the major television evening news and the morning programs. If the White House didn't call to suggest that he accept the numerous invitations to appear, Powell knew the rules. He told the shows no.

In April 2001, when an American EP-3E military spy plane off the coast of China was intercepted, forced down and taken hostage along with its 24 crew members by the Chinese government, the White House determined to keep Bush away from the issue, so that the president would not appear to be emotionally involved or the negotiator. It was important to behave as if there was no hostage crisis, mindful of how the Iranian hostage crisis had paralyzed President Carter and how the Lebanon hostage situation had become a consuming obsession for President Reagan in the mid-1980s.

The issue was turned over to Powell, who successfully won their release after 11 days. It was a big win, but even then the White House didn't want him on television to take credit.

Powell and Armitage would joke that Powell had been put in the "icebox" or the "refrigerator"—to be used only when needed.

Just the week before September 11, *Time* magazine had done a cover story on Powell with the headline, "Where Have You Gone, Colin Powell?" The story said he was leaving "shallow footprints" on policy and losing out to administration hard-liners. It was a very effective hit by the White House, where certain officials had cooperated with the writers to prove that Powell was operating, sometimes desperately, often in isolation, at the edges of the new administration.

Rove, for one, was saying privately that he thought Powell had somehow lost a step and that it was odd to see him uncomfortable in the presence of the president.

Powell and others in his circle had spent hours with the *Time* reporters unsuccessfully trying to talk them down from the story line. But Powell and Armitage knew the overwhelming power of perception in Washington where charting rise and fall is more than a parlor game. The problem was that the vivid story line would be seen as the truth, even if it wasn't. The larger problem was that it was in part true. Powell was not formulating a foreign policy. He was getting assignments and reacting to one minor crisis after another. But as he once said in private, "Survival at the top is pragmatics."

When he had been chairman of the Joint Chiefs, he had written out some of his favorite sayings and slipped them underneath the glass on his desk in the Pentagon. One said, "Never let them see you sweat."

2

PRESIDENT BUSH WAS reading to second graders at the Emma E. Booker Elementary School in Sarasota, Florida, when Rove brought him the news that a plane had hit the North Tower of the World Trade Center. At first, it seemed it might be an accident, pilot error or maybe, Bush thought, the pilot had had a heart attack.

He was sitting on a stool in the classroom in a dark suit, blue shirt and bright red tie. A small blackboard behind him said, "Reading makes a country great!"

Andrew H. Card Jr., 55, Bush's chief of staff and a former White House aide to Reagan and Bush senior, soon interrupted the president and whispered directly in his right ear, "A second plane hit the second tower. America is under attack."

A photo of that moment is etched for history. The president's hands are folded formally in his lap, his head turned to hear Card's words. His face has a distant sober look, almost frozen, edging on bewilderment. Bush remembers exactly what he was thinking: "They had declared war on us, and I made up my mind at that moment that we were going to war."

Bush decided that he needed to say something to the public. At 9:30 A.M. he appeared before the television cameras in the Booker school's media center to make a four-paragraph statement. He cautiously described what had happened as "an apparent terrorist attack." Looking shaken, his language oddly informal, he promised that the full resources of the federal government would be employed to investigate and find "those folks who committed this act.

"Terrorism against our nation will not stand," he said, echoing the famous "This will not stand" formulation his father had used 11 years earlier when he faced his greatest challenge after Iraq invaded Kuwait in August 1990.

Bush felt his father's declaration of resolve on the White House lawn several days after the invasion was among his finest moments as president. "Why I came up with those specific words, maybe it was an echo of the past," this president said later. "I don't know why. . . . I'll tell you this, we didn't sit around massaging the words. I got up there and just spoke.

"What you saw was my gut reaction coming out."

THE PRESIDENT'S MOTORCADE raced to the Sarasota Bradenton International Airport. He dashed up the steps and into his private front cabin and office on Air Force One.

"Be sure to get the first lady and my daughters protected," was his first order to the Secret Service agents.

"Mr. President," one of the agents said nervously, "we need you to get seated as soon as possible."

Bush strapped in, and the plane accelerated down the runway, almost standing on its tail as it climbed rapidly.

FIRST LADY LAURA Bush, in a bright red suit with a double string of pearls around her neck, was in the Caucus Room in the Russell Senate Office Building in Washington about to testify on children's early learning before Senator Edward M. Kennedy's committee.

Word of an "accident" came, and Mrs. Bush, Senator Kennedy and others left through a side door. When she learned some of the details, Mrs. Bush worked hard to control herself. Her face was soon quite ashen, her eyes tear-rimmed and her lips quivering.

Then the Pentagon was hit, and Secret Service and police cloistered around her. They explained the need to get her to a safe place. The group soon broke into an anxious trot. By 9:50, Mrs. Bush was awaiting an escort. In the traffic jam from the Capitol, it took 45 minutes to get her to Secret Service headquarters where she was taken into the basement to the Wood Conference Room.

Not until 10:51 A.M. did the Secret Service relocate Turquoise, the codename for Barbara Bush, a 19-year-old freshman at Yale, to their New Haven office. Twinkle, codename for the other Bush twin, Jenna, a freshman at the University of Texas in Austin, was relocated to the Driskill Hotel six minutes later.

IT WAS 9:39 A.M. when American Airlines Flight 77, a Boeing 757, slammed into the Pentagon.

Five minutes later, Bush reached his vice president, Dick Cheney, who had been whisked from his West Wing office by the Secret Service to the Presidential Emergency Operations Center, or PEOC, the emergency bunker beneath the White House grounds.

"We're at war," Bush said, and told Cheney to give the congressional leadership a briefing. When the president hung up, he turned to some of his staff on Air Force One who had heard his comment to Cheney. "That's what we're paid for boys. We're going to take care of this. And when we find out who did this, they're not going to like me as president. Somebody is going to pay."

Soon Cheney was on the phone again to the president urging that he authorize U.S. military aircraft to shoot down any additional commercial airliners that were controlled by hijackers. A hijacked airliner was a weapon. It would be a momentous decision, but Cheney, normally cautious, insisted that giving the American fighter pilots the authority to fire on commercial airliners, even if they were full of civilians, was the only practical answer.

"You bet," Bush said. He gave the authority.

At about 10:30 A.M. Cheney reached Bush again on Air Force One, which was still on its way to Washington. The White House had received a threat saying, "Angel is next." Since "Angel" was the codeword for Air Force One, it could mean that terrorists had inside information.

"We're going to find out who did this," Bush said to Cheney, "and we're going to kick their asses."

Card reported that First Lady Laura Bush was in a secure location with the Secret Service and that his daughters had been removed to safer locations.

A few minutes later, Cheney was back on the phone urging that the president not return to Washington. "There's still a threat," he said.

Signals intelligence and all kinds of reports were flooding in. Given what had happened—four hijackings—it wasn't prudent to come back. Cheney immediately clicked into the possibility that the terrorists might be trying to decapitate the government, to kill its leaders. He said they had a responsibility to preserve the government, its continuity of leadership. Bush recalled, "He was the man on the telephone who said, 'Do not come to Washington.' "

The president agreed to divert to Barksdale Air Force Base in Louisiana. Shortly after, those on the plane could feel it bank suddenly and sharply to the left in a westerly direction.

At 10:52 A.M. Bush spoke with his wife.

IT WAS A time of chaos and confusion that is reflected in the official documents of the day, some public, some classified. Various documents have Bush arriving in Louisiana at 11:48 A.M., 11:57 A.M., 12:05 P.M. and 12:16 P.M.—a range of 28 minutes. Somewhere around noon Air Force One landed at Barksdale under heavy security. At 12:36—this time is precise—Bush issued another statement before the television cameras.

It had been more than three hours since the president or any senior administration official had spoken publicly. The president's eyes were red-rimmed when he walked in. His performance was not reassuring. He spoke haltingly, mispronouncing several words as he looked down at his notes. He seemed to gain strength at the end of the 219-word statement, promising resolve. "But make no mistake," he said, "we will show the world that we will pass this test."

He told Card, "I want to go back home ASAP. I don't want whoever did this holding me outside of Washington."

But the Secret Service said it was too unsteady in Washington, and Cheney said it was not safe yet.

"The right thing is to let the dust settle," Card said.

Bush reluctantly acquiesced and reboarded Air Force One, which shortly after 1:30 P.M. zoomed into the western sky, this time for Offutt Air Force Base in Nebraska. Offutt is home to the Strategic Command, which controls the United States's nuclear weapons, and the base has a facility to protect the president. He could also meet with his National Security Council over a secure video link.

From the plane, Bush reached his secretary of defense, Donald H. Rumsfeld.

"Wow, it was an American airliner that hit the Pentagon," the president said in some wonderment. "It's a day of national tragedy, and we'll clean up the mess and then the ball will be in your court and Dick Myers's court."

Air Force General Richard B. Myers, the tall, gentlemanly vice chairman of the Joint Chiefs of Staff, was slated to move up to become chairman, the top U.S. military position, in three weeks.

Rumsfeld, a small-framed, almost boyish, former Navy fighter pilot who did not look his 69 years, had been expecting, even counting on, the order from the president putting the ball squarely in his court.

Earlier in the year, when Rumsfeld was in discussions about

becoming Bush's secretary of defense, he had had a talk with the president-elect, a little test of sorts. He told Bush that during the eight years of Clinton, the natural pattern when challenged or attacked had been a "reflexive pullback"—caution, safety plays, even squeamishness. The Clinton weapon of choice was the standoff cruise missile. Rumsfeld left no doubt in Bush's mind that when that moment came, as it surely would, that the United States was threatened, he, as secretary of defense, would be coming to the president to unleash the military. The president could expect a forward-leaning action plan.

Bush had replied, unambiguously in Rumsfeld's estimation, that that was precisely what he wanted. Rumsfeld believed they had a clear, common understanding.

RUMSFELD HAD BEEN one of the brightest Republican stars in the 1960s and 1970s—a JFK from the GOP—handsome, intense, well educated with an intellectual bent, witty with an infectious smile. Many in the party, including Rumsfeld himself, thought he might be headed for the presidency. But he never gained traction as a popular or national political figure, in part because of the brusque way he often treated people, especially subordinates. In addition, he made a political enemy of one of the party's rising stars, George H.W. Bush, who did make it to the presidency.

Rumsfeld's ascent to the inner circle of power is a story of intrigue, drive and luck. In 1962, at the age of 30, Rumsfeld was elected to his first of four terms in Congress representing the district of Chicago's North Shore suburbs where he had grown up. He resigned from Congress in 1969 to become director of the Office of Economic Opportunity, the anti-poverty organization that was a cabinet level post in the Nixon administration but not a flashy, high-visibility position.

By 1973–74 he was in Brussels, serving as U.S. ambassador to

NATO, dodging the Watergate bullet. According to Nixon's mem-
oirs, in July 1974, "Don Rumsfeld called from Brussels, offering to
resign as Ambassador to NATO and return to help work against im-
peachment among his former colleagues." Nixon resigned the next
month and Rumsfeld was asked to chair the presidential transition
team of his former House colleague Gerald Ford.

Ford asked Rumsfeld to become White House chief of staff,
but Rumsfeld wanted to stay at NATO. Rumsfeld agreed when Ford
promised to streamline the staff and give Rumsfeld full authority.

After a year in the White House, Ford told him he planned to
fire Defense Secretary James Schlesinger. Rumsfeld would move to
Defense. CIA Director William Colby was going to be replaced by
George Bush senior, then the U.S. representative in China. Rumsfeld privately called the China post "a crappy, irrelevant job." He
was opposed to the new assignments for both Bush and himself. He
told Ford that moving the two would put them on ice for Ford's upcoming presidential campaign. They were, he said, the only two
who could give effective political speeches in the coming election
year, 1976. But Rumsfeld saluted and took Defense.

Bush senior was convinced that Rumsfeld was secretly pushing him out to the CIA to end his political career. It seemed inconceivable at the time that the head of spying and dirty tricks abroad
could ever become president.

President Ford then elevated Rumsfeld's deputy, Dick Cheney,
to be White House chief of staff. At the time, over concerns about
politicizing the CIA, the Senate was refusing to confirm Bush senior
as director unless Ford pledged not to select him as his vice presidential running mate for the coming election. Rumsfeld told Ford
and Cheney that the president should not cave in to the Senate.
When Ford and Bush eventually made the pledge to the Senate anyway, Rumsfeld blamed Cheney in part, telling him in so many
words, You've screwed up on the first thing you've done.

Over the next year, 1976, there emerged a subtle rivalry between Secretary of Defense Rumsfeld and CIA Director Bush.

In their years in the House, Rumsfeld had found Bush to be a lightweight who was interested in friendships, public relations and public opinion polls more than substantive policy. In his view, Bush senior avoided controversy and sweat, except in the House gym. He went so far as to tell some that Bush had some of what Rumsfeld called the "Rockefeller syndrome"—available, wanting to serve, but not having clear goals. In Rumsfeld's world, having no larger purpose was almost a high crime.

Rumsfeld believed that Bush was a weak CIA director who seriously underestimated the Soviet Union's military advances and was manipulated by Secretary of State Henry Kissinger.

Rumsfeld went on to hold government appointments in the Reagan administration as Middle East envoy and in the Clinton administration as head of a commission to assess the ballistic missile threat to the U.S., but none in the administration of Bush senior.

Instead of being on a track to run for the presidency, Rumsfeld was now the secretary of defense for a second time, serving his longtime rival's son. In some respects, Rumsfeld was a walking example of what the novelist Wallace Stegner calls "resilience under disappointment," the persistence of drive, hard work and even stubbornness when ambition has not been fully realized.

In his first eight months back in the Pentagon, Rumsfeld struck two major themes. First, the military was hidebound and outdated, still equipped, trained and organized to fight old enemies, mainly the Soviet Union. He undertook what he called "transformation," to remake the force, and as he said somewhat presciently at his confirmation hearings, to "develop capabilities to defend against missiles, terrorism and new threats against our space assets and information systems."

Rumsfeld's second theme was surprise. He routinely handed out or recommended a book called *Pearl Harbor: Warning and Decision* by Roberta Wohlstetter. Rumsfeld particularly recommended the foreword, written by Thomas Schelling, who argued that Pearl Harbor was an ordinary blunder, the type government specializes in.

"There is a tendency in our planning to confuse the unfamiliar with the improbable. . . . The danger is in a poverty of expectations, a routine obsession with a few dangers that may be familiar rather than likely."

Rumsfeld's transformation plans met with something just short of organized resistance bordering on insubordination among a significant part of the senior uniformed officers. One four-star officer who worked with him said Rumsfeld was "an egomaniac cleverly disguised . . . a hip shooter who gives the impression he is not." Another said if anyone disagreed with Rumsfeld it was risky because the result might be an "ass chewing from him." The officer said, "I'd go up there [to Rumsfeld's office on the third floor] and when I disagreed with him I'd tell him I disagreed. Sometimes he was nice about it, sometimes he wasn't nice about it."

On occasion Rumsfeld bounced ranking generals out of his office, telling one, "Come back and brief when you know what you're talking about." Woe to the briefer who presented only a proposed solution. "Wait, let's back up," Rumsfeld would often say. I can read the answer. What I want to know is how you got there—the premise, the starting point, the full reasoning.

This baffled the senior military. It was humbling and off-putting too at times. Rumsfeld confronted them with tough questions that seemed excessive. What is it you know about this subject? What don't you know? What do you think about it? What do you think I ought to ask you about it? That's the only way I'm going to learn anything, he explained, adding, And for sure it's the only way that you are going to learn anything!

He seemed too confident in himself and too distrustful of his subordinates in the military. Working with a close-knit group, mostly civilians, he was a mystery to many in the building, especially the members of the Joint Chiefs of Staff, the uniformed heads of the Army, Navy, Air Force and Marine Corps.

Rumsfeld didn't like muddling along. He didn't like imprecision. He redid or had suggestions on most memos. He hated loose language. One memo had an obvious typographic error—"not" coming out as "ton"—and he asked, What does this "ton" mean? Why is "ton" in this sentence? What does it mean?

"Cambone!" was a familiar refrain when Rumsfeld wanted information or action. A 6-foot-3 defense intellectual who had worked on the space and missile defense commissions that Rumsfeld had headed, Steve Cambone was the dark, nonsunny, nonoptimistic side of Rumsfeld who had forebodings about something bad happening. He was civilian special assistant to the secretary, and he largely defined the relationships between Rumsfeld and the rest of the Pentagon. Cambone was the means by which, at least initially, Rumsfeld had extended his grasp around the throats of the military brass.

Army General Henry B. "Hugh" Shelton, the chairman of the Joint Chiefs of Staff since October 1997, grew despondent at times under the new civilian leadership, reporting to colleagues a real rupture with Rumsfeld. At one point Rumsfeld suggested that Shelton ought to give his military advice to the president through him. Shelton had to point out that the law made him the "principal military adviser" to the president, and he believed his advice should be given directly.

If Rumsfeld rubbed the chiefs and the brass raw at times, many had respect for his intelligence. One senior general said, "I admire the man greatly even though I don't necessarily like him. . . . He's got a weakness in wanting to have his hands around everything. Okay?"

AWARE OF THE attacks on the World Trade Center, Rumsfeld had been proceeding with his daily intelligence briefing in his office when the third hijacked plane struck the western face of the Pentagon. He felt the building shudder and darted to the window, but from his vantage it was unclear what had happened. He went outside and followed the rising cloud of smoke to the crash site, helping with the rescue effort before a security agent urged him to get out of the area.

"I'm going inside," Rumsfeld said, and hurried to the National Military Command Center, the large, heavily staffed Pentagon war room. It was filled with smoke, so he and his team went up to an isolated communications network room called "Cables" where the air was better.

General Myers urged Rumsfeld to leave. "The smoke is getting pretty bad," he said. "We've got a lot of support people here. It's actually worse for them than it is for us right here." The others would not leave as long as Rumsfeld was there. "We ought to think about moving."

Okay, Rumsfeld said, but kept on working.

The military, which seemed to have contingency plans for the most inconceivable scenarios, had no plans for Afghanistan, the sanctuary of bin Laden and his network. There was nothing on the shelf that could be pulled down to provide at least an outline. This was not a surprise for the secretary of defense. Now he turned to Myers with a message: When I've asked to see various plans, I've not been happy with what I've seen. They are neither imaginative nor creative. Clearly the plans are old and have been on the shelf for too long. I've just not been happy. We've got a long way to go. You need to know that.

"I understand, sir," Myers replied.

RUMSFELD FINALLY LEFT the war room and went to his office suite and set himself to working the problem.

"This is the defining moment," he told his top aides—Cambone, his military assistant, his general counsel and his spokesperson. The president is going to come back into town, he said, and I need to be ready to talk to him when he arrives. What are the things the president needs to think about? Rumsfeld asked. What does the president need to address?

He started jotting down ideas. He wanted thoughts from everyone, short concepts, statements of the problems. Get this old paper, this report, this memo, he said. Speak up. What did they have before them?

For Cambone, it was distill, distill, distill—digest, digest, digest.

Victoria A. "Torie" Clarke, assistant secretary of defense for public affairs, thought Rumsfeld was like a Vegas blackjack dealer, sitting in his massive office sorting through the paper, almost by instinct, setting out three stacks of memos, papers and notes: 1. This is what we know. 2. This is what we're dealing with right now. 3. This is what we've got to deal with next—tomorrow and into the long-term future.

How do we crystallize the problem for the president? Rumsfeld asked. He deemed it part of his responsibility to think on the president's behalf. We have to have the right thoughts, complete thoughts. Because, he said, the first full meeting of the National Security Council was going to be terribly important in setting the stage for how they moved forward. Paper kept flying from stack to stack, and the piles got smaller and smaller. He threw some of these notes and paper in the Burn Bag for classified trash. Clarke fished some out to recirculate.

After several hours, Rumsfeld had it all down on a single sheet of paper—nice, neat, no misspellings, no loose language—to take that night for a meeting at the White House with the president.

He had a final question for General Myers. "Where are those plans?"

AT OFFUTT AIR Force Base in Nebraska, President Bush convened the first meeting of the National Security Council for the terrorist crisis at 3:30 P.M.

Tenet reported with near certainty that bin Laden was behind the attacks. Passenger manifests showed three known al Qaeda operatives had been on American Airlines Flight 77, which had plowed into the Pentagon. One of them, Khalid Al-Midhar, had come to the CIA's attention the previous year in Malaysia. A paid CIA spy had placed him at an al Qaeda meeting. They had informed the FBI, who put him on a domestic watch list, but he had slipped into the United States over the summer and avoided detection by the bureau.

Al Qaeda was the only terrorist organization capable of such spectacular, well-coordinated attacks, Tenet said. Intelligence monitoring had overheard a number of known bin Laden operatives congratulating each other after the attacks. Information collected days earlier but only now being translated indicated that various known operatives around the world anticipated a big event. None specified the day, time, place or method of attack.

It was pretty obvious there had been some kind of screwup, and it didn't sound to the president like the FBI and CIA were communicating. "George, get your ears up," the president told Tenet, meaning listen in on everything.

Tenet said since all the attacks had taken place before 10 A.M. that morning, chances were that there would be no more that day, but there was no way to be sure.

FBI Director Robert S. Mueller III, who had only been in the job for a week, said they didn't know how the hijackers had taken over the planes. As a precaution, all air traffic over the U.S. had been grounded indefinitely.

The president said he wanted to get the airlines flying again.

"We need to understand the penetration of airport security before the planes take off," Tenet cautioned. It was a reasonable suggestion, but it seemed to shift the problem to airport security and away from intelligence lapses that may have allowed the hijackers to enter and live in the U.S. for months before their missions.

"I'll announce more security measures," the president said, "but we won't be held hostage," and he added impulsively, "We'll fly at noon tomorrow."

It would take three days before commercial airline flights resumed at a reduced schedule.

"The terrorists can always attack," Rumsfeld said defiantly. "The Pentagon's going back to work tomorrow."

Secret Service Director Brian L. Stafford addressed the president. "Our position is stay where you are," the director said. "It's not safe." Stafford thought he was making the obvious case. Bush knew the Secret Service could not guarantee perfect security—there was no 100 percent—but if the president followed their recommendations, they could provide him with the best security possible. If he ignored their recommendations, all bets were off.

"I'm coming back," Bush said.

Stafford was surprised.

About 4:30 P.M. the president reached his wife on the phone.

"I'm coming home," he said. "See you at the White House. Love you, go on home."

3

Aт CIA HEADQUARTERS, James L. Pavitt, the deputy director for operations (DDO) who headed the agency's clandestine service and covert operations, wanted to send a personal message to his troops. Pavitt, 55, a roly-poly, gregarious career spy, seemed an unlikely chief of the most secretive, subterranean latticework of undercover case officers, paid agents and secret-stealers in the world.

Pavitt's message was labeled a DOSB—a secret message for all Directorate of Operations Stations and Bases.

"The United States has been attacked again by resolute and committed foes readily willing to accept self-destruction in order to fulfill their mission of terror.

"I expect each station and each officer to redouble efforts of collecting intelligence on this tragedy. The Counterterrorism Center is the focal point for all information on this subject, and we anticipate that a good percentage of the most valuable information concerning the attacks and their perpetrators will come within the next 48 hours." They had to get information before the trail grew cold. He said they should be careful and protect their families. "I also ask all of you to join me in a silent prayer for the thousands who perished today and for their loved ones now so terribly alone."

• • •

BUSH WANTED TO give a speech that night to the nation on television, and his chief speechwriter, Michael Gerson, had come up with a draft. It included the sentences, "This is not just an act of terrorism. This is an act of war." This reflected what Bush had been saying all day to the NSC and his staff.

Take it out, Bush instructed Karen Hughes. "Our mission is reassurance." He wanted to calm already jumpy nerves.

"I did not want to add to the angst of the American people yet," Bush said later. He wanted to go on television and be tough, show some resolve but also find some balance—be comforting, demonstrate that the government was functioning and show the nation that their president had made it through. There had been some doubt as he had hopscotched most of the day from Air Force base to Air Force base.

About 6:30 P.M., the president was finally back at the White House dealing with the speech draft in the small study off the Oval Office. Drawing on a presidential campaign speech in 1999 at The Citadel military academy, Gerson had written that, in responding to terrorism, the United States would make no distinction between those who planned the acts and those who tolerated or encouraged the terrorists.

"That's way too vague," Bush complained, proposing the word "harbor." In final form, what would later be called the Bush Doctrine said, "We will make no distinction between those who planned these acts and those who harbor them." It was an incredibly broad commitment to go after terrorists and those who sponsor and protect terrorists, rather than just a proposal for a targeted retaliatory strike. The decision was made without consulting Cheney, Powell or Rumsfeld.

The president did consult with his national security adviser, Condoleezza Rice. She wondered if that kind of far-reaching declaration and policy pronouncement belonged in a speech that was meant to console the shaken nation. "You can say it now or you'll have other opportunities to say it," Rice advised him. It was her style not to commit herself unless the president pressed. But in the end she favored including it that night, because, she thought, first words matter more than almost anything else.

"We've got to get it out there now," Bush said. It had been a policy he had been inching toward. Might as well say it.

In the West Wing, there was debate about whether the president needed to make a firm declaration of the obvious—that this was war. White House communications director Dan Bartlett, 30, was deputized to suggest that to the president.

"What?" Bush barked. "No more changes."

Bartlett showed him a proposed change about being at war.

"I've already said no to that," the president replied.

Bartlett went back to his West Wing colleagues. "Thanks, you can take the message next time."

PRESIDENT BUSH SPOKE to the nation for seven minutes from the Oval Office. He declared his policy—go after terrorists and those who harbor them.

"None of us will forget this day," he said. "Yet we go forward to defend freedom and all that is good and just in the world."

After the speech, Bush chaired an expanded NSC meeting that turned out to be unwieldy. So at 9:30 P.M. he gathered his most senior principal national security advisers in the White House bunker. It was at the end of one of the longest and most chaotic days in each of their lives.

"This is the time for self-defense," the president said, making the somewhat obvious point. There was a sense it was not over, and they were meeting in the bunker not because it was comfortable—it wasn't—but because it was still dangerous. They had neither a handle on what had happened nor what might be next nor how to respond. "We have made the decision to punish whoever harbors terrorists, not just the perpetrators," he told them.

The president, Rice, Hughes and the speechwriters had made one of the most significant foreign policy decisions in years, and the

secretary of state had not been involved. Powell had just made it
back from Peru. And now, he said, "We have to make it clear to Pakistan and Afghanistan, this is showtime."

Afghanistan's ruling Taliban regime, an extreme Islamic fundamentalist militia group which came to power in 1996, was harboring al Qaeda terrorists in exchange for substantial bankrolling by
bin Laden. Neighboring Pakistan's powerful intelligence service,
the ISI, had had a giant role in creating the Taliban and keeping
them in power. The hard-line regime, whose strict interpretation of
Islamic law and draconian rule led to the oppression of women,
mass hunger and the flight of nearly one million refugees, earned
international condemnation for destroying the giant centuries-old
Buddha statues at Bamiyan.

"This is a great opportunity," Bush said, somewhat locating
the pony in the pile of manure. It was a chance to improve relations
especially with big powers such as Russia and China. "We have to
think of this as an opportunity."

The members of the war cabinet had lots of questions, none
more than Rumsfeld. On his single sheet of paper, he had the questions he thought the president and the rest of them needed to address and eventually answer: Who are the targets? How much
evidence do we need before going after al Qaeda? How soon do
we act?

The sooner they acted, Rumsfeld said, the more public support
they would have if there's collateral damage. He was being careful.
Since the military had no plan and no forces in the immediate area,
he wanted to keep expectations low. He dropped a bomb, telling
them that some major strikes could take up to 60 days to put together.

The notion of waiting 60 days for something major—until November 11 perhaps—just hung in the room.

Rumsfeld had more questions. Powell thought they were a
clever disguise, a way to argue rhetorically and avoid taking a position. Rumsfeld wanted others to answer his queries. It was a remarkable technique, Powell thought.

Still, the questions were good, and Rumsfeld went on. Are there targets that are off-limits? Do we include the American allies in any military strikes? Last, the secretary of defense said, we have to set declaratory policy, announce to the world what we're doing.

Cheney noted that Afghanistan would present a real challenge. A primitive country 7,000 miles away with a population of 26 million, it was the size of Bush's home state of Texas but had few roads and little infrastructure. Finding anything to hit would be hard.

The president returned to the problem of the al Qaeda terrorists and their sanctuary in Afghanistan. Since bin Laden relocated there from Sudan in May 1996, the Taliban had allowed al Qaeda to establish their headquarters and training camps in the country.

We have to deny al Qaeda sanctuary, Tenet said. Tell the Taliban we're finished with them. The Taliban and al Qaeda were really the same.

Rumsfeld said that they should employ every tool of national power, not just the military but legal, financial, diplomatic and the CIA.

Tenet said that al Qaeda, though headquartered in Afghanistan, operated worldwide, on all continents. We have a 60-country problem, he said.

"Let's pick them off one at a time," the president said.

Rumsfeld, not to be outdone in identifying difficulties, said the problem was not just bin Laden and al Qaeda, but other countries that supported terrorism.

"We have to force countries to choose," Bush said.

The meeting was adjourned. The president, untested and untrained in national security, was about to start on the complicated and prolonged road to war without much of a map.

CONDOLEEZZA RICE WENT to the national security adviser's office in the corner of the West Wing after the meeting. A former Stanford political science professor and then provost, she had worked on the NSC staff as a Russian expert during the presidency of Bush senior. Rice, 46, was perhaps the person in the upper reaches of Bush's national security team who was most alone. Her mother was dead and her father had died a year ago. Following the attacks that morning she called the only family she had, her aunt and uncle in Birmingham, Alabama, to tell them she was all right, then went back to work.

Beginning in the presidential campaign when she was Bush's chief foreign policy adviser, Rice had developed a very close relationship with Bush. Tall, with near perfect posture, a graceful walk and a beaming smile, she had become a permanent fixture in the presidential inner circle. The president and first lady had in a sense become her family.

That night, she acknowledged to herself that she was in a fog. She tried to focus on what had to be done the next day.

If it was bin Laden and al Qaeda—it almost surely was—there was another complication. The questions would sooner or later arise about what the Bush administration knew about the bin Laden threat, when they knew it and what they had done about it.

ABOUT A WEEK before Bush's inauguration, Rice attended a meeting at Blair House, across from the White House, with President-elect Bush and Vice President–elect Cheney. This was the secrets briefing given by Tenet and Pavitt.

For two and one half hours, Tenet and Pavitt had run through the good, the bad and the ugly about the CIA to a fascinated president-elect. They told him that bin Laden and his network were a "tremendous threat" which was "immediate." There was no doubt that bin Laden was coming after the United States again, they said, but it was not clear when, where or how. Bin Laden and the network were a difficult, elusive target. President Clinton had approved five separate intelligence orders, called Memoranda of Notification (MON), authorizing covert action to attempt to destroy bin Laden and his network, disrupt and preempt their terrorist operations. No authority had been granted outright to kill or assassinate bin Laden.

Tenet and Pavitt presented bin Laden as one of the three top threats facing the United States. The other two were the increasing availability of weapons of mass destruction—chemical, biological and nuclear, including weapons proliferation concerns—and the rise of Chinese power, military and other.

In April, the National Security Council deputies' committee, made up of the No. 2's in each major department and agency, recommended that President Bush adopt a policy that would include a serious effort to arm the Northern Alliance, the loose confederation of various warlords and tribes in Afghanistan that opposed the Taliban regime that harbored bin Laden.

The CIA estimated that the Northern Alliance forces were outnumbered about 2 to 1, with some 20,000 fighters to the Taliban's roughly 45,000 military troops and volunteers.

A CIA covert program of maintenance for the rebel forces of several million dollars a year was already in place. But worries about the Northern Alliance abounded. First, it was not really an alliance, because the various warlords could probably with some ease be bought off by the Taliban. The warlords flourished in a culture of survival—meaning they would do anything necessary. Several were just thugs, serial human rights abusers and drug dealers. In addition, the Russians and Iranians—who both supported the Alliance with substantial amounts of money—had strong influence with some of the warlords.

In the Clinton administration, the State Department had flatly opposed arming the Alliance because of these real concerns. It was Richard Armitage, Powell's deputy, who had agreed to lift State's objections that spring. Armitage had checked with Powell, who had agreed that bin Laden was a sufficient threat to justify arming the Northern Alliance on a large scale.

During July, the deputies' committee recommended a comprehensive plan, not just to roll back al Qaeda but to eliminate it. It was a plan to go on the offensive and destabilize the Taliban. During August, many of the principals were away. It was not until September 4 that they approved and recommended a plan that would give the CIA $125 million to $200 million a year to arm the Alliance.

Rice had a National Security Presidential Directive (NSPD) ready to go to the president on September 10. The door had been opened and they were ready to walk through it. The NSPD was numbered 9—meaning eight other matters had been formally assessed, vetted, agreed upon and signed off on as policy by the president before al Qaeda.

The question that would always linger was whether they had moved fast enough on a threat that had been identified by the CIA as one of the top three facing the country, whether September 11 was as much a failure of policy as it was of intelligence.

AT 11:08 P.M., September 11, the Secret Service awakened the Bushes and hurriedly escorted them to the bunker. An unidentified plane seemed to be heading for the White House. The president was in his running shorts and a T-shirt. Mrs. Bush was in her robe and without her contact lenses. Their dogs, Spot and Barney, scampered along. In the long tunnel leading to the bunker, they met Card, Rice and Stephen J. Hadley, the deputy national security adviser, who were racing along.

The errant plane was soon identified, but the Secret Service still wanted the president to spend the night in the bunker. Bush looked at the small bed and announced he was going back to the residence.

Rice had a Secret Service detail assigned to her, and an agent said they didn't want her to go home that night to her Watergate apartment. Maybe you ought to stay here, the agent said, so Rice agreed to sleep in the bunker.

"No," the president said, "you come stay in the residence."

Like his father during his White House years, the president tried to keep a daily diary of some thoughts and observations. He dictated that night:

"The Pearl Harbor of the 21st century took place today."

Bush would recall that he had two thoughts, "This was a war in which people were going to have to die. Secondly, I was not a military tactician. I recognize that. I was going to have to rely on the advice and counsel of Rumsfeld, Shelton, Myers and Tenet."

He was now a wartime president. Soldiers and citizens, the entire world, would pick up instantly on his level of engagement, energy and conviction. The widely held view that he was a lightweight, unconcerned with details, removed, aloof and possibly even ignorant would have to be dispelled. He had much work to do.

VICE PRESIDENT DICK Cheney, who had been the efficient, solid rock standing behind or to the side of President Bush during the first nine months of the administration, anticipated he would have a major role in the crisis. Heavyset, balding, with a trademark tilted head and a sly, knowing smile, the 61-year-old Cheney, a conservative hard-liner, had been training all his life for such a war. His credentials were impeccable—at 34, White House chief of staff to President Ford; congressman from Wyoming for 10 years, rising to become the No. 2 House Republican leader; defense secretary to the first President Bush during the Persian Gulf War.

Cheney had flirted with running for president himself in 1996, but decided against it after testing the waters—too much fundraising and too much media scrutiny. In the summer of 2000, Bush had asked Cheney to be his vice presidential running mate with these words, "If times are good, I'm going to need your advice, but not nearly as much as if times are bad. Crisis management is an essential part of the job."

On the morning of Wednesday, September 12, Cheney had a

moment alone with Bush. Should someone chair a kind of war cabinet for you of the principals? We'll develop options and report to you. It might streamline decision making.

No, Bush said, I'm going to do that, run the meetings. This was a commander in chief function—it could not be delegated. He also wanted to send the signal that it was he who was calling the shots, that he had the team in harness. He would chair the full National Security Council meetings, and Rice would continue to chair the separate meetings of the principals when he was not attending. Cheney would be the most senior of the advisers. Experienced, a voracious reader of intelligence briefing papers, he would, as in the past, be able to ask the really important questions and keep them on track.

Without a department or agency such as State, Defense or the CIA, Cheney was minister without portfolio. It was a lesser role than he had perhaps expected. But he, as much as any of the others, knew the terms of presidential service—salute and follow orders.

PRESIDENT BUSH, LIKE many members of his national security team, believed the Clinton administration's response to Osama bin Laden and international terrorism, especially since the embassy bombings in 1998, had been so weak as to be provocative, a virtual invitation to hit the United States again.

"The antiseptic notion of launching a cruise missile into some guy's, you know, tent, really is a joke," Bush said later in an interview. "I mean, people viewed that as the impotent America. . . . a flaccid, you know, kind of technologically competent but not very tough country that was willing to launch a cruise missile out of a submarine and that'd be it.

"I do believe there is the image of America out there that we are so materialistic, that we're almost hedonistic, that we don't have values, and that when struck, we wouldn't fight back. It was clear that bin Laden felt emboldened and didn't feel threatened by the United States."

Until September 11, however, Bush had not put that thinking into practice nor had he pressed the issue of bin Laden. Though Rice and the others were developing a plan to eliminate al Qaeda, no formal recommendations had ever been presented to the president.

"I know there was a plan in the works. . . . I don't know how mature the plan was," Bush recalled. He said the idea that a plan was going to be on his desk September 10 was perhaps "a convenient date. It would have been odd to come September the 10th because I was in Florida on September the 10th, so I don't think they would have been briefing me in Florida."

He acknowledged that bin Laden was not his focus or that of his national security team. "There was a significant difference in my attitude after September 11. I was not on point, but I knew he was a menace, and I knew he was a problem. I knew he was responsible, or we felt he was responsible, for the [previous] bombings that killed Americans. I was prepared to look at a plan that would be a thoughtful plan that would bring him to justice, and would have given the order to do that. I have no hesitancy about going after him. But I didn't feel that sense of urgency, and my blood was not nearly as boiling."

AT 8 A.M., September 12, Tenet arrived at the Oval Office for the President's Daily Brief, the TOP SECRET/CODEWORD digest of the most important and sensitive intelligence. This briefing included a review of available intelligence tracing the attacks to bin Laden and his top associates in al Qaeda. One report out of Kandahar, Afghanistan, the spiritual home of the Taliban, showed the attacks were "the results of two years' planning." Another report said the attacks were "the beginning of the wrath"—an ominous note. Several reports specifically identified Capitol Hill and the White House as targets on September 11. One said a bin Laden associate—incorrectly—"gave thanks for the explosion in the Congress building."

A key figure in the bin Laden financing organization called Wafa initially claimed that "The White House has been destroyed" before having to correct himself. Another report showed that al Qaeda members in Afghanistan had said at 9:53 A.M., September 11, shortly after the Pentagon was hit, that the attackers were following through with "the doctor's program." The second-ranking member of bin Laden's organization was Ayman Zawahiri, an Egyptian physician often referred to as "the Doctor."

A central piece of evidence involved Abu Zubayda, identified early as the chief field commander of the October 2000 attack on the Navy destroyer USS *Cole* that killed 17 sailors in the Yemeni port of Aden. One of the most ruthless members of bin Laden's inner circle, Zubayda, according to a reliable report received after September 11, had referred to the day of the attacks as "zero hour."

In addition, the CIA and the FBI had evidence of connections between at least three of the 19 hijackers and bin Laden and his training camps in Afghanistan. It was consistent with intelligence reporting all summer showing that bin Laden had been planning "spectacular attacks" against U.S. targets.

For Tenet, the evidence on bin Laden was conclusive—game, set, match. He turned to the agency's capabilities on the ground in Afghanistan.

As the president knew, the CIA had had covert relationships in Afghanistan authorized first in 1998 by Clinton and then reaffirmed later by him. The CIA was giving several million dollars a year in assistance to the Northern Alliance. The CIA also had contact with tribal leaders in southern Afghanistan. And the agency had secret paramilitary teams that had been going in and out of Afghanistan without detection for years to meet with opposition figures.

Though an expanded covert action plan had been in the works for months, Tenet told Bush an even more expanded plan would soon be presented for approval, and it would be expensive, very expensive. Though Tenet did not use a figure, it was going to approach $1 billion.

"Whatever it takes," the president said.

AFTER THE INTELLIGENCE briefing, Bush met with Hughes. He told her that he wanted a daily meeting to shape the administration's message to Americans about the fight against terrorism. Hughes, who was focused on details of the day ahead, proposed that the president make an early public statement and reminded him that he would need remarks for a scheduled visit to the Pentagon that afternoon.

"Let's get the big picture," Bush said, interrupting her. "A faceless enemy has declared war on the United States of America. So we are at war."

They needed a plan, a strategy, even a vision, he said, to educate the American people to be prepared for another attack. Americans needed to know that combating terrorism would be the main focus of the administration—and the government—from this moment forward.

Hughes returned to her corner office on the second floor of the West Wing to begin drafting a statement. Before she could open a new file on her computer, Bush summoned her.

"Let me tell you how to do your job today," he told her when she arrived at the Oval Office. He handed her two pieces of White House notepaper with three thoughts scratched out in his handwriting:

"This is an enemy that runs and hides, but won't be able to hide forever.

"An enemy that thinks its havens are safe, but won't be safe forever.

"No kind of enemy that we are used to—but America will adapt."

Hughes went back to work.

4

Bush CONVENED HIS National Security Council in the Cabinet Room and declared that the time for reassuring the nation was over. He said he was confident that if the administration developed a logical and coherent plan, the rest of the world "will rally to our side." At the same time, he was determined not to allow the threat of terrorism to alter the way Americans lived their lives. "We have to prepare the public, without alarming the public."

FBI Director Mueller began to describe the investigation under way to identify the hijackers. He said it was essential not to taint any evidence so that if accomplices were arrested, they could be convicted.

Attorney General John D. Ashcroft interrupted. Let's stop the discussion right here, he said. The chief mission of U.S. law enforcement, he added, is to stop another attack and apprehend any accomplices or terrorists before they hit us again. If we can't bring them to trial, so be it.

The president had made clear to Ashcroft in an earlier conversation that he wanted to make sure an attack like the ones on the Pentagon and World Trade Center never happened again. It was essential to think unconventionally. Now, Ashcroft was saying, the focus of the FBI and the Justice Department should change from prosecution to prevention, a radical shift in priorities.

After he finished with the NSC, Bush continued meeting with the half-dozen principals who comprised the war cabinet, without most of their deputies and aides.

Powell said the State Department was ready to carry the president's message—you're either with us or you're not—to Pakistan and the Taliban.

Bush responded that he wanted a list of demands for the Taliban. "Handing over bin Laden is not enough," he told Powell. He wanted the whole al Qaeda organization handed over or kicked out.

Rumsfeld interjected. "It is critical how we define goals at the start, because that's what the coalition signs on for," he said. Other countries would want precise definitions. "Do we focus on bin Laden and al Qaeda or terrorism more broadly?" he asked.

"The goal is terrorism in its broadest sense," Powell said, "focusing first on the organization that acted yesterday."

"To the extent we define our task broadly," Cheney said, "including those who support terrorism, then we get at states. And it's easier to find them than it is to find bin Laden."

"Start with bin Laden," Bush said, "which Americans expect. And then if we succeed, we've struck a huge blow and can move forward." He called the threat "a cancer" and added, "We don't want to define [it] too broadly for the average man to understand."

Bush pressed Rumsfeld on what the military could do immediately.

"Very little, effectively," the secretary replied.

Though Rumsfeld did not get into all the details, he was having a difficult time getting some military plans on his desk. General Tommy Franks, the commander in chief or CINC of the U.S. Central Command (CENTCOM), which was responsible for South Asia and the Middle East, had told him it would take months to get forces in the area and plans drawn up for a major military assault in Afghanistan.

"You don't have months," Rumsfeld had said. He wanted Franks to think days or weeks. Franks wanted bases and this and that. Afghanistan was halfway around the world. Al Qaeda was a guerrilla organization whose members lived in caves, rode mules and drove large sport-utility vehicles. Fearing a U.S. military strike, their training camps were virtually empty. Rumsfeld said he wanted creative ideas, something between launching cruise missiles and an all-out military operation. "Try again," Rumsfeld hammered.

Bush told his advisers what he had told British Prime Minister Tony Blair that morning in a secure phone call—that above all he wanted military action that would hurt the terrorists, not just make Americans feel better. He understood the need for planning and preparation but his patience had limits. "I want to get moving," he said.

Bush believed the Pentagon needed to be pushed. "They had yet to be challenged to think on how to fight a guerrilla war using conventional means," he recalled. "They had come out from an era of strike from afar—you know, cruise missiles into the thing."

He understood that his early actions on global climate change and national missile defense had rattled U.S. allies in Europe. America's friends feared the administration was infected with a new strain of unilateralism, a go-it-alone attitude, looking inward rather than engaging the world as the lone superpower might be expected to do.

In an interview, Bush later described how he believed the rest of the world saw him in the months leading up to the attacks of September 11. "Look," he said, "I'm the toxic Texan, right? In these people's minds, I'm the new guy. They don't know who I am. The imagery must be just unbelievable."

BEFORE 11 A.M., reporters were ushered into the Cabinet Room. Dressed in a dark blue suit, light blue dress shirt and blue striped tie, Bush sat slightly forward in his chair. He wanted to escalate his public rhetoric from the previous night.

"The deliberate and deadly attacks which were carried out yesterday against our country were more than acts of terror," he said. "They were acts of war."

He described the enemy as one America had never before encountered, an enemy who operated in the shadows, who preyed on innocent people, who hit and then ran for cover. "This is an enemy that tries to hide, but it won't be able to hide forever." The country would use all its resources to find those responsible. "We will rally the world. We will be patient, we will be focused, and we will be steadfast in our determination.

"This will be a monumental struggle between good and evil. But good will prevail."

MUCH OF THE work of assembling an international coalition was left to Powell, but Bush called Russian President Vladimir Putin and also spoke with the leaders of France, Germany, Canada and China.

"My attitude all along was, if we have to go it alone, we'll go it alone; but I'd rather not," Bush recalled.

At 11:30 A.M. the president met with the congressional leaders and told them, "The dream of the enemy was for us not to meet in this building. They wanted the White House in rubble." He warned of additional attacks. "This is not an isolated incident," he said. The public might lose focus. A month from now Americans will be watching football and the World Series. But the government would have to carry on the war indefinitely.

The enemy was not only a particular group, he said, but also "a frame of mind" that fosters hate. "They hate Christianity. They hate Judaism. They hate everything that is not them." Other nations, he added, would have to choose.

Senate Majority Leader Thomas A. Daschle, the South Dakota Democrat, cautioned the president to use care in his rhetoric. "War is a powerful word," he said. Daschle pledged bipartisan support but asked that the administration make Congress a full partner with ongoing consultations. During their first private meeting after Bush was declared the winner, the president-elect had surprised Daschle by saying, "I hope you'll never lie to me." Daschle had replied, "Well, I hope you'll never lie to me."

Near the end of the meeting, Senator Robert C. Byrd, the 83-year-old West Virginia Democrat president pro tempore of the Senate, took the floor and described his dealings with 10 presidents. He noted that Bush had said he did not want a declaration of war from the Congress but would be interested in a resolution endorsing the use of force. Byrd said Bush could not expect the kind of blank check Congress had given Lyndon Johnson in the Vietnam War with the 1964 Gulf of Tonkin resolution. We still have a Constitution, he said, pulling a copy from his pocket.

Byrd recalled the night he and his wife had dined with Bush at the White House. Bush had said grace before dinner, without asking. "It impressed me," Byrd said. The senator talked about Hollywood's negative influence on the culture, the slide America had taken toward permissiveness and materialism. "I'm praying for you," Byrd said. "Despite Hollywood and TV, there's an army of people who believe in divine guidance and the creator." His closing line brought silence to the room: "You stand there," he said. "Mighty forces will come to your aid."

That afternoon, Bush met privately with Bernadine Healy, the head of the American Red Cross, who said there was not enough blood if there was another terrorist attack.

"Keep collecting blood," the president said. "Get my drift?" He said he was not going to be on the run. "I'm in the Lord's hands." He had been told that an airliner flying up the Potomac River from National Airport could be steered off course and be at, and into, the White House in about 40 seconds. He had come to terms with that, he said.

· · ·

AT THE STATE Department, Richard Armitage was moving around his large suite of seventh floor offices like a fullback looking for a hole in the defensive line. President Bush had recently asked Armitage, who was well known for his obsessive weight lifting, what he was bench pressing these days. Armitage answered, "330/6," which meant 330 pounds, six repetitions in a row. At his peak, years earlier, Armitage had pressed 440.

That's good, the president had replied. I'm doing 205 pounds. Isn't that the best for any president?

Yes, Armitage had replied, he thought it must be.

Now, it was time for contact diplomacy. The president had declared the sweeping Bush Doctrine without formal input from State. The Pentagon was still burning; there was no time to coordinate with the other departments.

General Mahmoud Ahmad, the dignified-looking head of the Pakistani intelligence service, the ISI, was in Washington, by happenstance, visiting the CIA where he told Tenet and his deputies that Taliban leader Mullah Mohammad Omar was religious, a man of humanitarian instincts, not a man of violence, but one who had suffered greatly under the Afghan warlords.

"Stop!" the DDO Jim Pavitt said. "Spare me. Does Mullah Omar want the United States military to unleash its force against the Taliban? Do you want that to happen? Why would Mullah Omar want that to happen? Will you go ask him?"

Armitage invited Mahmoud to the State Department.

He began by saying it was not clear yet what the U.S. would ask of Pakistan but the requests would force "deep introspection. Pakistan faces a stark choice, either it is with us or it is not. This is a black and white choice with no gray."

Mahmoud said that his country had faced tough choices in the past but Pakistan was not a big or mighty power.

Pakistan is an important country, Armitage cut in.

Mahmoud returned to the past.

"The future begins today," Armitage said. Pass the word to General Musharraf, the Pakistani president—with us or against us.

• • •

AT 4 P.M., the NSC reconvened. The persistent question was the exact definition of the mission.

Rumsfeld insisted on a point he had made before. "Are we going against terrorism more broadly than just al Qaeda? Do we want to seek a broader basis for support?"

Bush again said his instinct was to start with bin Laden. If they could strike a blow against al Qaeda, everything that followed would be made easier. But Rumsfeld worried that a coalition built around the goal of taking out al Qaeda would fall apart once they succeeded in that mission, making it more difficult to continue the war on terrorism elsewhere.

Powell, agreeing with Bush, argued that it would be far easier initially to rally the world behind the specific target of al Qaeda. They could win approval of a broad U.N. resolution by keeping it focused on al Qaeda.

Cheney again focused on the question of state sponsorship of terrorism. To strike a blow against terrorism inevitably meant targeting the countries that nurture and export it, he said. In some ways the states were easier targets than the shadowy terrorists.

Bush worried about making their initial target too diffuse. Let's not make the target so broad that it misses the point and fails to draw support from normal Americans, he said. What Americans were feeling, he added, was that the country had suffered at the hands of al Qaeda.

Cheney countered that the coalition should be a means to wiping out terrorism, not an end in itself—a view that others shared. They wanted support from the rest of the world, but they did not want the coalition to tie their hands. The mission should define the coalition, not the other way around.

In that case, Rumsfeld argued, they wanted coalition partners truly committed to the cause, not reluctant participants.

Powell offered what one colleague later described as the "variable geometry" of coalition building. The coalition should be as broad as possible, but the requirements for participation would vary country by country. This would entail, as Rumsfeld put it, a coalition of coalitions.

Rumsfeld raised the question of Iraq. Why shouldn't we go against Iraq, not just al Qaeda? he asked. Rumsfeld was speaking not only for himself when he raised the question. His deputy, Paul D. Wolfowitz, was committed to a policy that would make Iraq a principal target of the first round in the war on terrorism.

Before the attacks, the Pentagon had been working for months on developing a military option for Iraq. Everyone at the table believed Iraqi President Saddam Hussein was a menace, a leader bent on acquiring and perhaps using weapons of mass destruction. Any serious, full-scale war against terrorism would have to make Iraq a target—eventually. Rumsfeld was raising the possibility that they could take advantage of the opportunity offered by the terrorist attacks to go after Saddam immediately.

Powell, who opposed striking Iraq at this point, countered that they were focusing on al Qaeda because the American people were focused on al Qaeda. "Any action needs public support. It's not just what the international coalition supports; it's what the American people want to support. The American people want us to do something about al Qaeda."

Bush made clear it was not the time to resolve the issue. He emphasized again that his principal goal was to produce a military plan that would inflict real pain and destruction on the terrorists.

"I don't want a photo-op war," he told them. He wanted "a realistic scorecard" and "a list of thugs" who would be targeted. Everyone was thinking about the Gulf War, he said, which was the wrong analogy. "The American people want a big bang," he said. "I have to convince them that this is a war that will be fought with many steps."

His reference was Vietnam, where the U.S. military had fought a conventional war against a guerrilla enemy. He later said he "instinctively knew that we were going to have to think differently" about how to fight terrorists. "The military strategy was going to take a while to unfold," he said. "I became frustrated."

LATER THAT AFTERNOON, Pavitt sent a second SECRET cable from CIA headquarters to all stations and bases around the world with the heading "Action Required: Your Thoughts."

The agency was continuing its massive worldwide effort to find the perpetrators of September 11, Pavitt wrote. "The CIA is also in the process of developing an unprecedented new covert action program with the clear goal of wreaking havoc upon and eliminating the sponsors and supporters of radical Islamic terrorism."

Pavitt pressed his clandestine officers in the Directorate of Operations, those on the street, closest to the action, to put forward their boldest, most radical thinking on how to conduct the massive terrorist manhunt. No restrictions. Think about "novel, untested ways" to accomplish the mission, he said.

"This covert action program will include paramilitary, logistical, and psychological warfare elements as well as classical espionage," the cable said. No holds barred, in other words.

The Directorate of Operations was back in business.

ABOUT 9:30 A.M., Thursday, September 13, the president met with the NSC in the White House Situation Room, one floor below the chief of staff's office in the southwest corner of the West Wing. Tenet brought counterterrorism chief Cofer Black to present more detail on the CIA proposals.

Tenet's concept called for bringing together expanded intelligence-gathering resources, sophisticated technology, agency paramilitary teams and opposition forces in Afghanistan in a classic covert action. They would then be combined with U.S. military power and Special Forces into an elaborate and lethal package designed to destroy the shadowy terrorist networks.

Tenet said the key concept was to fund and invigorate the Northern Alliance. The Alliance's roughly 20,000 fighters were decidedly a mixed bag dominated by five factions, but in reality probably 25 sub-factions. It was a strained coalition of sometimes common interests. The assassination two days before September 11 of its most charismatic leader, Ahmed Shah Massoud, was a major setback, leaving the Alliance more fractured than ever. But with the CIA teams and tons of money, the Alliance could be brought together into a cohesive fighting force, Tenet said.

The agency's paramilitary teams had periodically met clandestinely with Alliance leaders over the past four years. Tenet said he could insert paramilitary teams inside Afghanistan with each warlord. Along with Special Forces teams from the U.S. military, they would provide "eyes on the ground" for U.S. military bombing. American technological superiority could give the Northern Alliance a significant edge.

Cofer Black was next. Black had found at these meetings with the most senior officials that there was an unfortunate tendency to talk in generalities. They were not used to ordnance on target, so to speak, to hitting hard and directly. But he believed he knew what they craved.

He had a PowerPoint presentation and a narrative.

"Mr. President," he said, "we can do this. No doubt in my mind. We do this the way that we've outlined it, we'll set this thing up so it's an unfair fight for the U.S. military."

Black faced Bush, who was at the head of the table. "But you've got to understand, people are going to die. And the worst part about it, Mr. President, Americans are going to die—my colleagues and my friends.

"So there should be no misunderstanding that this is going to be a bloodless activity."

"That's war," Bush said.

"We've got to accept that we're going to lose people in this deal. How many, I don't know. Could be a lot."

"All right," the president said. "Let's go. That's war. That's what we're here to win."

Black was theatrical as he described the effectiveness of covert action. He kept popping up and down from his chair as he made his points, throwing paper onto the floor as he described putting forces on the ground in Afghanistan.

Black wanted the mission to begin as soon as possible. He had no doubt that it would succeed. "You give us the mission," he said, "we can get 'em." Echoing the president's public language about smoking out the terrorists from their caves, he said, "We'll rout 'em out."

Now, he noted, the desired end was to capture the al Qaeda and render them to law enforcement so they could be brought to justice. With regret, however, he had learned the al Qaeda do not surrender, and they would not negotiate. The great martyred Northern Alliance leader Massoud had once told him, "We've been fighting these guys for four years and I've never captured one of these bastards." The reason was that anytime one of their units was overrun, they bunched up together and detonated a hand grenade. So the task would be killing the al Qaeda, Black said.

"When we're through with them, they will have flies walking across their eyeballs," he said. It was an image of death that left a lasting impression on a number of war cabinet members. Black became known in Bush's inner circle as "the flies-on-the-eyeballs guy."

Black also said that they were going to have to go not only after al Qaeda but the Taliban because the two were joined at the hip. The CIA had been unable to come up with a covert action plan that, for love or money, would allow them to keep the Taliban at bay so the al Qaeda could be engaged.

How much do we know about the individual Northern Alliance leaders? Bush asked.

Black provided some thumbnail sketches, and then noted some glaring weaknesses too, to show that the agency wasn't all rosy scenario. One key Alliance general, Abdurrashid Dostum, had been on everyone's payroll—Russia, Iran and Pakistan.

Bush asked how long it would take to get the paramilitary teams inside Afghanistan.

Pretty quick, Black said. It would be escalatory—once one team was in, the second would follow more easily and so forth.

"How long will it take?" the president asked—the "it" meant victory.

Once we're on the ground, Black said, it should go in weeks.

No one else in the room, including Tenet, believed that was possible.

It was nonetheless a memorable performance, and it had a huge effect on the president. For two days Bush had expressed in the most direct way possible his determination to track down and destroy the terrorists. Now, for the first time, he was being told without reservation that there was a way to do this, that he did not have to wait indefinitely, that the agency had a plan.

Black's enthusiasm was infectious, though certainly optimistic. It would never be as quick or as simple as he made it sound, but at that moment it was what the president wanted to hear. It also sounded logical—using the CIA, the Northern Alliance and the American military as a kind of triad.

Powell, for one, saw that Bush was tired of rhetoric. The president wanted to kill somebody.

"It became clear to me that we were going to be able to fight a different war than the Russians fought," Bush commented later. Invading Afghanistan with a traditional army, as the Soviet Union had unsuccessfully done in the 1980s, would not be the United States's only military option. "I was impressed by their [the CIA's] knowledge of the area. We've had assets there for a long period of time. They had worked, had been thinking through things."

• • •

SHORTLY BEFORE 11 A.M., White House aides ushered the press pool into the Oval Office for a scheduled conference call with New York Mayor Rudolph W. Giuliani and New York Governor George E. Pataki.

The previous day, the White House communications team, Hughes and company, had decided to televise the conversation. They wanted the president to be seen reaching out to the families of the thousands of victims who had died when the towers collapsed, as well as the rescue workers who were struggling around the clock in a desperate search for survivors. Since Bush didn't plan to get to New York that week, the televised conference call was seen as the next best gesture.

When he got on the phone, however, Bush told the mayor and governor that he would fly to New York the next afternoon, immediately after a prayer service at Washington National Cathedral.

Bush appeared uncomfortable, almost distracted as he talked on the televised conference call. "I wish I was visiting under better circumstances," he said in closing. "But it will be a chance for all three of us to thank and hug and cry with the citizens of your good area." When the call was over, Bush decided to take questions from the reporters who were standing only a few feet away.

"Mr. President," one asked, "could you give us a sense as to what kind of prayers you are thinking and where your heart is, for yourself, as you—"

"Well I don't think about myself right now," Bush said, and it was instantly obvious that he was struggling with his emotions. "I think about the families, the children." He turned his head and his eyes filled with tears.

"I am a loving guy," he said, as he started to regain his composure, but only partially, "and I am also someone, however, who has got a job to do, and I intend to do it. And this is a terrible moment. But this country will not relent until we have saved ourselves and others from the terrible tragedy that came upon America."

Still with tears in his eyes, Bush ended the session with a slight nod of his head, and the pool reporters were escorted out.

"Presidents don't particularly like to cry in front of the American public, particularly in the Oval Office, but nevertheless I did," Bush said later. But he believed his "mood reflected the country in many ways. People in our country felt the same way I did."

The public tears were perhaps very important. For two days Bush had been responding as president, genuinely but still within the norms of expected presidential behavior. It was perhaps too detached and impersonal. What he had been saying didn't seem quite like him. He had assumed the aura of president, had imposed it on himself. Standing there in the Oval Office and crying made it clear that human emotions trumped even the office of president.

BEFORE NOON, BUSH left with his wife for a tour of the burn unit at Washington Hospital Center, where some survivors from the Pentagon attack were being treated. Men and women were bathed in oils and swathed in bandages, some almost unrecognizable. Many who were burned over large percentages of their bodies talked about crawling through fire.

It was another emotional wallop, and at about 12:30 P.M. when his limousine pulled into the White House driveway, the president was in no mood for quibbles. Before he could get out of the car, Andy Card put his hands up, motioning the president back down in his seat.

"Mr. President," Card said, "sit back down for a minute. I've got to tell you something." He climbed into the back seat next to Bush and closed the door.

"We've got another threat on the White House," the chief of staff said. "We're taking it seriously." The CIA had just sent over a warning from the Indian intelligence service saying that Pakistani jihadists—Muslim extremists—were planning an imminent attack on the White House.

"Why are you telling me in here?" snapped Bush, irritated that Card had unnecessarily risked a scene that could be observed by the press pool just down the driveway. "You could have waited until I got into the Oval Office."

Bush stepped out of the car, and he and Card walked directly to the Oval Office, where Secret Service Director Stafford and the head of Bush's personal Secret Service detail were waiting for them.

"We need to evacuate you," Stafford said. The threat was credible and consistent with other intelligence that established an immediate danger. The Indian intelligence service was well wired into Pakistan. Stafford wanted to take Bush to the Presidential Emergency Operations Center, the bunker beneath the White House.

"I'm not leaving," Bush said. He wanted more information if they got it. For now, he wasn't going anywhere. "And by the way," he added to no one in particular, "I'm hungry." He located Ferdinand Garcia, the Navy steward on duty in the West Wing. "Ferdie," he said, "I want a hamburger."

Card knew that Bush was a bit of a fatalist. If something was going to happen they could only do so much. And hiding in the bunker was just not an option. Prior to the attacks, Bush had been eating lighter—fruit and other healthy foods—to lose weight.

"Well," said Hughes upon hearing the hamburger order, "you might as well have cheese."

RICE HAD JOINED the group and they all agreed that, even if the president wasn't prepared to leave, they had an obligation to the rest of the employees in the White House. Many on the staff, particularly some of the younger, lower-level aides, were still suffering from anxiety after the trauma of September 11, when the White House had been evacuated.

The president and his advisers decided they should allow all nonessential employees to go home that afternoon. Card relayed the information at a senior staff meeting and announced that the Secret Service would implement additional measures to protect the building, such as expanding the secure perimeter around the White House complex.

Card said the vice president would be moved to an undisclosed location as a precaution against having the president and vice president together in the event of another attack. Continuity in government—ensuring the survival of someone in the constitutional line of succession to the presidency—was an essential priority.

The decision to move Cheney was the clearest indication of how seriously they were taking the threats of another attack. It would lead to questions about the vice president's whereabouts and his health—he had had four heart attacks—but he insisted on staying away from the White House when threats were high.

"We have got the responsibility to make sure that the government can go on," Cheney told the president.

5

At the State Department, Powell and Armitage were focused on Pakistan—the linchpin for any strategy to isolate and eventually attack al Qaeda and the Taliban in Afghanistan. Pakistan was one of only two major nations in the world that formally recognized the Taliban as the official government of Afghanistan. The radical Islamic movement had a substantial following within its borders.

The United States did not have good relations with General Pervez Musharraf, who had come to power in a bloodless military coup in 1999, one year after the U.S. had imposed sanctions on Pakistan for conducting a nuclear test.

Powell had already told Bush that whatever action he took, it could not be done without Pakistan's support. So the Pakistanis had to be put on notice. Squeezing Musharraf too hard was risky, but not squeezing him at all was riskier. Powell had in mind a pitcher's brushback pitch to a particularly dangerous batter—high, fast and hard to the head.

"Do what you have to do," the president had said.

Let's make it up, Powell said to Armitage. What do we want out of these guys?

They started a list:

First: "Stop al Qaeda operatives at your border, intercept arms shipments through Pakistan and end ALL logistical support for bin Laden."

Second: "Blanket overflight and landing rights."

Third: Access to Pakistan, naval bases, air bases and borders.

Fourth: Immediate intelligence and immigration information.

Fifth: Condemn the September 11 attacks and "curb all domestic expressions of support for terrorism against the [United States], its friends or allies." Powell and Armitage knew that was something they couldn't even do in the United States.

Sixth: Cut off all shipments of fuel to the Taliban and stop Pakistani volunteers from going into Afghanistan to join the Taliban.

The seventh demand was the one that Powell thought would trip up the Pakistanis or cause Musharraf to balk: "Should the evidence strongly implicate Osama bin Laden and the al Qaeda network in Afghanistan AND should Afghanistan and the Taliban continue to harbor him and this network, Pakistan will break diplomatic relations with the Taliban government, end support for the Taliban and assist us in the aforementioned ways to destroy Osama bin Laden and his al Qaeda network."

In so many words, Powell and Armitage would be asking Pakistan to help destroy what its intelligence service had helped create and maintain: the Taliban.

Armitage called the Pakistani intelligence chief, General Mahmoud, with whom he had met the previous day, and invited him to the State Department.

This is not negotiable, Armitage told the general, handing him a single sheet of paper with the seven demands. You must accept all seven parts.

At 1:30 P.M. Powell called Musharraf. "As one general to another," he said, "we need someone on our flank fighting with us. Speaking candidly, the American people would not understand if Pakistan was not in this fight with the United States."

Musharraf to Powell's surprise said that Pakistan would support the United States with each of the seven actions.

• • •

THE PENTAGON PRESS briefing that day was conducted by Deputy Defense Secretary Paul Wolfowitz, who had been a senior defense official under Cheney during the first Bush administration. Wolfowitz often voiced the views of an outspoken group of national security conservatives in Washington, many of them veterans of the Reagan and senior Bush administrations. These were men who believed that there was no greater menace in the world than Iraqi President Saddam Hussein, and they argued that if the president was serious about going after those who harbor terrorists, he had to put Hussein at the top of that list.

Iraq posed nearly as serious a problem for the president and his team as Afghanistan, they held. If Saddam, a wily and unpredictable survivor, decided to launch a terrorist attack or even a limited military strike on U.S. facilities after September 11 and the president had failed to move against him, the recriminations might never end.

Rumsfeld had raised Iraq during the previous day's national security meetings with the president. Now Wolfowitz wanted to issue a public warning to terrorist states. It was another effort to prod the president to include Iraq in his first round of targets.

"It's not just simply a matter of capturing people," he said, "and holding them accountable, but removing the sanctuaries, removing the support systems, ending states who sponsor terrorism.

"It will be a campaign, not a single action. And we're going to keep after these people and the people who support them until it stops."

In a benign reading, this was merely a more provocative restatement of the Bush Doctrine from the night of September 11. Wolfowitz wasn't really innovating but he did get his tongue twisted. His comment would be big headlines and certain to alarm many U.S. allies. "Ending states who sponsor terrorism"—regime change—was implied in what Bush had said, but not explicitly stated.

Powell publicly distanced himself. "Ending terrorism is where I would like to leave it, and let Mr. Wolfowitz speak for himself," he said.

Army General Hugh Shelton, who would be chairman of the Joint Chiefs of Staff for another two weeks before Myers took over, firmly opposed bringing Iraq into the military equation at this early stage. In his analysis, the only justification for going after Iraq would be clear evidence linking the Iraqis to the September 11 attacks. Short of that, targeting Iraq was not worth the risk of angering moderate Arab states whose support was crucial not only to any campaign in Afghanistan, but to reviving the Middle East peace process.

Earlier in the week, Powell had approached Shelton and rolled his eyes after Rumsfeld had raised Iraq as a potential target.

"What the hell, what are these guys thinking about?" asked Powell, who had held Shelton's job as chairman of the Joint Chiefs. "Can't you get these guys back in the box?"

Shelton could not have agreed more. He had been trying, arguing practicalities and priorities, but Wolfowitz was fiercely determined and committed.

AT THE NATIONAL Security Council meeting that afternoon in the Situation Room, the president said he was going to approve the CIA proposal for an expanded covert operation to give paramilitary and financial support to the Northern Alliance.

"I'd like to tell you what we told the Pakistanis today," Powell said, getting out a copy of the seven demands he had presented to them. He knew the president didn't like to sit still for long readings, but he was proud of what they had done unencumbered by a long interagency debate. So he read the seven demands aloud. When he finished, Powell reported that Musharraf had already accepted them.

"It looks like you got it all," the president said. He thought it was the State Department at its best, no striped-pants formality.

"Can I have a copy of that?" some of the others asked.

Treasury Secretary Paul H. O'Neill reported on the effort to draft an executive order to allow Treasury to go after the finances of the terrorists. In pre–September 11 deliberations about what to do with bin Laden during the spring and summer, Treasury officials had resisted efforts to go after terrorists' financial assets, and there was continuing institutional resistance to imposing sanctions. The chief problem was that many terrorist groups used private charitable organizations as cover, and the effort to freeze their assets could make the United States look punitive, bring loud protests and the threat of lawsuits.

Bush noted that some bureaucrats were nervous about this new authority but he dismissed concerns that the moves might be unsettling to the international financial order. "This is war, this isn't peace. Do it. [Bin Laden] needs money and we need to know whoever is giving him money and deal with them."

Shelton offered a pessimistic assessment of the immediate military options. The contingency plans on the shelf were only cruise missiles against training camps. "It's just digging holes," he said.

Rumsfeld said they needed new tasks for the military if they wanted to go after states harboring bin Laden. "We've never done that before."

Bush was concerned that the war cabinet had not had sufficient time to really debate and evaluate their course of action, consider the options and plans. The NSC meetings were too rushed and short, sometimes lasting 60 to 90 minutes, sometimes much less. His time was being chopped into small pieces to accommodate the demands of both his private and public roles in the crisis. They had not had time to chew on the issue the way he wanted, so he asked his advisers to come to Camp David with their spouses that weekend.

"This is a new world," Bush said insistently. "General Shelton should go back to the generals for new targets. Start the clock. This is an opportunity. I want a plan—costs, time. I need options on the table. I want Afghan options by Camp David. I want decisions quick."

Rumsfeld was trying to push the Pentagon, and he applauded Bush's decisiveness and sense of urgency, but he reminded the president of the embarrassments of some earlier attacks—the bombing of the Chinese Embassy in Belgrade during the 1999 Kosovo conflict, the missile attack on the Sudan chemical plant in 1998 that was part of an unsuccessful operation on bin Laden.

"We owe you what can go wrong," Rumsfeld said, "things that can take wind out of our sails. For example, hitting camps with no people."

"Tell the Afghans to round up al Qaeda," Bush said. "Let's see them, or we'll hit them hard. We're going to hurt them bad so that everyone in the world sees, don't deal with bin Laden. I don't want to put a million-dollar missile on a five-dollar tent."

A note-taker at the meeting wrote down snatches of dialogue that captured the sense of urgency and the lack of focus, a blizzard of random ideas.

"We need new options," Rumsfeld said at one point. "This is a new mission."

The president seemed to agree. "Everything is on the table," Bush said. "Look at the options." He also said that the British really wanted to participate. "Give them a role. Time is of the essence. By the time we get to Camp David, we need a clear timetable for action—but I want to do something effective."

IT WAS ABOUT midnight that third night of the crisis when Rice finally returned home to her apartment at the Watergate. She had spent the first night of the crisis at the White House in fitful sleep. Wednesday night's sleep had been no better. She had been operating, like everyone, on adrenaline. Now she had a few moments at home to unwind. She flipped on her television for the first time since the crisis began, and the screen showed a familiar scene—the changing of the guard at Buckingham Palace in London. But it was the music that caught her attention. In a gesture of solidarity and sympathy with the United States, the band of the Coldstream Guards was playing "The Star-Spangled Banner." Rice listened for a few seconds, and then she started to weep.

EARLY THE MORNING of Friday, September 14, a mid-level officer at the National Military Command Center, the Pentagon war room, called the White House to confirm that the president did not want a fighter escort accompanying Air Force One when he flew to New York that afternoon.

Rice, her deputy, Steve Hadley, and White House Chief of Staff Card conferred. It had to be Rumsfeld's decision, they all agreed. The threat conditions were still off the charts, and no one knew what might be out there. If something happened because there was no fighter escort, it would be Rumsfeld who would have to explain to the country, and the world.

One of Rice's deputies called the Pentagon and the issue was presented to Rumsfeld that the NMCC had called the White House to ask about fighter escort.

Rumsfeld went nuts. Somebody in my building is talking to the White House without my knowledge or permission, he vented. "I will not have that!" Rumsfeld was under immense pressure. He had no military plans and the president was going to war. A search was immediately launched to identify the officer who had called the White House. In the meantime, Rumsfeld refused to address the question of whether he was going to put a fighter escort on Air Force One.

THAT MORNING THE full cabinet, meeting at the White House for the first time since the terrorist attacks, stood and applauded when the president entered the room. Caught by surprise, Bush choked up for a moment, the second time in two days he had lost his composure in front of others.

Bush liked to open every cabinet meeting with a prayer, and he had asked Rumsfeld to prepare one for this gathering. Among the things Rumsfeld prayed for was the "patience to measure our lust for action."

Powell was worried about Bush's show of emotion. In a few hours, the president would be speaking at Washington National Cathedral, and Powell thought the country and the world needed to see a strong president. Sitting by tradition as senior member of the cabinet next to the president, he jotted a note. Dear Mr. President, what I do when I have to give a speech like this, I avoid those words I know will cause me to well up such as Mom and Pop. Then, with some trepidation, he slid the note along the table.

Bush picked up the piece of paper, read it, and smiled. "Let me tell you what the secretary of state told me," Bush said, holding up the note. "Dear Mr. President, don't break down!" The room erupted in laughter, shared by both Powell and the president.

"Don't worry, I've got it out of my system," Bush said. He assured them that he and the war cabinet were developing plans for a military response that would be effective, and then went around the table asking for updates.

Powell described the diplomatic offensive. Like the president, Powell saw the attacks as an opportunity to reshape relationships throughout the world. But, he told the cabinet, this was coalition building with clear definitions of what was expected from the partners, including sharing intelligence, freezing the terrorists' finances and assistance in the military campaign.

"This is not just an attack against America, this is an attack against civilization and an attack against democracy," Powell said, sounding presidential. "This is a long war, and it's a war we have to win. We are engaging with the world. We want to make this a long-standing coalition."

By that morning, Powell had made 35 calls to world leaders,

with another 12 ahead of him that day. "I have been so multilateral the last few days, I'm getting seasick," he joked.

There was laughter.

Rumsfeld updated the group on the damage to the Pentagon and announced that the military alert status had been reduced one notch, to DefCon 4. On September 11, the Pentagon had moved to DefCon 3 for the first time since the 1973 Arab-Israeli war. The highest possible alert status, DefCon 1, is used in time of all-out war.

Transportation Secretary Norman Y. Mineta said air travel was resuming that day but at just 16 percent the normal rate, a measure of the impact of the attacks.

Bush concluded with a reminder that while the focus of the administration now was the war on terrorism, they should not ignore domestic priorities such as an education bill, a patients' bill of rights and legislation giving him greater authority to negotiate trade agreements.

AROUND LUNCHTIME, THE presidential motorcade left the White House in a driving rain for a ride of about 12 minutes north to the National Cathedral.

An extraordinary group waited at the cathedral for the service. The speakers included a Protestant minister, a rabbi, a Catholic cardinal, a Muslim cleric and the Reverend Billy Graham. Former Presidents Bill Clinton and Jimmy Carter were there, as was former Vice President Al Gore. The audience included the cabinet, much of the Senate, many members of the House, Federal Reserve Chairman Alan Greenspan and many other top officials. Seated next to the president and his wife were his mother and father.

Condi Rice thought the trip to the cathedral had been like a funeral procession. When opera singer Denyce Graves led the congregation in singing the Lord's Prayer, she wondered, How is he going to hold together after that?

"We are here in the middle hour of our grief," Bush began. So many suffered so great a loss from the attacks, he said, and the nation would linger over them and learn their stories and weep. "But our responsibility to history is already clear: To answer these attacks and rid the world of evil." The president was casting his mission and that of the country in the grand vision of God's master plan.

"It is said that adversity introduces us to ourselves." He spoke of the acts of bravery and sacrifice that showed Americans' commitment to one another and love for their country. "Today we feel what Franklin Roosevelt called the warm courage of national unity," a unity that was a "kinship of grief and a steadfast resolve to prevail against our enemies."

There was much in the speech intended to comfort, but the most memorable line—which had originated with his team of speechwriters and was quickly adopted by the president—came when Bush spoke confidently about what was to come. "This conflict was begun on the timing and terms of others," he said. "It will end in a way, and at an hour, of our choosing."

A war speech in a cathedral was jarring, even risky, but it delivered the message Bush wanted. When he returned to his seat in the front row, his father reached across Laura Bush and squeezed his son's hand.

At the end of the service, the congregation stood and sang "The Battle Hymn of the Republic." Rice felt the whole church stiffen with determination.

When the presidential party walked out of the cathedral, the grayness and rain of the morning had lifted, replaced by brilliant sunshine and blue skies.

Bush would recall the speech as less a pivot point toward war than a religious expression. "I saw it as a moment to make sure that I helped comfort and helped get through the mourning process," he said. "I also really looked at it from a spiritual perspective, that it was important for the nation to pray." He agreed that some of the language was "very tough," and said it "reflected my mood." But he added, "To me, the moment was more, it really was a prayer. I didn't view it as an opportunity to set the stage for a future speech. I believed that the nation needed to be in prayer."

THE PENTAGON WAS still waiting for Rumsfeld's decision about whether to send a fighter escort with the president, who was going to leave soon for New York City. The secretary was stewing. He saw it as an issue that went right to the heart of the chain of command and his legal authority. Information regularly flows between the Pentagon and the White House, but the decision to deploy forces, even a fighter escort, is his alone by law. "The national command authority is the president to me," Rumsfeld said later. "And to the extent you get people down below sending instructions into the building that people then act off of, then the president can't be sure that, that the actions are going to be consonant with what he's wanted me to do.

"And to the extent people talk to other people and someone then says, 'Oh, let's send up an escort or let's send up a CAP [Combat Air Patrol] or let's not,' it may very well be completely opposite of what the president wants or of what I want. . . . This is something you do not want to mess around with."

About 15 minutes before Air Force One left, the secretary gave his order. There would be an escort.

He then turned to editing the draft of the TOP SECRET intelligence order that the CIA wanted the president to sign. In his view, it was sloppy and carelessly done. The language was vague and open-ended, the authority too broad and sweeping. He marked up his copy with proposed revisions, cuts and clarifications. Authority that ought to be reserved for the president or the CIA director was being given to subordinates.

• • •

"DO YOU SMELL something?" Hughes asked as a helicopter carrying White House staff members approached New York on the final leg of the trip. They were 20 or 25 miles from Lower Manhattan.

The others nodded. Press secretary Ari Fleischer thought it must be from the helicopter. But looking out their windows to one side, they saw a giant plume of smoke. What they smelled was the burning rubble of the World Trade Center.

The helicopters put down at the Wall Street heliport, and an enormous motorcade—55 vehicles, the largest motorcade that anybody on the presidential advance team had ever seen—was formed. The president drove past cheering, flag-waving crowds to Ground Zero.

For Bush, the sight of the enormous, dark wasteland of wreckage left an indelible impression, one that he would recall as "very, very, very eerie." Though he had talked with many others about the devastation, he still was not prepared for what he found. It was "a nightmare, a living nightmare." Along with destruction far worse than anything he had seen on television or heard about from his advisers, he encountered a crowd of rescue workers hungry for revenge. It was an "unbelievably emotional" crowd demanding justice, he recalled.

As he walked through the area, the president faced a wild scene. "I cannot describe to you how emotional" the workers were. "Whatever it takes," they shouted.

One pointed to him as he walked by and yelled out: "Don't let me down." Bush was stunned. He thought that the words and look on the man's face would perhaps stay with him forever—"Don't let *me* down." This was so personal, he thought. It was as if he were in some ancient arena. The rescue workers began chanting "U-S-A, U-S-A, U-S-A."

"They want to hear him," Nina Bishop, a member of the advance team, shouted at Karl Rove as the president was working his way through the crowd. "They want to hear their president!"

For once, the ever-ready White House communications team

was totally unprepared. Since there was no plan for Bush to address the group, there was no sound system. Could she find a bullhorn, Rove asked.

Nearby, Bob Beckwith, a somewhat frail-looking 69-year-old retired New York firefighter, stood on a charred fire truck that had been pulled from the rubble. A Bush aide asked him if the president could use it as a platform and if Beckwith, a gas mask dangling around his neck, could bounce up and down on it a few times to make certain it was stable. At the base of the fire truck was a large slab of paving or concrete. Some in the advance team thought they should move it, until rescue workers told them there might be human remains underneath.

At 4:40 P.M., someone placed a white bullhorn in the president's hands and helped him up on the wreckage. Beckwith wanted to step down but Bush asked that he stay by his side. Another round of chants began: "U-S-A, U-S-A."

"Thank you all," Bush began. "I want you all to know . . ." and the gigantic canyon of rubble and humanity seemed to swallow up the words from his tinny bullhorn.

"Can't hear you," a rescue worker shouted.

"I can't go any louder," Bush said with a laugh. "America today is on bended knee in prayer for the people whose lives were lost here. . . ." Another voice erupted from the crowd: "I can't hear you." Bush paused for an instant, then with his arm around Beckwith's shoulder, shouted back: "I can hear you. The rest of the world hears you. And the people who knocked these buildings down will hear all of us soon!"

Hughes, off to the side, was absolutely beaming. This was an amazing moment, she thought—eloquent, simple, the perfect backdrop, a moment for the news magazine covers, the communications hall of fame and for history. And she had had nothing to do with it.

• • •

AFTER A BRIEF stop to allow the president to thank teams of work-ers, the motorcade rolled up the West Side Highway to the Jacob K. Javits Convention Center, which was being used as a staging ground for the rescue efforts. The president's schedule called for him to spend 30 to 45 minutes with families of the victims. It was to be private—no press, no photographers, not even members of the congressional delegation that accompanied Bush.

The organizers had used draperies to turn a cavernous room into a more intimate area, and Bush's aides set up a human wall to give the group even more privacy. About 250 people awaited the president, many carrying photographs of missing relatives. Children now without a parent clutched teddy bears and other mementos.

The families applauded the arrival of the president, then sud-denly it was so silent that only the ventilation system could be heard whirring. It was a potentially awkward moment for Bush, who wasn't sure how to approach the families. Finally, he waded into the crowd. "Tell me about yourself," he said to one person, and then another and another. Each time he heard the same story. It was a crushing realization. Each of them, he recalled, "believed that their loved one was still alive."

They wanted autographs and Bush began to sign his name to photos or pieces of paper or treasured items. He would say to the families, he recalled, " 'I'm going to tell you something, I'm going to sign this, and when you see Jim, or you see Bill, you tell them this is truly my autograph, that you didn't make this up.' And that's the only way I knew how to help, just use that moment to be able to say, 'I share your hope too, and we pray Jim comes out.' "

Many in the room were weeping. The president was teary-eyed as he made his way from one family to the next. One man, cradling a child in his arms, was carrying a picture of his brother, a fire-fighter who had been killed. The child pointed at the photograph and said simply, "My uncle." An hour or so into the session, Bush seemed to regain some of his buoyancy. There were bursts of laugh-ter from some of the relatives as he continued, for two hours, to move among them. He spoke with every family. Toward the end of his visit, Bush met Arlene Howard, the mother of George Howard, an off-duty Port Authority policeman who was killed attempting to save others. She was carrying her son's police shield and she offered it to the president, asking him to take it in her son's honor. The president accepted the shield.

On the way back to the heliport, Bush's motorcade drove through Times Square, which was filled with people holding candles and American flags and applauding as the cars passed by. Back at McGuire Air Force Base in New Jersey, a spent Bush parted with his staff who were returning to Washington.

If it was possible to live a whole life in a single day, this was the day.

INSTEAD OF BOARDING Air Force One, Bush climbed aboard a C-20 aircraft small enough to land in Hagerstown, Maryland. From there he would head for Camp David. The video of the president emerging from his helicopter shows him dead tired, drained, almost staggering.

The president had asked his most senior national security advisers—Cheney, Powell, Rumsfeld and Rice—to go to Camp David ahead of him to prepare for the next day's meeting. They gathered in the vice president's cabin to eat a dinner of buffalo.

The dinner gave them the chance to compare notes in a more relaxed setting, to update each other and tee up the issues for the meetings the next day. They talked about the continuing pressure for speedy action, about the length of the struggle ahead and the differences between the coming conflict and the Persian Gulf War, when there was a long buildup and a relatively short military campaign—38 days of massive bombing and a four-day ground war. This would be the opposite, they thought, and the more they talked, the more they realized how much harder this war would be and how enormous the consequences would be if they got it wrong.

Powell thought it was like a rehearsal dinner the night before a wedding, but one that concealed some serious differences within the family.

When Bush got to his cabin, he checked in with Rice, who reported that there were no significant new developments. After a day in the public spotlight as mourner in chief, he was about to begin the most critical discussions he would have with his war cabinet. In his own mind, he had already come to some conclusions.

"What was decided was that this is the primary focus of this administration," he recalled later. "What was decided is, it doesn't matter to me how long it takes, we're going to rout out terror wherever it may exist. What was decided was, the doctrine is, if you harbor them, feed them, house them, you're just as guilty, and you will be held to account. What was decided was that . . . this war will be fought on many fronts, including the intelligence side, the financial side, the diplomatic side, as well as the military side. What was decided is, is that we're going to hit them with all we've got in a smart way."

Bush knew there was much still to be addressed. "What wasn't decided was, was the team stitched up to the same strategy, did the team sign off on it? Because one of the things I know that can happen is, if everybody is not on the same page, then you're going to have people peeling off and second-guessing and the process will not, will really not unfold the way it should, there won't be honest discussion."

These were the team management problems, but far more than that was before the president. He had been swimming in a sea of broad concepts and rhetoric, fueled by the rawness, the surprise and the carnage of the terrorist attacks and by his own instincts. The real gut calls in the presidency get down to when and where and how to use force—both covert action and military strikes, putting ordnance on target. There would be times the next day when Bush's advisers wondered if they would ever find a way to end the talking—to emerge from the sea of words and pull the trigger.

6

THE PRESIDENT WAS on a war footing when he walked into Camp David's Laurel Lodge early Saturday morning, September 15, but first he was going to have to listen and make sure he was decisive without being rash.

"One way you're not impulsive," he explained later, "is to make sure you listen to an experienced group of national security advisers." He saw his advisers as a useful check on his own inclinations. "If I have any genius or smarts, it's the ability to recognize talent, ask them to serve and work with them as a team." By conservative count, the team together had close to 100 years of full-time experience dealing with national security. The president had not even a year.

"When they give advice," he said, "I trust their judgment. Now sometimes the advice isn't always the same, in which case my job—the job is to grind through these problems, and grind through scenarios, and hopefully reach a consensus of six or seven smart people, which makes my job easy."

He was about to find out that, indeed, the advice might not only be different, but that it could come dressed in language that was not always straightforward. He also was going to see that grinding through was not always easy.

He had been up about four hours, when at 9:19 A.M., he invited reporters into the conference room to tell them how little he would have to say in public. "This is an administration that will not talk about how we gather intelligence, how we know what we're going to do, nor what our plans are."

The war cabinet filed into the wood-paneled conference room and took their seats around the large table that accommodates about two dozen people. Tenet had brought his deputy, John E. McLaughlin, and counterterrorism chief, Cofer Black. Rumsfeld had brought his deputy, Paul Wolfowitz. Powell had understood it was supposed to be principals only so he did not have Armitage with him. All were dressed informally, many wearing jackets because of the chilly temperature. Bush, in a blue shirt and green bomber jacket, sat front and center, flanked on his right by Cheney and his left by Powell. Rumsfeld sat next to Powell.

They began with a prayer, and routine updates from Powell and Treasury Secretary O'Neill.

Tenet spoke next. The CIA director had come to Camp David carrying a briefcase stuffed with TOP SECRET documents and plans, more than four years of work on bin Laden, al Qaeda and worldwide terrorism. He distributed a briefing packet with the attention-grabbing title "Going to War." In the upper-left-hand corner was a picture of bin Laden inside a red circle with a slash superimposed over his face, the CIA's adaptation of the universal symbol of prohibition.

Tenet flipped open to the first page, "Initial Hook: Destroying al Qaeda, Closing the Safe Haven"—Afghanistan, bin Laden's operating base and home. CIA paramilitary teams would be deployed with the Northern Alliance. They could eventually link up with U.S. military Special Forces units, bringing firepower and technology to the opposition fighters in Afghanistan to create a northern front.

The plan called for a full-scale covert attack on the financial underpinnings of the terrorist network, including clandestine computer surveillance and electronic eavesdropping to locate the assets of al Qaeda and other terrorist groups that were hidden and laundered among various charitable fronts and so-called nongovernmental organizations, NGOs.

Another component was titled "CIA, FBI Focus on the Large Afghan Community in the U.S." The CIA and FBI would coordinate to track down and smoke out bin Laden supporters—a clear, glaring weakness before the attacks.

Tenet referred to propaganda efforts, mentioning that they had some mullahs on the payroll.

At the heart of the proposal was a recommendation that the president give what Tenet labeled "exceptional authorities" to the CIA to destroy al Qaeda in Afghanistan and the rest of the world. He wanted a broad intelligence order permitting the CIA to conduct covert operations without having to come back for formal approval for each specific operation. The current process involved too much time, lawyering, reviews and debate. The CIA needed new, robust authority to operate without restraint. Tenet also wanted encouragement from the president to take risks.

Another key component, he said, was to "use exceptional authorities to detain al Qaeda operatives worldwide." That meant the CIA could use foreign intelligence services or other paid assets. Tenet and his senior deputies would be authorized to approve "snatch" operations abroad, truly exceptional power.

Tenet had brought a draft of a presidential intelligence order, called a finding, that would give the CIA power to use the full range of covert instruments, including deadly force. For more than two decades, the CIA had simply modified previous presidential findings to obtain its formal authority for counterterrorism. His new proposal, technically called a Memorandum of Notification, was presented as a modification to the worldwide counterterrorism intelligence finding signed by President Reagan in 1986. As if symbolically erasing the recent past, it superseded five such memoranda signed by President Clinton.

The CIA chief came to a page headed "Heavily Subsidize Arab Liaison Services." He explained that with the additional hundreds of millions of dollars for new covert action, the CIA would "buy" key intelligence services, providing training, new equipment, money for their agent networks, whatever they might need. Several intelligence services were listed: Egypt, Jordan, Algeria. Acting as surrogates for the United States, these services could triple or quadruple the CIA's resources, an extended mercenary force of intelligence operatives.

Like much in the world of covert activity, such arrangements carried risks. It would put the United States in league with questionable intelligence services, some of them with dreadful human rights records. Some had reputations for ruthlessness and using torture to obtain confessions. Tenet acknowledged that these were not people you were likely to be sitting next to in church on Sunday. Look, I don't control these guys all the time, he said.

Bush said he understood the risks.

Tenet added that the United States already had a "large asset base" in the region, given the work the CIA had been doing in countries near Afghanistan. The agency had been operating un-manned aerial vehicles—the so-called Predator drones—on surveillance missions out of Uzbekistan for more than a year to provide real-time video of Afghanistan. The Predator could be equipped with remotely controlled Hellfire missiles and used for lethal missions too, to take out bin Laden or his top lieutenants for example.

The United States should seek to work closely with Tajikistan, Turkmenistan and Pakistan, Tenet said, to stop the travel of al Qaeda leaders and "close all border crossings" to them. He called for initiating intelligence contact with some rogue states such as Libya and Syria that he said might be helpful in trying to destroy al Qaeda. For the CIA to obtain helpful information against the terrorists, they might have to get their hands dirty.

Tenet turned to operations within Afghanistan. He described a role for the opposition tribes in the southern part of Afghanistan, groups hostile to the Northern Alliance but crucial to a campaign against al Qaeda and the Taliban. The CIA had begun working with about a dozen tribal leaders in the south the previous year. Some would try to play both sides, he said, but once the war began, they could be enticed by money, food, ammunition and supplies to join the U.S.-led campaign.

Tenet then expanded on his earlier briefing to the president about how they could effectively employ the Northern Alliance, which the CIA believed was potentially a powerful force but which was desperate for money, weapons and intelligence.

The CIA director turned then to another TOP SECRET document, the "Worldwide Attack Matrix," which described covert operations in 80 countries either underway or that he was now recommending. Actions ranged from routine propaganda to lethal covert action in preparation for military attacks. Included were efforts to disrupt terrorist plots or attacks in countries in Asia, the Middle East and Africa. In some countries, CIA teams would break into facilities to obtain information. What he was proposing represented a striking departure for U.S. policy. It would give the CIA the broadest and most lethal authority in its history. He referred to this as the "outside piece," beyond Afghanistan. He walked the group rapidly through the 80 countries—here's where we are, here's what we could do, here's what we want to do. It was stunning in its sweep—a secret global war on terror.

Because the CIA had been working aggressively against terrorism for years, Tenet said, the agency had done extensive target development and network analysis. What it needed was money, flexibility and broad authority—so that it could move quickly, instantly, if it discovered targets.

Rumsfeld was enthusiastic about the broad concept, but he still wanted the order to be more carefully written and restrictive.

The president made no effort to disguise what he thought of Tenet's proposals, virtually shouting "Great job!"

"OKAY, MUELLER," BUSH said, turning to the FBI director, "give me a brief. Where are we on what's happening?"

Robert Mueller was a former federal prosecutor who had spent years working on the 1988 terrorist bombing of Pan Am Flight 103, and he knew that the worst thing that can happen to an FBI director is to have a major domestic terrorist incident on his watch. Perhaps the second is being called on by the president when unprepared. The brand-new director had been surprised by the invitation to attend the war-planning session. He had expected to be called on much later, if at all.

Not used to the company, intimidated by the presence of the nation's top leadership, Mueller gave a routine summary of the investigation into the hijackings. He realized he was almost babbling and quickly yielded the floor.

Attorney General Ashcroft provided an update on his efforts to develop a legislative package to expand the powers of law enforcement to fight terrorism. He warned that it was important to disrupt the terrorists now but added, "We need to remember these are patient people," reminding them that eight years passed between the two attacks on the World Trade Center. The administration needed a new long-term strategy, "because that's the kind of strategy they have in place."

The final presentation of the morning was by General Shelton, who had also brought a big briefcase to Camp David. Bush had ordered the Pentagon to come to the meeting with plenty of options, and Shelton was prepared to talk about military action against both Afghanistan and, if pressed, Iraq.

He had three general options for Afghanistan.

Option One was a strike with cruise missiles, a plan the military could execute quickly if speed was the president's overriding priority. The missiles could be launched by Navy ships or Air Force planes from hundreds of miles away. The targets included al Qaeda's training camps.

The problem, he noted, as they all knew, was that the camps were empty. Clearly, Shelton, Bush and Rumsfeld were not enamored of this idea, nor were the others. It might as well have been labeled the Clinton Option. There was palpable disgust at the mere mention of cruise missiles only.

The second option combined cruise missiles with manned bomber attacks. Shelton said Bush could initially choose a strike lasting three or four days or something longer, maybe up to 10 days. The targets included al Qaeda training camps and some Taliban targets. This too had limits.

Shelton described the third and most robust option as cruise missiles, bombers and what the planners had taken to calling "boots on the ground." This option included all the elements of the second option along with elite commando units of U.S. Special Forces, and possibly the Army and Marines, being deployed inside Afghanistan. But he said it would take a minimum of 10 to 12 days just to get initial forces on the ground because bases and overflight rights would be needed in the region for search and rescue teams to bring out any downed pilots.

Veterans of the Gulf War, certainly Powell and Cheney, were struck by how the military situation in Afghanistan was shaping up as far different from Desert Storm. On Saturday, August 4, 1990, in the same lodge at Camp David, General Norman Schwarzkopf, then the commander in chief of the Central Command, had presented a detailed, off-the-shelf proposal for military action. It was called Operations Plan 90-1002, and it was the basic military plan that would be executed over the next seven months to oust the Iraqi army from Kuwait.

Now there was no off-the-shelf military plan. One would have to be devised fast and from scratch, once the president had decided the shape of the war, the initial focus of the campaign and the relationship between the CIA and the Pentagon.

At one point, someone said this was not likely to be like the Balkans, where ethnic hatreds had occupied the Clinton administration for nearly eight years. "We're going to wish this was the Balkans," Rice said, the problems of Afghanistan and the surrounding region were so complicated. She looked at a map and just thought "Afghanistan." It evoked every negative image: far away, mountainous, landlocked, hard.

Bush said that the ideal result from this campaign would be to kick terrorists out of some places like Afghanistan and through that action persuade other countries that had supported terrorism in the past, such as Iran, to change their behavior.

Powell asserted that everyone in the international coalition was ready to go after al Qaeda, but that extending the war to other terrorist groups or countries could cause some of them to drop out.

The president said he didn't want other countries dictating terms or conditions for the war on terrorism. "At some point," he said, "we may be the only ones left. That's okay with me. We are America."

Powell didn't reply. Going it alone was precisely what he wanted to avoid if possible. He thought that the president's formulation was not realistic. Without partners, the United States could not launch an effective war even in Afghanistan, certainly not worldwide. He believed the president made such statements knowing they might not withstand a second analysis. Tough talk might be necessary, but it shouldn't be confused with policy.

Cheney, in contrast, took Bush at his word. He was convinced that the president was serious when he said the United States would go it alone if necessary.

Rumsfeld raised another problem. Although everyone agreed that destroying al Qaeda was the first priority, any singling out of bin Laden, particularly by the president, would elevate him the way Iraqi President Saddam Hussein had been during the Gulf War. He said that the worst thing they could do in such a situation was to misstate their objective. It would not be effective to succeed in removing or killing bin Laden or Taliban leader Mohammad Omar without solving the basic problem of terrorism. Vilification of bin Laden could rob the United States of its ability to frame this as a larger war. In other words, the "No bin Laden" sign that graced every page of the CIA briefing pack was off-message and shouldn't be repeated in public.

Another puzzle was the Taliban. The United States was clearly going to apply pressure in the hope that it would break with al Qaeda and give up bin Laden. They didn't think this was likely but they agreed they had to make the effort.

Afghanistan's history nagged at the president's advisers. Its geography was forbidding and its record of rebuffing outside forces was real. Despite the options that had been presented earlier that morning, several advisers seemed worried. Bush asked them: What are the worst cases out there? What are the real downside risks?

One was triggering chaos in Afghanistan that would spill over into Pakistan. Rice and Cheney in particular viewed this as a great danger. Afghanistan was already a mess, Cheney said. If Pakistan went, they would have unleashed a whole other set of demons. He was worried that Pakistan's choice to support the United States could lead its extremists to try to bring down Musharraf's government. That could give Islamic fundamentalists access to Pakistan's nuclear weapons.

Everyone understood that President Musharraf was the crucial barrier between stability and a worst-case scenario.

Have the Pakistanis fully thought through the risks of supporting us? Bush asked.

Powell said he believed they had. First, Musharraf had seen how serious the administration was. Second, he said, Musharraf realizes he has gradually been losing control of his country, and he may see this as an opportunity to stop the slide into extremism. Musharraf did not want Pakistan to turn into a rogue state, Powell believed. He sought a more secular, westernized country.

President Musharraf is taking a tremendous risk, the president said. We need to make it worth his while. We should help him with a number of things, including nuclear security. Put together a package of support for Pakistan, he directed.

Another risk they faced was getting bogged down in Afghanistan, the nemesis of the British in the 19th century and the Soviets in the 20th. Rice was wondering whether it might be the same for the United States in the 21st.

Her fears were shared by others, which led to a different discussion: Should they think about launching military action elsewhere as an insurance policy in case things in Afghanistan went
bad? They would need successes early in any war to maintain domestic and international support. The United States's rapid victory
in the 1991 Gulf War, and the immediacy of watching it unfold live
on CNN, had redefined people's expectations about warfare, which
the Clinton administration's occasional cruise missile attacks had
done nothing to alter.

Rice asked whether they could envision a successful military
campaign beyond Afghanistan, which put Iraq back on the table.

Deputy Defense Secretary Paul Wolfowitz perked up. Mild in
manner but hard-line in policy, Wolfowitz, 57, believed that the
abrupt end to the Desert Storm ground campaign in 1991 which
left Saddam in power had been a mistake.

Since taking office, Bush had been seeking ways to undermine
Hussein, with Wolfowitz pushing efforts to aid opposition groups,
and Powell seeking support for a new set of sanctions. The fear was
that Saddam was still attempting to develop, obtain and eventually
use weapons of mass destruction, and without United Nations inspectors in the country, there was no way to know the exact nature
of the threat they faced. The terrorist attacks of September 11 gave
the U.S. a new window to go after Hussein.

Wolfowitz seized the opportunity. Attacking Afghanistan
would be uncertain. He worried about 100,000 American troops
bogged down in mountain fighting in Afghanistan six months from
then. In contrast, Iraq was a brittle, oppressive regime that might
break easily. It was doable. He estimated that there was a 10 to 50
percent chance Saddam was involved in the September 11 terrorist
attacks. The U.S. would have to go after Saddam at some time if the
war on terrorism was to be taken seriously.

Andy Card thought Wolfowitz was just banging a drum, not
providing additional information or new arguments.

During a break, Bush joined a side discussion that included

Cheney, Cheney's chief of staff, I. Lewis "Scooter" Libby, and Wolf-owitz. He told them that he had found some of Shelton's military options unimaginative.

Wolfowitz expanded on his arguments about how war against Iraq might be easier than against Afghanistan.

The president asked why he didn't present more of this at the meeting.

"It is not my place to contradict the chairman of the Joint Chiefs unless the secretary of defense says to," said Wolfowitz, knowing Shelton was opposed to an attack on Iraq.

When the group reconvened, Rumsfeld asked, Is this the time to attack Iraq? He noted that there would be a big buildup of forces in the region and he was still deeply worried about the availability of good targets in Afghanistan.

Powell objected. You're going to hear from your coalition part-ners, he told the president. They're all with you, every one, but they will go away if you hit Iraq. If you get something pinning September 11 on Iraq, great—let's put it out and kick them at the right time. But let's get Afghanistan now. If we do that, we will have increased our ability to go after Iraq—if we can prove Iraq had a role.

Bush had strong reservations about attacking Iraq, but he let the discussion continue. He was concerned about two things, he said later. "My theory is you've got to do something and do it well and that . . . if we could prove that we could be successful in [the Afghanistan] theater, then the rest of the task would be easier. If we tried to do too many things—two things, for example, or three things—militarily, then . . . the lack of focus would have been a huge risk."

Bush's other concern was one that he did not express to his war cabinet but that he would say later was part of his thinking. He knew that around the table were advisers—Powell, Cheney, Wolf-owitz—who had been with his father during the Gulf War delibera-tions. "And one of the things I wasn't going to allow to happen is, that we weren't going to let their previous experience in this theater dictate a rational course for the new war." In other words, he didn't want them to use the war on terror as an excuse to settle an old score.

At another point during the morning, Wolfowitz interrupted his boss, Rumsfeld, and expanded on a point he had made earlier about Iraq. He may have taken the president's remark during the break as encouragement.

There was an awkward silence. Rumsfeld seemed to ignore the interruption but his eyes narrowed. Some thought he might be annoyed; others thought he was just listening.

Bush flashed a pointed look in Card's direction. During another break in the meeting, the chief of staff took Rumsfeld and Wolfowitz aside.

"The president will expect one person to speak for the Department of Defense," Card told them.

Sometime before lunch, Bush sent a message to the group that he had heard enough debate over Iraq. "There wasn't a lot of talk about Iraq in the second [afternoon] round," he later recalled. "The second round of discussion was focused only on Afghanistan, let me put it to you that way."

LUNCH WAS SERVED at 12:45, and Bush told his advisers that they should take some time to exercise or rest. Then, I want everybody back here at four o'clock, and I want to hear what you think we ought to do.

Rice was concerned about the lack of focus during the last part of the morning. The NSC meetings usually were more structured, with the principals reporting on their departments or agencies, and then together they would work through the problems—"noodle it around," she once said—and come up with options. The morning meeting had started well, but then had become repetitious, unusually freewheeling. She didn't know where the morning discussion had left them. How are we going to get a plan out of this? she wondered. Have we got anything here? She knew the president wanted to come away from the meeting with a plan of action.

Rice convened the principals—Powell, Rumsfeld, Tenet, Card—without the president. She expressed her concerns. We need to bring more discipline to the discussion in the afternoon, she said, urging them to be specific.

Powell went back to his cabin, where his wife, Alma, was reading a book. As he saw it, the big questions were still on the table: what to do, when to do it, and do you go after this one thing—al Qaeda and Afghanistan—that they knew was out there, or do you expand the war at this time? He sat down in a chair and closed his eyes for half an hour.

Tenet and McLaughlin went out on a golf cart for a ride. McLaughlin wondered how the president was going to take the discussion, which had sprayed all over, and bring it together.

Rice went back to her cabin, returned some phone calls and went off to exercise. About 3:45 P.M., she ran into the president outside his cabin. He had worked out on the elliptical machine and lifted weights. Now he told his national security adviser that he had a plan for the afternoon. "I'm going to go around the table and I'm going to ask people what they think," the president said. "What do you think about that?"

"That's fine," she replied. "Do you want me just to listen?"

"I want you to listen," Bush said. She could offer her thoughts after they had heard everyone out.

I WANT TO hear recommendations from the principals—Powell, Rumsfeld, Tenet, Card, and the vice president—said the president when the group reconvened in Laurel Lodge at 4 P.M.

Okay, who will start? He looked at Powell.

Powell had expected more general discussion but plunged ahead. "In the first instance, it's about al Qaeda and UBL," he said, using the common government shorthand for bin Laden, based on the spelling "Usama." Make them the target, their camps and their infrastructure. "Beyond that, there are other networks, but not the FARC," the left-wing guerrilla group in Colombia. They needed a sustained air campaign in places where bin Laden was known to hide, he said, and they should issue a warning to the Taliban 48 hours before the campaign starts that they will be held responsible. If not, they would start to pay a price.

"Don't go after the leadership in their capital," Powell continued, "go after the things that keep them in power like their air force. Start with the bottom of the loop first, rather than the top down."

He had several other ideas. "Stay away from CNN," he suggested. Instantaneous battlefield coverage could create unnecessary pressure. He also said it would be desirable to leave somebody in the Taliban to negotiate with, and it might be possible to work with the Saudis to try to get to the Taliban, since the Saudis were the only other major government besides Pakistan that formally recognized the Taliban as the legitimate rulers of Afghanistan.

"All the states that supported terror, you can do at a time of your choosing," Powell said, repeating Bush's phrase from the cathedral speech the day before. "They are not going anywhere." Don't go with the Iraq option right away, or we'll lose the coalition we've been signing up. "They'll view it as bait-and-switch—it's not what they signed up to do."

If we weren't going after Iraq before September 11, why would we be going after them now when the current outrage is not directed at Iraq, Powell asked. Nobody could look at Iraq and say it was responsible for September 11. It was important not to lose focus. "Keep the Iraq options open if you get the linkages," he said. "Maybe Syria, Iran"—the chief state sponsors of terrorism in the 1980s—"but doubt you'll get the linkages."

Though the U.S. military claims to be designed and equipped to fight two full-scale conflicts simultaneously, Powell thought the Defense Department was overestimating its ability to do two things at the same time from the same command, with the same commander and staff. Military attacks on both Afghanistan and Iraq would be under the jurisdiction of CENTCOM.

He didn't articulate that point, but he figured it was his ace in the hole. No military plan had been presented for Iraq. No one, neither Rumsfeld nor Wolfowitz, had told the president precisely what should be done in Iraq and how it might be done. Nobody had taken it to the next step and said, This is what we're talking about. The absence of a plan was a gaping hole.

A public case had to be made that bin Laden was the guilty one, Powell said. That was important. Evidence mattered.

Rumsfeld was next. We must not undercut our ability to act over the long term, he said, which meant they should keep thinking about what to do about terrorism in general. Patience was important. Rooting out bin Laden would take very different intelligence than they had. The doctrine of "hit, talk, hit," in which the United States would strike, pause to see the reaction, and then hit again, sounded much like Vietnam.

"The military options look like five or ten years ago," he said, a direct swipe at the uniformed military planners. Rumsfeld said there was a need for unconventional approaches, especially the Special Forces operations, in gathering intelligence on the ground. "Get a group functioning fast. Lift out of conventional mind-set."

Responding to Powell's comment that the coalition would dissolve if Iraq were attacked, Rumsfeld said that any "argument that the coalition wouldn't tolerate Iraq argues for a different coalition." But significantly, he did not make a recommendation on Iraq.

"We have to do a better job at target selection," he said. "This will be a sustained campaign. We need an operational cell that doesn't exist at present."

He offered some thoughts on controlling information. "Need tighter control over public affairs. Treat it like a political campaign with daily talking points. Sustaining requires a broad base of domestic support. Broad, not narrow. This is a marathon, not a sprint. It will be years and not months." In a war that was going to be remote, lengthy and relatively secret they would need message discipline.

"The people who do this don't lose," Rumsfeld said, "don't have high-value targets. They have networks and fanaticism." It was a somewhat obvious but important point that got to the heart of the problems they were facing—lack of good targets, lack of inside intelligence sources, the worthlessness of a deterrence strategy.

"We need to stress homeland defense," the president said. "One, we need an early blueprint for response." He assigned that task to Cheney. "Have to coordinate public affairs," he agreed. "Have to update our communications." For months Bush had been complaining about crappy communications systems, which had deteriorated in recent years from lack of investment. On the morning of September 11, the phones didn't work well.

Tenet summarized. "Seems to be a three-part strategy," he said. First would be the demands on the Taliban and others. Second would be "strike and strangle." Third would be "surround and sustain."

He added a depressing thought. "Our situation is more like that of the Israelis," he said. The United States could be entering a period of routine domestic terror attacks. The problem isn't going to go away. "We need a strategy at home that disrupts."

"Start Taliban military options." Tenet agreed with Powell that initially they should pursue military targets rather than their leadership. "Meet at least the al Qaeda target. Take out the majority of Taliban military structure."

He mentioned his own plans for a global approach but supported the position that the initial military focus should be exclusively on Afghanistan.

Card was next. He did not have much foreign policy experience, so he began by speaking generally. "What is the definition of success?" he asked. He said it would first be proving that this was not just an effort to pound sand—as the president had repeatedly made clear. "People are either with us or against us. If the line isn't clear and there aren't clear consequences, people migrate to the wrong side of the line." Echoing Powell and Rumsfeld, he said, "Don't define it as UBL. Al Qaeda can be the enemy."

"*An* enemy," Bush said, interrupting his chief of staff, reminding them all it was war way beyond al Qaeda.

Card said consideration should be given to simultaneous actions in other parts of the world such as Indonesia, the Philippines, Malaysia, Yemen or Somalia. "If you had 15 SEAL teams hitting 10 different targets on the same day, all at once, around the world that would send a message that we're reaching out globally."

Card also proposed they "build up troops big-time" in the Persian Gulf. It would show they were there to stay and would put them in a ready position to strike Iraq later on. But he said he did not think the case had been made that Iraq should be a principal, initial target.

Tenet interjected that he was concerned about what he called "the failure blame game," knowing there would be all kinds of finger-pointing and investigations like the endless rehashing of Pearl Harbor, trying to find a culprit, someone who had dropped the ball. "People are working their butts off," he said. His people were, as were others. "They've saved thousands of lives." It was essential to give them support. Then Tenet did something unusual. He looked at the president and said, "The men and women who are doing the job need to know you, Mr. President, believe in them."

Bush made it clear he did.

The vice president went last. We need to do everything we can to stop the next attack. Go after anyone in the U.S. who might be a terrorist. Are we being aggressive enough? We need a group now that's going to look at lessons learned from where we've been. And in going after bin Laden we need to consider the broader context. A week ago, before September 11, we were worried about the strength of our whole position in the Middle East—where we stood with the Saudis, the Turks and others in the region. Now they all want to be part of our efforts, and that's an opportunity. We need to reach out for that opportunity.

Building a coalition to take advantage of the opportunities, he said, suggests that this may be a bad time to take on Saddam Hussein. We would lose momentum. "If we go after Saddam Hussein, we lose our rightful place as good guy."

Cheney thus joined Powell, Tenet and Card in opposing action on Iraq. Rumsfeld had not committed. To anyone keeping a tally, it was 4 to 0 with Rumsfeld abstaining.

Still, the vice president expressed deep concern about Saddam and said he was not going to rule out going after Iraq at some point.

Cheney said the CIA must push every button it could. "One disappointment are the NGOs, bin Laden's one real asset"—the charitable groups and nongovernmental organizations that helped finance al Qaeda. He recommended strengthening the Northern Alliance and hitting the Taliban—but not necessarily in a massive way at first. We need to knock out their air defenses and their airpower at the start, he said. We need to be ready to put men on the ground. There are some places only Special Operations Forces will get them, he added. And we need to ask: Do we have the right mix of forces?

Finally, Cheney returned to the question of homeland defense. They must do everything possible to defend, prevent or disrupt the next attack on America. The issue was very worrisome. He had reviewed the work of five government commissions that had recently studied terrorism. The president had assigned him the task of coming up with a homeland security plan back in May. It's not just borders and airline security, but biological and other threats that they had to think about.

At the end of the meeting, Bush went around the table and thanked everyone. It was not clear where things stood.

"I'm going to go think about it, and I'll let you know what I've decided," he said.

• • •

POWELL AND RUMSFELD left Camp David, but most of the others and their spouses stayed over for dinner. Rice led the group in a sing-along of American standards including "Old Man River," "Nobody Knows the Trouble I've Seen" and "America the Beautiful." The president spent some time at a table nearby, joining others trying to assemble an elaborate wooden jigsaw puzzle.

7

AT HIS HOME in the Washington suburbs the next morning, Tenet took out a pen, some paper and began writing in longhand. He was pumped up, and wanted to send a message to his own team of advisers. He wrote at the top: "We're At War."

It was an all-fronts war on al Qaeda, he wrote. "There can be no bureaucratic impediments to success. All the rules have changed. There must be an absolute and full sharing of information, ideas and capabilities. We do not have time to hold meetings or fix problems—fix them quickly and smartly. Each person must assume an unprecedented degree of personal responsibility." Any problems with other agencies, the military or law enforcement must be "solved now.

"We must all be passionate and driven—but not breathless. We must stay cool.

"Together we will win this war and make our president and the American people proud. We will win this war on behalf of our fallen and injured brothers and sisters in New York and Washington and their families."

He sent it over the secure fax in his home to headquarters to be typed and distributed. The memo was a call to action but it was also an acknowledgment that his agency had some problems, a tendency to deal with problems by holding meetings.

• • •

THE PRESIDENT ARRIVED back at the White House at 3:20 P.M.
from Camp David, made a brief statement to the press on the South
Lawn and took five questions. He referred to "evil" or "evildoers"
seven times and three times voiced amazement at the nature of the
attacks.

"We haven't seen this kind of barbarism in a long period of
time," Bush said. "No one could have conceivably imagined suicide
bombers burrowing into our society and then emerging all in the
same day to fly their aircraft—fly U.S. aircraft into buildings full of
innocent people and show no remorse.

"This crusade, this war on terrorism is going to take a while,"
he added. The characterization of the war as a "crusade" would be
recognized as a blunder because of its serious negative connota-
tions in the Islamic world, where it is still associated with invading
medieval European Christian armies. Aides would later have to take
back the comment and apologize.

BUSH WAS AWARE of the monumental communications problem he
and the administration faced. September 11 was not only the dead-
liest attack on the American homeland, surpassing Pearl Harbor in
body count, but the most photographed and filmed violent assault
in history. Who could forget the crystal-clear video reruns of the
gently banking United Airlines Flight 175 plowing into the 80th
floor of the South Tower of the World Trade Center, depositing its
lethal fireball and nearly emerging from the other side. Or the
image of the smoking Twin Towers. Or the video of the collapsing
towers, one then the other, and the cloud of debris and smoke suf-
focating Lower Manhattan. Or the pictures of the people jumping
from the uppermost floors to their deaths to escape the unbearable
heat inside. Or the despair on the faces of all Americans. It was almost as if the terrorists had a perfect sense of the American thirst

for the theatrical and the dramatic. It seemed they realized that the country had a news media and value system that would push all these images back in every face time and time and time again.

Bush sensed that he was not going to be able to offer an equivalent spectacular event in response. Much of his war and his response would be invisible, and a long time in coming.

He summoned Rice, Hughes, Bartlett and press secretary Ari Fleischer to join him in his office on the second floor of the residence, known as the Treaty Room.

Bush told Hughes, "You're in charge of how we communicate this war." How the White House explained its goals and thinking about the war effort would be critical to the overall success of the campaign. It would be central to retaining public confidence in his leadership, to holding together the international coalition. The problem was that the communications team was not going to know the details, especially about the covert CIA operations, and the American response was going to be delayed.

"I knew full well that if we could rally the American people behind a long and difficult chore, that our job would be easier," Bush said later. "I am a product of the Vietnam era. I remember presidents trying to wage wars that were very unpopular, and the nation split." He pointed to a portrait of Abraham Lincoln that hung in the Oval Office. "He's on the wall because the job of the president is to unite the nation. That's the job of the president. And I felt like, that I had the job of making sure the American people understood. They understood the severity of the attack. But I wasn't sure if they understood how long it was going to take and what a difficult process this would be."

Bush told his advisers, We're going to be entering missions where U.S. military personnel will be at risk. We need to be careful. He wanted Defense and State and other agencies all operating from the same plan. Make sure the left hand knows what the right hand is doing.

For nearly an hour, they talked about what the president expected from his communications team. His advisers remember the conversation as mostly one-way. Bush stressed the unconventional aspects of the war—the role of law enforcement, of intelligence sharing, of disrupting the terrorists' financial network, the role of the CIA and the overriding imperative that much of the war be invisible.

He asked his advisers to think about how to explain the mission, the risks and the time it might take to complete the tasks ahead. There would be parts of the campaign that they could not talk about, he said again, and they should think of ways to showcase all elements of the war they *could* talk about, particularly the financial piece, the effort to squeeze the money out of the terrorists' networks.

We cannot tolerate leaks, the president said insistently. Lives will be at stake. Rumsfeld and the Pentagon would talk about operations; White House officials would not. We will not be able to confirm some actions or operations. Your jobs will not be easy.

Later, Bush recalled being very certain and clear about what they needed to say at the time: "We're in for a difficult struggle; it is a new kind of war; we're facing an enemy we never faced before; it is a two-front war initially—Afghanistan and at home.

"I also had the responsibility to show resolve. I had to show the American people the resolve of a commander in chief that was going to do whatever it took to win. No yielding. No equivocation. No, you know, lawyering this thing to death, that we're after 'em. And that was not only for domestic, for the people at home to see. It was also vitally important for the rest of the world to watch." He was particularly concerned about how world leaders would interpret his actions. "These guys were watching my every move. And it's very important for them to come in this Oval Office, which they do, on a regular basis, and me look them in the eye and say, 'You're either with us or you're against us.' "

Twice Bush was interrupted for calls with foreign leaders, including one with Mexican President Vicente Fox, whose ranch he had visited shortly after taking office. As the two ranchers spoke,

Bush slipped into the vernacular of the Old West. "Wanted dead or alive. That's how I feel," Bush said.

Bush excused his communications team and asked Rice to stay behind.

"I know what I want to do and I'm going to do it tomorrow at the NSC," he told her. He dictated a list of actions he would order the next morning.

Rice returned to her office to draw up a one-page summary of 11 items, a war plan on a single sheet of paper.

MONDAY, SEPTEMBER 17, at 9:35 A.M., Bush and the NSC reconvened in the Cabinet Room. Overlooking the Rose Garden, the room looks like the library of a venerable law firm. It is dominated by a large, sturdy oval mahogany conference table which was a gift from President Nixon in 1970.

It was not clear to the others what the crucible of Camp David had yielded. This morning, Bush opened. "The purpose of this meeting is to assign tasks for the first wave of the war against terrorism," he said. "It starts today."

He was approving every one of Tenet's requests for expanding the role of the agency, rejecting most of Rumsfeld's efforts to scale back. CIA subordinates would have authority to act covertly.

"I want to sign a finding today," the president said. "I want the CIA to be first on the ground.

"The attorney general, the CIA and the FBI will assist in protecting America from further attacks." The new policy would stress preemption of future attacks, instead of investigation, gathering evidence and prosecution. He directed Ashcroft to request new legal authority from Congress for the FBI to track, wiretap and stop terrorists—a project already under way.

He told Rumsfeld, "We need plans for protection of U.S. forces and installations abroad.

"The secretary of state should issue an ultimatum against the Taliban today," he addressed Powell, almost barking orders. He wanted something "warning them to turn over bin Laden and his al Qaeda or they will suffer the consequences.

"If they don't comply, we'll attack them," Bush said. "Our goal is not to destroy the Taliban, but that may be the effect.

"We'll attack with missiles, bombers and boots on the ground," he said, choosing the most extensive of Shelton's options. "Let's hit them hard. We want to signal this is a change from the past. We want to cause other countries like Syria and Iran to change their views. We want to hit as soon as possible."

The Pentagon should develop and present a detailed plan, he said, but it was clear some basic questions about the operation—raised six days before by Rumsfeld—had not been resolved. Bush repeated them: What targets, how soon? What allied forces do we want? When? How? What's in the first wave? What's later?

Putting men on the ground before bombing in Afghanistan would be a good idea. "We are going to rain holy hell on them. You've got to put lives at risk. We've got to have people on the ground."

Powell had been slightly taken aback that Bush wanted to give the Taliban an immediate ultimatum. It was nighttime in South Asia. Since the United States did not have diplomatic relations with the Taliban, any private message would have to be issued through the government of Pakistan.

There were complications. Powell had to write the ultimatum. Everyone had to understand the consequences. He was concerned about what might happen in Pakistan. They would have to button up their embassies and talk to the allies. "I'd like an hour to think it through, whether we should delay until tomorrow morning," the secretary said.

Bush agreed, but he wanted the language to be tough. "I want to have them quaking in their boots."

Bush said he wanted a plan to stabilize Pakistan and protect it against the consequences of supporting the U.S.

As for Saddam Hussein, the president ended the debate. "I believe Iraq was involved, but I'm not going to strike them now. I don't have the evidence at this point."

Bush said he wanted them to keep working on plans for military action in Iraq but indicated there would be plenty of time to do that. Everything else, though, had to be done soon.

"Start now," the president said. "It's very important to move fast. This is a new way."

Shelton said it should take four days to a week to set up the airlifting of troops and supplies so they could be moved near the Afghan border. It would take longer to get the Special Forces troops in place.

"This is chess, not checkers," Rumsfeld said. "We must be thinking beyond the first move." He thought it was more like three-dimensional chess. It reminded him of the old 25-cent game at the gas station, the one that involved a set of multiple joints and handles that had to be manipulated to win the prize.

What's after the 10-day bombing campaign? What can happen that could change their minds? What were the worst things that could happen? What were the best things? Sometimes an operation could move too fast, so they had to be ready to react if things went better than they thought.

These were good questions, but Rumsfeld's tendency to intellectualize masked a practical frustration. As his top aides knew, he was worried that the military, particularly General Franks, was not, as one aide put it succinctly, "looking aggressively enough at aggressive options."

THE PRESIDENT NEXT went to the Pentagon for a detailed briefing on special operations. He had been scheduled to visit Fort Bragg in North Carolina, home of the Special Forces and Delta, the elite hostage rescue unit, but the trip had been scrubbed because of worries that his presence could signal the direction his plans were taking.

A two-star general had been sent from that command to brief Bush, Rice and Frank Miller, the senior NSC staffer for defense. Miller, who had worked for Cheney in the Pentagon on nuclear war plans, knew that special operations officers were a breed apart. He went ahead to review the classified slide presentation.

One slide about potential operations in Afghanistan was labeled: "Thinking Outside the Box—Poisoning Food Supply."

Miller almost gagged. He showed it to Rice. The United States doesn't know how to do this, he reminded her, and we're not allowed. It would be a chemical or biological attack, clearly banned by treaties the United States had signed.

Rice took the slide to Rumsfeld. "This slide is not going to be shown to the president of the United States," she said. A poison attack was exactly what they feared from bin Laden. How was it conceivable that someone could imagine adopting bin Laden's tactics and presenting the idea to the president?

"You're right," Rumsfeld said. Pentagon officials said later that their internal review had caught the offending slide and it never would have been shown. But the briefing was only minutes away when Miller saw it.

Afterward, the president addressed some of the 35,000 reservists who were being called up, and answered questions from reporters.

"Do you want bin Laden dead?"

"There's an old poster out West, as I recall, that said, 'Wanted Dead or Alive,' " Bush replied.

He was to sign a document that day authorizing covert and overt action designed to capture or kill bin Laden. He said later that he used the language to let the public know where he was heading.

"A lot of times you get out here and you know something is going to happen or you're thinking about something," he recalled. "And you get asked a question and it just, it pops out. I'm not very guarded in that sense sometimes. . . . It was a little bit of bravado, but it was also an understanding that in self-defense of America, that I had made that decision in self-defense of America that 'Dead or Alive,' that it's legal."

When Laura Bush saw the news accounts, she was not happy at all. "Tone it down, darling," she told him.

But, she said, he didn't tone it down. "Every once in a while, I had to say it again."

LATER IN THE afternoon at the White House, the president was presented with two documents to sign. One was a Memorandum of Notification modifying the finding that President Ronald Reagan had signed on May 12, 1986.

The memorandum authorized all the steps proposed by Tenet at Camp David. The CIA was now empowered to disrupt the al Qaeda network and other global terrorist networks on a worldwide scale, using lethal covert action to keep the role of the United States hidden.

The finding also authorized the CIA to operate freely and fully in Afghanistan with its own paramilitary teams, case officers and the newly armed Predator drone.

The second document, two and a half pages long, consisted of the orders and action steps to the war cabinet and agencies that Bush had presented earlier that morning. The orders called for financial pressure, diplomatic action, military planning and covert action. It was classified TOP SECRET/PEARL. The codeword PEARL had been selected at random as the name of the special access compartment for the early phases of the war, and only those on a restricted list were supposed to see the documents.

In the middle of the third page the president scribbled in his distinctive longhand, "George W. Bush."

• • •

TUESDAY, SEPTEMBER 18, President Bush and Vice President Cheney marked the seventh day since the terrorist attacks with a moment of silence on the White House lawn, then met with the National Security Council. Tenet told the group that the agency was sending its first paramilitary team to Afghanistan to work with the Northern Alliance. It would take eight days before the team landed in Afghanistan but Tenet said, "We are launching our plan."

Rumsfeld reported that military planning was proceeding. Keeping options open is important but not the primary focus, Bush told him. "The top priority is shaking bin Laden's tree."

After the NSC meeting, the president met with Hughes and the speechwriting team about the address he was to deliver to a joint session of Congress. He wasn't satisfied with a first draft. He wanted to conclude with a personal pledge to the American people, an ending along the lines of: This is my mission, my purpose, this is the nation's purpose. "This is what my presidency is about."

He told his team he wanted to convey that the war on terrorism would consume him throughout his presidency, and that he was making a personal commitment to the American people to see it through, however long.

The speech had become the rhetorical vehicle to describe, at least in veiled language, the scope of a total war on terrorism.

Rice brought in the State Department's draft of the ultimatum to the Taliban. When Bush read it, he began to think it made more sense to include the ultimatum in his speech, rather than have it issued by State. An ultimatum would carry more weight if it came directly from the president and it would produce a headline.

That night at about 9:30 P.M., Bush called his chief speechwriter, Michael Gerson. Gerson had just pulled into his driveway in suburban Virginia. It was unusual for the president to call this late in the evening, but for a half hour they went through the draft. Bush proposed two dozen changes.

• • •

ARMITAGE AND COFER Black flew to Moscow to seek help from top Russian diplomatic and intelligence officials.

"We're in a war," Black told the Russians. "We're coming. Regardless of what you do, we're coming anyway." He knew Afghanistan was their sphere of influence and they would be queasy. "At the very least, we want you to look away." He did not want the Russians trying to gum up CIA operations. "From my humble position, I think this is a historical opportunity. Let's get out of the last century into the new one."

The Russians indicated they would help and certainly not obstruct. One noted that Afghanistan was ambush heaven, where the guerrilla fighters had demolished the Russian army. "With regret," the Russian said, "I have to say you're really going to get the hell kicked out of you."

"We're going to kill them," Black said. "We're going to put their heads on sticks. We're going to rock their world."

The Russians soon sent a team to the CIA to provide extensive on-the-ground intelligence, especially about topography and caves in Afghanistan.

THE NSC MET Wednesday morning, September 19, in the White House Situation Room. Bush asked for assurances that U.S. officials had clearly insisted that the Taliban regime release two young American female aid workers who were being held hostage.

He also urged Powell and Rumsfeld to emphasize in their briefings that the international coalition would change with the requirements of the war effort, that different countries would be asked for different contributions, that this would not be a single, grand, unchanging coalition.

"We won't demand from our coalition partners what they can't give, but states can't say they are anti-terror here and pro-terror at home," Powell replied.

He said they needed to build a case that al Qaeda was behind the attacks.

"Not a legal case," countered Rumsfeld. "It's not event-related." The issue was not specific acts of terrorism. They knew al Qaeda believed in terrorism. Bin Laden and the others had said so publicly and repeatedly. Indictments and federal criminal charges had been filed against them in the past. "Some countries are fearful—they have different perspectives. The press will say the coalition is coming apart if the evidence doesn't support our case."

"Is Iran in the coalition?" asked Steve Hadley.

"It's not a single coalition," said Rumsfeld.

"Silence may sometimes be more threatening," Tenet said. Saying nothing might worry the Iranians more than anything.

THAT MORNING, HUGHES asked Card and Rice if they thought the president had decided that the speech draft was in good enough shape. She thought it still needed a lot of work. Rice agreed, and said she would send two of her senior staff members to work with Hughes.

Despite his impassioned statements throughout the week, the president felt his speechwriters had not incorporated the directness and simplicity he was looking for in the conclusion.

"Is anybody listening?" he asked.

About 11:30 A.M., Gerson called Hughes to say he was bringing a revised draft over to her office. They went over it line by line before deciding they were ready to show it. About 1:15 P.M., they walked into the Oval Office.

"You're all smiling," Bush noted. "That's good."

As he began reading the speech aloud, he got to the first addition and asked: "Are you just putting things in and out of the speech?" He came to another one. This is different, he said. Who put this in? Are you just willy-nilly adding things to this speech?

"No," Hughes replied. "I had to use my judgment. You were in a meeting."

Bush made a few suggestions as he read, but when he finished he said, "Great job. Let's go tell the Congress."

Then, at 6:25 P.M., dressed in a nylon jogging jacket, Bush went to the White House theater and practiced.

AT 7 P.M., Bush met with his war cabinet. Rumsfeld said the speech shouldn't single out bin Laden. It risked elevating bin Laden and narrowing the base of support for the anti-terrorist campaign. Rice responded that the decision had been made to mention bin Laden once.

There was one other issue to resolve. More than anything else, Bush's advisers had debated the section warning states that supported terrorism. They had searched for language that would clarify the doctrine Bush had laid out in his statement on the night of the attacks, that the U.S. would not distinguish between terrorists and those who harbor them.

What other states might they be targeting beyond their initial campaign? What were the new rules to measure the behavior of countries with a history of sponsoring terrorism?

Rice and Powell believed the present language was too strident. They wanted to give countries the opportunity to break with the past. They agreed that by adding the words "continue to" to the sentence, they held out a carrot. Without the change, Powell thought, the United States would be declaring war on everybody.

"WE HAVE THREATS of an imminent terrorist attack," announced Tenet at the start of Thursday morning's NSC meeting. It was alarming news, especially with the president scheduled to address

Congress that night. Intelligence showed that very senior members of al Qaeda, including key bin Laden lieutenants, were indicating there would be a big attack in the next couple of days. It was the same kind of intelligence chatter that had bedeviled them before July 4 when there had been no attacks, and before September 11.

Tenet told the president that the first CIA paramilitary team would be in Uzbekistan by Friday, and in northern Afghanistan by Sunday.

"Beware of raising false expectations, defeating them versus defeating their ability to threaten our way of life," Rumsfeld said. This was a careful, even subtle formulation. There was no way to stop all terrorism but it could be curtailed to such a level that the American way of life would continue. With that standard it would be easier to clear the bar in both the short and long run. He was worried about sounding too ambitious.

But Bush insisted he would not soft-pedal America's determination to win the war. We will defeat our enemies, we will set a tone for future presidents, he said. "Two years from now only the Brits may be with us."

Rumsfeld raised the possibility that weapons of mass destruction could be used against the United States. "It's an energizer for the American people," he said. "It's a completely different situation from anything we've ever faced before." Should the president address the issue in his speech?

"I left it out," Bush said flatly. "It could overwhelm the whole speech. At some point we have to brief the nation, absolutely. But I took it out. It's going to stay out. I thought long and hard about it."

Bush, clearly fearful of alarming people just nine days after the shocking attacks, said they would address it later, perhaps when they had better information.

"Do it in the context of an overall strategy," he said. "Need to be sure. Need to be honest," he added, "but I don't know about being brutally honest."

Rumsfeld mentioned that a routine request to hit some Iraqi targets in the decade-long effort to enforce the no-fly zone set up after the Gulf War was still pending. Now, nothing about military action or Iraq could be considered routine.

"If you strike close to Baghdad, which turns on all the warnings in Baghdad, then the clarity of the mission becomes confused," Bush replied. Iraq and the world might think a strike was related to a September 11 response. "We have to be patient about Iraq."

BUSH TOOK A short nap in the late afternoon while awaiting the arrival of British Prime Minister Tony Blair. He had invited Blair to the White House for dinner and as a distinguished guest at his speech to Congress. Blair had accepted the invitation despite concerns at home about what one official called "the poodle factor"— the fear that the prime minister might appear to have become an appendage of the U.S. president. Blair saw it as another chance to express his solidarity with Bush and, more important, to hear first-hand how U.S. planning for the war had evolved.

Bush and Blair went off alone to the Blue Room for 20 minutes. Bush laid out his plan, including the use of U.S. force in Afghanistan. "Full force of the U.S. military," he told Blair, and "bombers coming from all directions."

"You don't seem the least bit concerned or nervous," Blair said, according to Bush. "Don't you need some time alone?"

"I know exactly what I need to say, and how to say it, and what to do," Bush told Blair.

"I think it surprised him a little bit," Bush said later. "You know, you've got to remember, every speech is now 'the speech of my life.' . . . I've had about six of those from some of my trusted advisers. So I'm immune to the 'speech of your life' speech."

More than 80 million Americans watched on television.

• • •

"TONIGHT WE ARE a country awakened to danger and called to defend freedom," Bush said as fighter jets circled over the Capitol. "Our grief has turned to anger and anger to resolution. Whether we bring our enemies to justice or bring justice to our enemies, justice will be done.

"We will direct every resource at our command," he said, "every means of diplomacy, every tool of intelligence, every instrument of law enforcement, every financial influence, and every necessary weapon of war, to the disruption and to the defeat of the global terror network."

He described the unusual nature of the campaign to demonstrate that U.S. policy had undergone important changes. "Our response involves far more than instant retaliation and isolated strikes," he said. "Americans should not expect one battle but a lengthy campaign, unlike any other we have ever seen. It may include dramatic strikes visible on TV, and covert operations, secret even in success." He urged Americans "to live your lives and hug your children" and asked for "patience" for the long struggle ahead.

He made the pledge he had worked to perfect. "I will not forget this wound to our country and those who inflicted it," he said. "I will not yield; I will not rest; I will not relent in waging this struggle for freedom and security for the American people."

The applause was thunderous.

From the podium, it was impossible to tell how the speech was being received, Bush recalled. "I don't know how these things go. You know, I'm in the middle of the whirlwind, as they say, in speeches.

"When I really realized the extent to which America wanted to be led was when they stopped the hockey game in Philadelphia," he said. Fans had demanded they be able to watch the president's speech on the stadium's overhead video screens. Officials called the game, and the players huddled around their benches to watch also.

"It was unbelievable," Bush said. "And they wanted, they didn't want the game to go on. They wanted to hear what the commander in chief, the president of the United States, had to say during this moment."

Bush called Gerson. Both remember the president's words: "I have never felt more comfortable in my life."

Bush was about to learn how less comforting and more difficult it was going to be to implement his bold declarations.

8

"THE LEAKS WILL kill us and they will undermine our coalition," thundered Tenet at the beginning of the 9:30 A.M. NSC meeting, Friday, September 21. He was particularly concerned about Uzbekistan, which was secretly allowing the CIA to fly Predator drones from its territory. President Islam Karimov could easily use a leak as justification for bailing out.

Other countries that were helping or would be asked to help in the war could become skittish or refuse to assist, leaving the CIA and the Pentagon out in the cold.

In the 10 days since the attacks on New York and Washington, the news media had thrown unprecedented resources at covering every angle of the story. Reporters, editors and producers were tapping old and new sources, pursuing back channels to land a scoop. The hunger for even a morsel of new information was made more acute by the pressures of the 24-hour news cycle—now punctuated by a nonstop news ticker crawling across the bottom of a half-dozen cable news channels. Intelligence or secret military plans or diplomatic moves made the best scoops.

"I'm gonna read the riot act to our workforce," Tenet said.

"We'll just have to put some of the most sensitive stuff not on paper," said Bush. History be damned. So what if the record was incomplete. He was not going to jeopardize the undertaking.

The group turned to a discussion about the latest intelligence on the location of bin Laden. Though the administration was trying to play down his importance, Bush understood the symbolism of getting him. He wanted bin Laden badly.

Once again the intelligence was thin gruel. Tenet really had nothing of consequence.

The president told them they needed to find a way to show visible progress in the war on terror, on their terms. He wanted a "scorecard," a way to measure and demonstrate what they had and would accomplish. They were in the implementation phase, and though they weren't going to talk about plans and operations, he wanted to talk results. He wanted something up on the scoreboard. "I want the people involved with the operations to know that I am going to be watching."

No one doubted that.

Treasury Secretary Paul O'Neill was present at the meeting because of plans to disrupt terrorist finances worldwide.

"We need to get operational on this," Bush said, turning his fire hose on the treasury secretary. "Disruption of financial networks needs to be a tool in our arsenal. It's important. We must use it."

There were nods. He was assured in a chorus of "Soon, Mr. President, coming Mr. President" that a public announcement of plans would be ready in days.

Rice raised an equally difficult subject. The CIA was circulating a TOP SECRET/CODEWORD Threat Matrix each day listing the freshest and most sensitive raw intelligence about dozens of threatened bombings, hijackings or other terrorist plans. It was chilling, at times containing 100 specific threats to U.S. facilities around the world or possible targets inside the country—embassies, shopping complexes, specific cities, places where thousands gather. Some were anonymous phone or e-mail threats that looked potentially serious; some were just nut cases. But many came from the most sensitive human sources and overseas communications intercepts.

The deputies had been meeting each day specifically on homeland security. Rice had been closely watching their work and found that their progress was minuscule. This was because they were trying to do more, solve the big problems of security, truly harden America. Well, that was impossible, she realized.

She summarized this conclusion for the NSC. "Make sure the best is not the enemy of the good," she said. "Do what you can right now to help reduce the risk to the United States." Steps that might be unsatisfactory in the long run had to be taken in the short run, now.

The chance that the United States would be hit again in the near term was real. Rice recognized that as the shock of 9/11 subsided, the natural tendency would be to begin methodical, wholesale improvements to the systems and procedures that had been exploited by the terrorists, especially airport security. That could take months or years. The focus needed to be primarily on whatever short-term measures might prevent, disrupt or delay another attack.

"Don't wait for the long studies. We'll have time enough to do studies," Rice continued. "Sixty to 70 percent of what you need to do, you know you need to do right now. Just go do it." She suggested that they simply employ brute force, beef up screening and security everywhere. Putting the National Guard in the airports lent an aura of heightened security. As many packages or containers as possible coming into American ports should be examined.

The reality was that the country was open and vulnerable.

Bush returned to the issue of terrorist financing. It was something that could be done immediately. They needed international cooperation to disrupt the networks of funding, he said. "Look, if countries are reluctant, let us know. Put it on my call list."

As operations in the war on terror were commencing—or soon would—Bush wanted his advisers to feel they could call on him for help. He had offered his office, his phone, his influence, whatever they needed to move through their work lists. "Get us the top ten things you want us to do, and we'll do it," he directed.

They shifted to the economy, another worry. Stock prices had plunged all week since the market reopened Monday, sending all the major indexes to their lowest levels in more than two years. The Dow Jones Industrial Average had sunk below 8,400 points—dropping 13 percent in less than a week.

They also touched on where the U.S. was headed with the United Nations General Assembly, which had been scheduled to meet in New York the next week, with President Bush delivering a welcome address. The U.N. had postponed the meeting indefinitely because security personnel in New York were already stretched to the max.

Toward the close, Powell turned to one of his favorite subjects—the coalition of nations that were helping and would help. It was clear from the meeting that the war on all fronts—military, intelligence, financial and diplomatic—hinged on having partners. And he agreed the U.S. would not bend to adapt to what other nations wanted. "The coalition doesn't constrain our operations," he said, sounding one of Rumsfeld's themes.

"The war is as I defined it last night," Bush replied. In his speech he had sounded more as if he would go it alone, if necessary. But the unilateralist in him seemed to be giving way. "It requires a coalition, it can't be done without one," he conceded.

But he quickly turned to what was primarily on his mind, adding, "And we've got to start showing results."

He was pressuring them, he realized. The president said later that he was also trying to protect them. "I told our team, I said, 'Look, don't get pressured into making irrational decisions. And don't worry about me second-guessing what you do.' I said, 'Make the best decisions you can, and I'll protect our team as best as I can by explaining to the public that this is going to take a long time.' "

OUT AT LANGLEY, Tenet called in the agency's top Afghanistan experts—operators and analysts—for a free-for-all in his conference room.

How do we launch the covert action in Afghanistan? he asked.

Tribalism is important, a dominant feature of Afghan life, someone said. Everyone agreed. The Afghan population is comprised of a half-dozen sizable ethnic groups and many smaller ones whose histories, claims on land and conflicts traced back centuries. Hostility among rival groups is often fierce. Ethnic Pashtuns, who make up two-fifths of the country's inhabitants, live mostly in the south. The ethnic Tajiks, the next largest group, and the ethnic Uzbeks are mostly in the north. Warring between the southern Pashtuns and the northern Tajiks and Uzbeks had kept the country mired in conflict since the end of the Soviet occupation in 1989.

This was the vacuum that had allowed the Taliban and bin Laden to take over the country.

Even within ethnic groups, tribal and religious differences had sparked internecine feuds. The two dominant tribes of Pashtuns had been fighting each other since the 16th century, with one tribe most recently supporting Mullah Omar's Taliban militia and the other backing the former Afghan monarch, King Mohammed Zahir Shah.

Second, the CIA experts said it was important to make the war Afghan versus Arab, not some Westerners versus Afghans. It was critical to frame the war as one of liberation. Afghans remembered the 10-year failed effort of the Soviets who wanted authoritarian rule. The thousands of foreign-born Arabs who had come to Afghanistan to train in al Qaeda camps were the outsiders, the invaders. The war was against them, not against native Afghan tribesmen. Tenet found near unanimity on this point also.

How could they use tribalism to their advantage? The answer: Getting Afghans to fight, not just to talk.

An Afghanistan operation furthermore had to be geared so it would not make things harder on Pakistani President Musharraf. The U.S. could accomplish that in several ways, they said, foremost by avoiding large refugee flows from Afghanistan into Pakistan and by showing the Pakistanis the benefits of cooperating. Already that week, there had been talk that in return for their assistance in the war on terror Pakistan could expect a lifting of economic sanctions imposed after their 1998 nuclear tests and a generous package of aid and debt relief. The undersecretary of state for political affairs, Marc Grossman, was on Capitol Hill that day to inform congressional leaders of the president's intention to waive the sanctions on Pakistan.

Several said the United States had to emphasize public diplomacy, a nice term for a propaganda war. The key themes should be: 1) this was not a war against Islam, and 2) this was not a war against the Afghan people.

The general rule was to study what the Soviets had done and do the opposite.

AT 5:30 P.M. the principals convened via secure video teleconference without the president. Condi Rice and Andy Card were at Camp David, where they would be spending the weekend with the president. The others were gathered in the White House Situation Room.

Running through a checklist of countries, they reported on where the U.S. stood with the basing, access and overflight rights that were necessary before military operations could begin. The more they examined Afghanistan the more difficult it looked. Iran was to the west, three former Soviet republics and China to the north, Pakistan to the east and south. The nearest accessible body of water was the Indian Ocean, 300 miles away. They had no strong allies in the immediate region; they didn't have diplomatic relations with Iran. So they turned to the small Persian Gulf nations of Bahrain, the United Arab Emirates and Oman, hoping they would provide territory from which bombing sorties or other offensive military action could be launched.

Oman was the best prospect. About the size of Kansas and strategically located on the east end of the Arabian Peninsula, Oman has 1,000 miles of shoreline on the Gulf of Oman and the

Arabian Sea—within striking distance of Afghanistan, some 700 miles away. Omani leader Sultan Qaboos bin Said, who had gone to Britain's Sandhurst military academy, had seized power in 1970 from his father. In 1980 he had made the country available as a staging area for the unsuccessful 1980 Desert One hostage rescue mission into Iran. In 1998 he allowed U.S. bombers to strike Iraq from his country.

The initial report on Oman, however, was inconclusive—it was still unclear whether they would allow combat operations to be staged from its strategically located island of Masira in the Arabian Sea.

It was clear Russia would play a central role. The principals split up responsibility on working the Russians over basing issues in Central Asia. The strategy was "Everybody plays." They would all reach out to their Russian counterparts. Powell was to deal with foreign minister Igor Ivanov; Rumsfeld with the defense minister, Sergei Ivanov; Rice with Kremlin security adviser Vladimir Rushailo.

It was tricky Rice realized. Some of the Central Asian states, former Soviet republics, would be offended that the United States was going through Russia. Uzbekistan was alienated from Russia. On the other hand, Tajikistan was thoroughly in the Russian camp and wouldn't move without its approval.

Rice reminded them of the president's desire to also play. "If you need the president to call Putin, you do that."

ON SATURDAY, SEPTEMBER 22, the president asked what the score-card was showing.

Mueller reported that the FBI had conducted interviews with 417 persons as part of its terrorist sweep and that they had a staggering 331 people on their watch list.

Three hundred and thirty-one. The number weighed on their minds. Mueller was saying that as many as 15 times the number of terrorists who carried out the September 11 attacks could be in the United States? They had to assume some were capable of carrying out deadly plots.

A big number, Rice thought. Her heart almost sank. Before September 11, they had been warned about al Qaeda abroad. But no equivalent warning or detail about terrorists in the U.S. had been provided by the FBI, which had responsibility for domestic counterterrorism.

"I was floored," Bush later recalled. "It was a lot. I remember that. It's an incredible number."

He said he kept trying to get numbers on the size of their army—in Afghanistan, the rest of the world and in the United States.

Though he was dropping numbers in public all the time to report progress, the president decided the 331 number was one scorecard figure that was going to stay secret. He said later, "That is a number which says to the American people that have just come off a traumatic moment in our history, and there's still a lot of trauma in our society, there really was. People—you know it as well as I know it. And the idea of saying, there's 331 al Qaeda–type killers lurking, to the point where they made a list, would have been a—just wasn't necessary.

"On the other hand, what was necessary was for our FBI to realize that all throughout the system, their mind-set had to change," Bush said, recalling his concern. "This enemy is elusive, very sophisticated. These aren't a bunch of poor people that are desperate in their attempt. These are cold, calculating killers."

Powell reported on the status of basing negotiations. Uzbekistan was still holding out. "Our chargé will see Karimov at 11 this morning. If we don't get a yes from him, I will call." He asked the president to call the Russian president and ask him to call the Uzbeks to encourage them to allow the U.S. in.

Rice thought that might have the opposite effect, but a call to Putin on related matters could be useful.

Bush was eager for the public announcement of an executive

order freezing terrorist finances. He was told it was essentially finished. Rice was going to work on it that afternoon.

BUSH CALLED PUTIN that weekend.

"We are going to support you in the war on terror," Putin said. Using translators, the two spoke for 42 minutes.

Putin said that Russia would grant the U.S. overflight clearance, but for humanitarian purposes only. "We can't put any Russian troops on the ground in Afghanistan," he said, according to the White House translation. "That makes no sense for you or for us." He didn't need to mention the disaster of Soviet intervention. "But we are prepared to provide search and rescue if you have downed pilots in northern Afghanistan. We are prepared to do that."

Bush asked if the Russian president would use his influence with the Central Asian states to help the U.S. obtain basing rights in the region.

"I am prepared to tell the heads of governments of the Central Asian states that we have good relations with that we have no objection to a U.S. role in Central Asia as long as it has the object of fighting the war on terror and is temporary and is not permanent. If it is that, then we will have no objection and that is what I will tell people." He said that Russia would be doing more for the U.S. than its traditional allies.

Rice was surprised. It was a significant concession. She had expected that Putin would tell Bush, Be careful, this was a region of Russian interest. Normally, the Russians would suspect hidden motives behind any U.S. presence there.

The big downside was that Russia did not have good relations with Uzbekistan, the key Central Asian state.

Rice thought Putin saw an opportunity to change relations between the U.S. and Russia. The Cold War was over and national security was no longer a zero-sum game. It seemed that Putin wanted not just to move from being enemies to neutral, but all the way to embracing a sense of common security. Putin seemed to see the anti-terror war as a strategic opportunity to break through to the U.S. president instantly. If Bush was looking to solidify a friendship by asking a favor, Putin was doing so by granting it. "I'm here to help" was the message being sent. You've got a friend in this time of enormous personal challenge. Rice thought it was smart on Putin's part.

THE PRESIDENT SAW the Putin relationship in deeply personal terms. In an interview, he described his first meeting with Putin on June 16, 2001, in Ljubljana, Slovenia:

"And in comes Putin, and he sits down, and it's just me, Condi, Putin, whatever that guy—Rashilov, and the interpreter from both sides. And he wants to get started. And I said, 'Let me say something about what caught my attention, Mr. President, was that your mother gave you a cross which you had blessed in Israel, the Holy Land.' And he said, 'It's true.' I said that amazed me, that here you were a Communist, KGB operative, and yet you were willing to wear a cross. 'That speaks volumes to me, Mr. President. May I call you Vladimir?' " So it became Vladimir and George after that, he said.

"And he said, 'The rest of the story is, is that I was wearing my cross. I hung it on a dacha. The dacha burned down, and the only thing I wanted recovered was the cross.' And he said, 'I remember the workman's hand opening, and there was the cross that my mother had given me, as if it was meant to be.' And I think I told him then, I said, 'Well, that's the story of the cross as far as I'm concerned. Things are meant to be.'

"He then immediately went to Soviet debt, how unfair it was that Russia is saddled with Soviet Union debt, and can we help. I was more interested in, who is this person I'm dealing with. I wanted to make sure that the story of the cross was a true story." It was Reagan's old motto, "Trust, but verify," but under an entirely new set of circumstances.

Putin showed the cross to Bush a month later at a meeting in Genoa, Italy.

"We had a very successful meeting. And I had convinced him that I no longer viewed Russia as an enemy, and I viewed him, on a personal level, as somebody with whom we could deal."

The phone call that weekend in September was important. "What he is saying is, 'Go get them, we want you to be successful.' However, in his tone it was clear that he needed reassurance that this was not a play to establish a long-term military presence in what was his former territory"—an assurance Bush said he readily gave.

KAREN HUGHES WAS at church on Sunday, September 23, when her pager went off, the president calling from Camp David. He was snappish.

"You all don't get it," he said.

Her draft statement on the president's Executive Order freezing the financial assets of terrorists completely missed the point. This was no ordinary bit of business to be handled by the treasury secretary in a routine press conference—it was big news, and they had to make it so.

"This is the first bullet in the war against terrorism. This is the first strike. It's not with guys in uniform. It's guys in pinstripes. This will hone in on the fact that this is a completely different kind of war. I should be making this announcement."

Hughes called Dan Bartlett.

"You know anything about this?"

Bartlett said yes. Normally the secretary of the treasury announced when assets were frozen.

They quickly realized that normal did not apply. Bush had repeatedly told them it would be up to them to communicate why and how this war was different. They had dropped the ball.

LATER THAT SUNDAY, the principals met again—Cheney, Powell, Rumsfeld, Tenet and Shelton. Rice presided, and laid out the agenda. "I want to hear from George Tenet on the chief of station report," she said. "I want to talk about our strategy on Afghanistan, and then I want to talk about the Putin/Ivanov conversations."

Tenet's chief of station in Islamabad, Pakistan, a very experienced regional expert, Bob,* had cabled an eight-page SECRET "Field Appraisal" that Tenet wanted to summarize.

"I asked the chief of station, how do we use covert action? How do you think about military targets? How do you think about sequencing?"

Mullah Omar, the supreme spiritual leader of the Taliban, would throw his lot in with bin Laden and the Taliban would "fatalistically" join in that support, the appraisal said. Tribal elders and ardent Afghan nationalists—of which there were no shortage among the Taliban—were growing increasingly skeptical of Mullah Omar for his hard-line fundamentalist brand of Islam and for his support of bin Laden and the Arab terrorists. The station chief suggested that the U.S. could play to those differences.

"The threat of U.S. action has provoked fissures within the Taliban that can be exploited," Tenet recounted. "There are tribal contacts with thousands of fighters. Our message: It's the Afghans against the Arabs. . . . Omar defied the elders, he picked the wrong side."

The warlords and opposition commanders were plentiful in both the north and south, according to the station chief. The cable did not identify them by name, but indicated that one had several

* CIA officers who are still operating undercover are identified by their first names only.

thousand fighters and a few others had 500 or 1,000 men. A half-dozen commanders had about 200 fighters, which he said might seem small but were important.

"September 11 was a heinous crime not consistent with the Koran. Choosing sides is a zero-sum game," Tenet said. "We need to encourage the king."

The king, Mohammed Zahir Shah, a moderate, pro-Western ethnic Pashtun, ruled the country from 1933 to 1973, a period of relative prosperity and stability. In exile in Rome since being deposed by his prime minister in a bloodless coup, he had many supporters in Afghanistan and internationally. There was hope that the 86-year-old monarch might inspire a revolt against the ruling Taliban and perhaps assume a leadership role in an interim government.

The main point in Bob's cable was that the war had to be cast as Afghans against the foreigners. "We need to brand these folks as outsiders. We need to go after Arab facilities and destroy the Arab infrastructure," Tenet said.

"We need to go after the Taliban leadership and then go after the Taliban more generally." Bob had stressed the importance of public diplomacy—the propaganda war—and suggested two themes. First, remind everyone about the successful CIA effort to drive the Soviets out of Afghanistan in the 1980s by supporting the native resistance movement. Second, underscore that the U.S. had no desire for territory or permanent bases in the region.

"We need to push the tribals into combat," Tenet said. The best opportunity for success was to get the opposition forces to do the work. "We need to give them reconnaissance, we need to help target the al Qaeda leadership, we need to have Afghans fighting Arabs and striking Arab targets. There should be quick, surgical ground attacks. We're passing money, we have got to pass communication equipment."

The U.S. action would not succeed if the Northern Alliance took over or even seemed to take over the country. The Pashtun majority would not accept that. It would lead to civil war and tribalism as bad as what we have inherited, Tenet said. "Let's ask the Pakistanis for everything they have on al Qaeda." The appraisal expressed confidence in President Musharraf.

"We want to hold off on the Taliban," Tenet continued, "so as not to destabilize Pakistan and our relationship with Pakistan." There was still sufficient support for the Taliban in Pakistan that a military campaign conspicuously against the Taliban could undermine Musharraf. "We want to get al Qaeda moving into enclaves, which may allow us to target them and exploit them."

"How does the strategy work domestically?" Rumsfeld asked. "We don't want to look like we are pounding sand." Rumsfeld knew that was loaded. "Pounding sand" was Bush's derisive expression for the weak efforts of the Clinton administration—cruise missiles into tents and so forth. "That's why we had Taliban military targets in our target set," Rumsfeld continued. The Taliban had the military assets, limited as they were, a few aircraft and radars. "We have to have something to hit. There is not a lot of al Qaeda to hit." The intelligence so far on al Qaeda largely showed tents and mud huts and empty training camps.

Looking for something actionable in the station chief's largely conceptual report, Rumsfeld lobbed a key question: What is my target set?

"We might focus on the Arab brigade up north," replied Tenet, "because there are defined Arab units." The Arab brigade—also known as Brigade 055—was the Taliban's elite fighting force. Trained in bin Laden's terror camps and so loyal that anyone who dared to retreat in battle was shot, the roughly 1,000 brigade members were the core of the Taliban/al Qaeda army. The best 100 or so soldiers served as bin Laden's personal security detail; the others fanned out across key cities in the north, spurring on the rank-and-file troops.

Target the brigade at the start, Tenet suggested, and whatever they did would just be a beginning. Tenet mentioned some Muslim commentators who might support what the U.S. wanted to do.

"Maybe we should put some people on the ground," Rumsfeld

said, "to conduct humanitarian operations both in the north and the south. Small units. It will help mute some criticism of our operations.

"We need actionable intelligence to let us work through this program," he said. He was not satisfied with the intelligence he was receiving. "We also need to think through our declaratory policy to divide Taliban from the al Qaeda and to divide other Taliban from Mullah Omar."

Propaganda and diplomatic pressure on the Taliban should be the focus, Powell said. "It is not the goal at the outset to change the regime but to get the regime to do the right thing." They could wait to see how the Taliban responded. "We hit al Qaeda targets because they were used for terrorism in the past." He understood that it was difficult to separate the two. "We'll sneak up on the Taliban issue," he proposed.

Uzbekistan had not yet responded to the U.S. They needed to reevaluate. What was its importance? How much did they need it?

The answer was they needed it a lot.

Rice said they needed to get on the ground in Afghanistan to gather intelligence about the enemy.

"Where do you want boots on the ground?" Powell asked.

"The north is more secure," offered Tenet, but they ultimately agreed that it would be best to get people in the north and the south.

"Boots on the ground has a value in and of itself," said Rumsfeld. "It gives a different image for the United States." Leaning forward. "We're not invading, we're not going to stay. But we need to start creating an environment in which Afghanistan becomes inhospitable to the al Qaeda and the Taliban."

Rice wanted to settle on how they would present all of this to the president the next day. She liked to deliver the president clear, unambiguous summaries that reflected their thinking. The best way frequently was to orchestrate and script the next day's NSC meeting. They agreed on who was going to say what, and in what order.

• • •

IN A MORNING intelligence briefing with Tenet during this period, the president was going over the threats—threats to malls, buildings, cities, businesses, individuals, bridges, tunnels, sporting events, any large gathering place.

"We can't chase everything," he said. He wanted a risk analysis. "Let's prioritize, let's assess risk and then let's figure out the strategy necessary to deal with each risk."

Bush recalled in an interview, "It was the continuation of understanding the frame of mind of the enemy. In order to win a war, you must understand the enemy.

"What I was very worried about at the time was the psychological effect of a dirty type of bomb." A so-called crude radiological bomb could be made by taking highly radioactive material, such as spent reactor fuel rods, and wrapping the material around conventional explosives. "Whether you're alone or with your National Security Council, you begin to think about and talk about worst case scenarios, and how to deal with them. You know there are some pretty devastating worst case scenarios that we've got to think through."

Bush, Tenet and Rice tried to think through the possibilities. Clearly, bin Laden and his network liked spectacular. Maybe they would hit monuments, maybe the entertainment industry in some form because of their hatred of American values. Everything was a potential target, from the White House to a small school in the Midwest prairie.

"We're going to have to make some bets about what's likely," Bush said. Make some lists, a report, almost assess the odds and likelihood. He was serious, ordering Tenet to get after it right away, at once.

Tenet went to a phone in the White House and called his deputy, John McLaughlin, at CIA headquarters.

"We have to put down on paper what we think the targets are," Tenet said.

Huh? McLaughlin thought. Maybe they could send in the telephone books from every place in the world.

"We don't know," Tenet conceded, "because there is not the specificity." He realized the difficulty. "But place your bets." Yes, this had to be on paper. Get the best heads around the table—do it now. Try to figure out what motivates these guys. What are they trying to achieve? What would help them achieve what they are trying to achieve? "Place your bets."

McLaughlin, a soft-spoken, professorial CIA veteran who had risen to the No. 2 position at the agency through the analytical side, was intrigued. Certainly there was a way to think about all of this— intelligence analysis was in part about placing the best bets possible.

SHORTLY AFTER 9:30 on Monday morning, September 24, Bush stepped out into the Rose Garden to speak to reporters.

"At 12:01 this morning, a major thrust of our war on terrorism began with the stroke of a pen," Bush said. "Today we have launched a strike on the financial foundation of the global terror network." He had signed an Executive Order last night—just after midnight, well past his usual bedtime—that immediately froze the financial assets of several terrorist organizations, several leaders, a front corporation and several nonprofit organizations—27 in all.

It meant that U.S. banks had to freeze the assets of the 27 groups and named individuals. The tough order, which went into effect before the start of the banking day, also put pressure on banks and financial institutions overseas, where the U.S. had no jurisdiction but where most terrorist money was believed to be held. If those banks failed to share information and freeze terrorist-linked assets themselves, the Treasury Department could prohibit them from conducting transactions or accessing their assets in the U.S. It gave Treasury sweeping authority which Bush pledged would be exercised responsibly.

"We have developed the international financial equivalent of law enforcement's 'Most Wanted' list," he said. The list of 27 was just a beginning.

9

THE PRESIDENT MOVED briskly from the Rose Garden down to the White House Situation Room for the scheduled 9:45 A.M. NSC meeting.

"Mr. President," Cheney began, following the script, "you directed us to discuss the chief of station memo at principals level. We've done that. We've generally adapted our plans to reflect the input from the chief of station memo. Our priority is first to go after the al Qaeda camps, to start narrowing their freedom of action.

"We're going to focus on Omar, to encourage the current Taliban leadership to replace him with someone more amenable to what we need done with respect to al Qaeda.

"Then we will focus on the Taliban military and are also going to go after that al Qaeda brigade in the north."

Cheney was presenting the rough game plan and sequence. But the timing was almost totally up in the air.

The principals had different thoughts on whether to go after the Taliban up front. This had been reflected the day before on the Sunday television talk shows. Powell had said, "That is not uppermost in our minds right now." Rice had hinted otherwise, "It's a very repressive and terrible regime. The Afghan people would be better off without it. We will see what means are at our disposal to do that."

"We're going to crank it up this week," Tenet said. One of his secret paramilitary teams would soon be going into Afghanistan with the Northern Alliance. "We're providing intelligence and surveillance on soft targets. We're going to give them some time to consider."

Tenet turned to the core concepts that he and the CIA leadership had developed with agency experts and from the Islamabad station chief's appraisal. "We want to structure it as Afghanistan versus the outsiders," he said, repeating himself. "We are not invading. We are not occupying. Mullah Omar betrayed the Afghan people. He let in these outsiders. That's the problem."

He said it was important to delay a direct attack on the Taliban. Their missiles and radars would have to be hit initially for defense of the U.S. bombers. "But we'll hold off going hard on the Taliban to see if we get traction on the notion of either a change in Taliban leadership or some other way to break with al Qaeda." And if they didn't get traction, then they would go hard against the Taliban troops and leadership.

Cheney agreed. "We don't want to hit the Taliban up front, for we don't want to discourage them from changing leadership and breaking with al Qaeda."

Rice voiced her concern that it might unite the Afghans against the United States.

"Are there any doubts about the station chief's assessment?" asked Cheney.

"All my Afghan people agree with the station chief," Tenet said.

"This should be a template for our strategy. We should use the Afghans in the struggle," Bush said.

"The chief of station and Tommy Franks will discuss this," Tenet replied.

"You need to be exactly clear on what it is you are asking of the Uzbeks," Powell said. "The bases, the number of people, what are they going to do, how long they are going to be there."

"Look," Rumsfeld said, "we have to say things in a general

way, because we don't know what we're going to do until we get there." The Pentagon was still coming up dry on war plans. Privately, Rumsfeld was furious and beating on Franks incessantly.

The Pentagon and the State Department faced a familiar problem of how to secure overflight and basing rights from foreign countries for operations that were not fully knowable until the conflict was under way. Nations that are considering what kind of rights to grant want specific information about the type, length and size of planned operations before granting any permissions. But defense officials had no idea whether a conflict might escalate and demand larger operations. So the military tended to over-request, pushing for as much as possible and thus delaying or prolonging negotiations.

They turned to the question of what the Uzbeks would want in return if an agreement could be reached.

Powell said that they had to be careful about what the cost would be. The initial forays suggested that it would become real rug-merchant work, no first offer would be accepted.

Rice knew that President Karimov wanted action against his internal opposition, the extreme fundamentalist Islamic Movement of Uzbekistan (IMU). One of the dangers was to let every opposition figure be characterized as a terrorist who would then be subject to the U.S. terrorism war. "We have to make sure we know what we're buying into," she cautioned.

"We need to get al Qaeda before they get us," said Cheney. He was as worried as anyone that they would attack again. "We have to be willing to deal with the Russians to that end."

Several around the table who had worked with Cheney were surprised. They knew how deeply distrustful he had been of the former Soviet Union and the current Russian government. His willingness to work with the remnants of the former "Evil Empire" spoke volumes.

Bush would recall, "I think Dick began to realize that Putin was different, because he had heard from my discussions with Putin." Cheney "clearly understood that we were evolving toward a relationship that was going to be significantly different, that the Cold War was in fact over."

Powell gave his formulation. "We want Afghanistan to be terrorist-free. If the Taliban can do that, fine. If not, we will work with someone else as long as they make it terrorist-free. Our rhetoric should avoid suggesting we are trying to determine who runs Afghanistan at the end of the day."

The president turned to what was increasingly on his mind. "I want a humanitarian aid drop in the north and the south. I want it coordinated with the military. Can we have the first bombs we drop be food?"

Anyone with a basic understanding of military strategy might have smiled at the question. The noisy, slow-moving transport planes used for food drops are sitting ducks until air defense installations are wiped out. Politely, Shelton replied, "Well, you know, you have to be concerned about air defense." He knew it would be negligent to go in there with the first humanitarian assistance plane and have it shot down.

"How are we coming on Pakistan?" Bush asked.

Hadley reported on a large aid package for Pakistan.

Cheney was less concerned with humanitarian or Pakistani aid than he was with weapons of mass destruction. "We need to be targeting WMD and drug labs in our initial strikes," the vice president said.

Toward the end Rumsfeld said, "We need to get a list of requests of what we want to ask from each country and break it up into individual pieces."

THE SURPRISE FOR Rice was when the president raised the issue of humanitarian aid. It had not really been discussed among the principals, the deputies or sub-deputies. What was this? Where was it coming from?

For Bush, it was fundamental to what he sees as the moral

mission of the United States. I explored the issue with him at length in a later interview. "I was sensitive to this [accusation] that this was a religious war, and that somehow the United States would be the conqueror. And I wanted us to be viewed as the liberator," the president said. The idea of feeding the poor Afghan people appealed to him. He said he didn't believe the people supported the Taliban, and were at best pawns. "The idea of bombing a people into submission, therefore causing the government to fall, was not a relevant thought in this war." Bombing the people might make the Taliban stronger. That was the practical consideration. The moral one, he said, was, "We've got to deal with suffering."

Bush had seen satellite pictures of starvation, torture and prison camp brutality on a massive scale in North Korea. He also knew of forced starvation in Iraq. "There is a human condition that we must worry about in times of war. There is a value system that cannot be compromised—God-given values. These aren't United States–created values. There are values of freedom and the human condition and mothers loving their children. What's very important as we articulate foreign policy through our diplomacy and military action, is that it never look like we are creating—we are the author of these values.

"It leads to a larger question of your view about God." And the lesson, he said, was, "We're all God's children." He wanted war with both practical and moral dimensions.

After he had proposed that the first bombs be food, the president remembered, everyone got it. "Rumsfeld grasped it, Mr. Hard Guy, who is not a hard guy. He's a very softhearted man in many ways. He understood it immediately." The military might have been bemused at first, he said, but they understood.

The principals met without the president later that afternoon via video teleconference. After routine reports from Ashcroft and Powell, Rice raised the issue of state sponsorship of terrorism. "What is our strategy with respect to countries that support terrorism like Iran, Iraq, Libya, Syria and Sudan? How do we define the hurdles they have to jump over to get on the right side of the war on terrorism?" The United States needed some benchmarks by which to evaluate states' terrorist leanings.

"We need a small group, deputies and principals, to look at the next phase in the war on terror," she said.

"TRYING TO ANTICIPATE the Next Attack" was the title of the highly classified three-page paper that arrived in the president's inbox the morning of Tuesday, September 25. It was the report that Bush had requested several days earlier. It was distributed to him and a limited number of his key advisers with the President's Daily Brief (PDB), the most restricted document in Washington.

The report was put together by a "Red Cell" team that Tenet and McLaughlin had set up. The team of experienced CIA analysts and operatives saw all incoming intelligence on bin Laden, al Qaeda and other relevant international terrorism. Their job was to think like bin Laden and his lieutenants and say what the other side—what Bush and Tenet called "the Bad Guys"—might be thinking or doing.

A notation on the paper said that since Red Cell had been directed to think "unconventional" and "out of the box," their thoughts should not be taken as conclusive. The Red Cell had been tasked to consider the "limitless" number of possible terrorist targets, and then to attempt to narrow that down to the most likely future domestic targets given the past practices of al Qaeda. In other words, to place their bets.

The Red Cell had come up with nine categories:

1. Political centers—Washington, D.C., or federal offices anywhere
2. Infrastructure facilities—airports, roads, harbors, railroads, dams, tunnels, bridges
3. Economic systems—Wall Street, Chicago trading centers
4. Energy infrastructure—refineries, oil platforms

5. Military targets—areas of large troop concentrations, Army, Navy, Air Force or Marine bases, weapons storage sites
6. Global telecommunications—electronic communications transit points, Internet computer routing centers, banking nodes
7. Educational centers—Harvard and the Massachusetts Institute of Technology (MIT) in the Boston area
8. Cultural centers—Hollywood, sports stadiums
9. Monuments and other symbols of national identity

"UBL tends to go back after targets they considered or previously attacked," the paper said, noting that some possible targets have "multiple values."

The White House had such multiple value as both a political center and a symbol of national identity. Bush was living and working at a designated Ground Zero.

THE NATIONAL SECURITY Council met again on Tuesday, September 25, at the White House. The president spoke first. "We can't define the success or failure in terms of capturing UBL."

Tenet reported on the Northern Alliance. "The people are ready to go. They are not Pashtuns, but they are anti-Taliban. We won't be able to hold them back. They will hit both al Qaeda and Taliban targets, because they are all intermixed." A CIA team was about to go in. "We will encourage them to go to the targets. They've got communications gear to give us intelligence. We'll give them money. We will have to decide whether to pay for the Soviet weapons we're going to be provided."

The Northern Alliance controlled a part of the northeast quadrant of the country. "It is a potential base of operations," Tenet said. "We want to push as much pressure from the north and from the south. We'll have meetings with district leaders. We want to seal the borders and make sure the Arabs don't flee."

"Do we want to pay the Russians for Soviet weapons?" Powell asked.

"Does it help advance the mission?" asked Bush.

"Yes," Tenet said.

Bush wanted it done.

"There is little change from the chief of station approach," Rice said, referring to the ideas suggested in the cable from Islamabad. "Do we need to change the target list?"

"Well, we are going to hit the SAM and air defense up front," said Tenet, referring to the surface-to-air missile sites. The CIA director was directly involving himself in military discussions because it was his men who were ready to go in on the ground while the Pentagon was lagging. "Are there any other Taliban targets we want to strike in the north?"

It remained an open question. Once the U.S. exhausted the target set of Taliban air defenses, operations would be hamstrung without men on the ground to scout out targets and relay precise coordinates. There was enough space in southern Afghanistan to begin inserting ground forces, though the situation was not optimal. In the north, however, they would have to explore alternative approaches since Uzbekistan had not yet committed on basing rights.

"Can we base in the Northern Alliance areas?" asked Cheney. Another possibility was to launch from Tajikistan, which had agreed to support the U.S. But the flight path from there into northern Afghanistan was treacherous and involved climbing over a tall mountain range.

"We have a deadline on Uzbekistan as 4 P.M.," said Franks. "If we can't get it, we'll have to drop the north, do it later, and do the south now. In the south, we'll have to operate off carriers" in the Indian Ocean, Franks said, what they called a "lily pad" strategy, using the carriers as oceangoing stepping-stones.

They reviewed comments that some Islamic scholars had made about the Pentagon's name for the operation. "Operation Infinite Justice" had been quickly criticized for its insensitivity to the Muslim faith, which holds that only Allah can mete out infinite justice. The name was shelved. Rumsfeld said he had decided on "Enduring Freedom."

But the Pentagon's image problem was a minor worry for Rumsfeld compared to the major overhaul of the armed services he had begun, and was now executing while trying to conduct a war. Skeptics were saying that he could not transform the military and fight a war. But Rumsfeld's thinking was, If you're fighting a different kind of war, the war transforms the military.

We're changing our Special Operations Forces so they have a global role, he said. They won't be tied to individual geographic areas under the CINCs any longer, that is, not limited to certain operational theaters.

Tenet saw the transformation as not limited to the Pentagon; the CIA was thinking anew as well. "And we're working between the military and our covert people side by side," he added, "with transparency between them, deconflicting and viewing both in a global context." Deconflicting meant keeping their forces from shooting each other.

They discussed whether to issue a white paper, designed to prove that bin Laden and al Qaeda were behind the September 11 attacks.

Did they want or need a white paper? Rumsfeld asked. It could set an awful precedent. Suppose they wanted to launch a preemptive military attack on terrorists or some state sponsor? They could create an expectation that some white paper would follow. That might not be possible. National security decisions about military action often had to be made on the best available evidence and that might fall far short of courtroom proof. They could be setting themselves up.

While American and allied intelligence services were beginning to unravel the trail of the September 11 attacks, the evidence was circumstantial and somewhat fragmentary, though there were some hard nuggets. The danger of issuing a white paper that presented evidence was that it could condition people to view the war on terror as a law enforcement operation, within the model of the judicial system with its evidentiary standards, burden of proof on the government and proof beyond a reasonable doubt—things that could not possibly be met.

Powell wanted some kind of white paper if possible. He had to deal with European and Arab states where the leaders wanted evidence and proof.

Turning to the outline of the war, Rumsfeld said, "We ought to have a broad beginning and an ending. It ought to focus on al Qaeda—it shouldn't focus on UBL. . . . It's not over if we get his head on a platter. And the failure to get his head on a platter is not failure."

The president asked about international participation in the first phase of the operation.

"Look, we're not able to define a special operations role for our own forces," Rumsfeld replied. "Until we can do that, how can we talk about including others?"

"We need to plan as if things won't go well," Bush said. What was the scenario if there was no split in the Taliban? "We need to war-game it out, figure out how to keep the pressure on them and effect change, even if things don't go the way we want."

When he commented later in an interview about why he, the perennial optimist, wanted to examine bad scenarios, Bush said, "I think my job is to stay ahead of the moment. A president, I guess, can get so bogged down in the moment that you're unable to be the strategic thinker that you're supposed to be, or at least provide strategic thought. And I'm the kind of person that wants to make sure that all risk is assessed. There is no question what the reward is in this case. But a president is constantly analyzing, making decisions based upon risk, particularly in war, risk taken relative to the—what can be achieved." He had advisers "who have seen war, who have been in situations where the plan didn't happen the way it was planned."

Whether it was trying to stay ahead of the moment, assessing risk or reaching a consensus, he said, "I just think it's instinctive. I'm not a textbook player. I'm a gut player."

He and the others were increasingly discovering there was no textbook for this war.

At the meeting, Rumsfeld said, "Look, as part of the war on terrorism, should we be getting something going in another area, other than Afghanistan, so that success or failure and progress isn't measured just by Afghanistan?"

It was becoming clearer and clearer that the defense secretary didn't want success to hinge on Afghanistan. The targets were meager. What could they actually accomplish?

But Bush's focus remained Afghanistan, he recalled. "Obviously, there were some who discussed Iraq. That's out of the question at this point. I mean, I didn't need any briefings." Rumsfeld wanted to show that the war on terror was global, the president said. "Rumsfeld wanted to make sure that the military was active in other regions. My point was that the degree of difficulty had to be relatively small in order to make sure that we continued to succeed in the first battle."

Cheney's biggest concern was still the possibility that bin Laden or other terrorists would acquire and use weapons of mass destruction. Nothing had suggested that al Qaeda possessed any nuclear devices, but there was a concern about biological and chemical weapons.

"Can we do a good enough job of identifying targets in Afghanistan that relate to BW/CW?" Cheney asked. "It should be a top priority.

"We need to have a deliberate strategy but also we need to hit him before he hits us. Give additional targets."

"We need to ratchet down my trip to the Far East," Bush said. The president was scheduled to travel to Shanghai for the Asia-Pacific Economic Cooperation (APEC) summit later in October and then visit Beijing, Tokyo and Seoul. They should cancel the latter three cities. "I need to be here."

Later that morning Bush welcomed Japanese Prime Minister Junichiro Koizumi to the White House. In a private meeting, he told Koizumi the problem of terrorism was theirs together. "In this new war," Bush said, "cutting off funding is just as important as dropping a bomb. Aid to Pakistan is just as important as landing troops." He was going to be deliberate, patient, because the consequences would be great. "We're angry, but we're not stupid."

10

ABOUT 4 A.M. Washington time the next morning, Wednesday, September 26, a husky 59-year-old man with a round, cheerful face and glasses was huddled in the back of a Russian-made, CIA-owned Mi-17 helicopter that was going to have to strain to climb 15,000 feet to clear the Anjoman Pass into the Panjshir Valley of northeastern Afghanistan. It was 12:30 P.M. there.

Gary was leading the first critical wave of President George W. Bush's war against terrorism. With him was a team of CIA covert paramilitary officers with communications gear that would allow them to set up direct classified links with headquarters. Between his legs was a large strapped metal suitcase that contained $3 million in United States currency, nonsequential $100 bills. He always laughed when he saw a television show or movie where someone passed $1 million in a small attaché case. It just wouldn't fit.

Several times in his career, Gary had stuffed $1 million into his backpack so he could move around and pass it to people on other operations. He had signed for the $3 million as usual. What was different this time was that he could dole it out pretty much at his own discretion.

Gary had been an officer in the Directorate of Operations of the CIA for 32 years, the type of CIA clandestine operative that many thought no longer existed. In the 1970s, he had been an undercover case officer in Tehran and then Islamabad. He had re- cruited, developed, paid and run agents who reported from within the host governments. In the 1980s, he served as chief of the CIA base in Dubai, United Arab Emirates, and later as chief of station for Kabul. The American Embassy in Kabul was closed due to the Soviet invasion, so he operated out of Islamabad. In the 1990s, he served as deputy chief of station in Saudi Arabia, then chief of a se- cret overseas station that operated against Iran. From 1996 to 1999, he had been chief of station in Islamabad, and then deputy chief of the CIA's Near East and South Asia operations division at Langley.

On September 11, Gary had been almost out the door, weeks away from retirement and in the agency's 90-day retirement transi- tion program. Another officer had taken over as deputy division chief. His wife was delighted.

Gary had been pulled back inside the door on the Saturday that President Bush had the day-long meeting with his war cabinet at Camp David, September 15. That day, he had received a call from Cofer Black, the head of the agency's counterterrorism center, ask- ing him to come into headquarters.

Black told him, "I know you're ready to retire. But we want to send a team in right away. You're the logical person to go in." Not only did Gary have the experience, he spoke Pashto and Dari, Af- ghanistan's two main languages.

The team would be a small group of CIA operatives and para- military officers working out of the super-secret Special Activities Division of the Directorate of Operations.

"Yeah, I'll go," Gary said. When he was Islamabad station chief he had made several covert trips into Afghanistan, meeting with the Northern Alliance leaders, bringing in cash, normally $200,000—a bag of money on the table. He had known Ahmed Shah Massoud. Massoud had held the rival warlords together, and his assassination was surely designed to rid the opposition Northern Alliance of that glue and leadership.

Go in, Black told Gary, convince the Northern Alliance to work with us, which shouldn't be too hard given the situation and the fact that Massoud was just assassinated by the same people who attacked New York and the Pentagon. Prepare the ground in Afghanistan to receive U.S. forces, to give them a place to come in and stage operations.

The post-Massoud situation among the Northern Alliance was unclear. Gary's team would be the first in. No backup. Minimal available search and rescue teams to get them out if something went wrong.

Four days later, on September 19, Black called Gary back to his office. The team, formally called the Northern Afghanistan Liaison Team (NALT), was given the codeword "Jawbreaker." They were to deploy the next day, proceed to Europe and then into the region and into Afghanistan as fast as possible.

Jawbreaker had another assignment. The president had signed a new intelligence order, the gloves were off.

"You have one mission," Black instructed. "Go find the al Qaeda and kill them. We're going to eliminate them. Get bin Laden, find him. I want his head in a box."

"You're serious?" asked Gary. Black had a penchant for dramatizing and Gary knew the presidential restraints on direct killing and assassination. He was the guy who had told CIA assets, the GE/SENIOR bin Laden tracking teams, that they could not ambush bin Laden's convoy because it would be deemed assassination.

"Absolutely," Black said. The new authority was clear. Yes, he said, he wanted bin Laden's head. "I want to take it down and show the president."

"Well, that couldn't be any clearer," Gary replied.

Gary left Washington the next day, and the team hooked up in Asia. There was a maddening wait for visas and clearances to get into Uzbekistan and Tajikistan.

Now in the helicopter, he had to worry through the two-and-a-half-hour overflight into Afghanistan. A CIA man in Tashkent, Uzbekistan, was in regular radio contact with the Northern Alliance and had radioed that the team was heading in. But the radio link was not secure, and though the territory they were flying over was supposed to be controlled by the Northern Alliance, any Taliban or al Qaeda with a Stinger missile or a Z-23 antiaircraft gun on a hilltop could have shot the Mi-17 out of the air.

The CIA had purchased the reliable Russian helicopter more than a year earlier for $1.5 million. The Mi-17 is a workhorse, not a handsome machine, but it provided good cover. The U.S. had upgraded theirs with better avionics, night vision capability and a paint job to match the Northern Alliance fleet.

Because the copter would have to climb 15,000 feet to clear the mountains, Gary had consolidated their equipment, weapons and other packages to lighten the load. They had brought lots of food because they had no idea what conditions they would find, or whether they would have to live off the land.

Jawbreaker comprised 10 men—Gary, a senior deputy, a young Directorate of Operations case officer who had four years in Pakistan and spoke excellent Farsi and Dari, an experienced field communications officer who had worked in tough places, a former Navy SEAL, another paramilitary operative, a longtime agency medic, two pilots and a helicopter mechanic. The men spanned nearly 30 years in age, different shapes and sizes. They wore camping clothes and baseball caps.

Jawbreaker touched down in a landing field about 70 miles north of Kabul, in the heart of Northern Alliance territory at about 3 P.M. local time.

Two Northern Alliance officers and about 10 others greeted them. They loaded the gear on a big truck and drove about a mile to a guest house that Massoud had fixed up in a tiny village. The village had been cordoned off with a checkpoint at each end. The Alliance officers were nervous and wanted the team out of sight.

Their quarters were in a primitive building with a concrete floor covered with a pseudo-carpet. The roof consisted of tree trunks across, then packing crate material on top, followed by a mud layer. The air was dusty as hell, and the dirt never went away.

The toilet was a hole in the floor that they could urinate into or squat over.

By about 6 P.M., they had their secure communications up. Gary sent a classified cable asking for some resupplies. In the exuberance of the safe arrival and mindful of Cofer Black's request about bin Laden's head, he added a line to the cable requesting some heavy-duty cardboard boxes and dry ice, and if possible some pikes.

GARY'S FIRST MEETING that evening was with Engineer Muhammed Arif Sawari, who headed the Alliance's intelligence and security service. Arif had argued to his commander Massoud that he not receive the two men who assassinated him, though they had come as journalists with letters of introduction. Nonetheless, because he had been in charge of security, and because the assassination had taken place in his office, he was under immense pressure to help pull the Alliance together.

Arif recognized Gary from the previous December, when as deputy division chief, he had met with Massoud in Paris. Arif seemed to relax. "You were there," he said.

Gary nodded and placed a bundle of cash on the table: $500,000 in 10 one-foot stacks of $100 bills. He believed it would be more impressive than the usual $200,000, the best way to say, We're here, we're serious, here's money, we know you need it.

"What we want you to do is use it," he said. "Buy food, weapons, whatever you need to build your forces up." It was also for intelligence operations and to pay sources and agents. There was more money available—much more. Gary would soon ask CIA headquarters for and receive $10 million in cash.

The Northern Alliance welcomes you, Arif said.

The plan, Gary said, was to prepare the way for the U.S. military forces. "We don't know how they're coming or how many, but we're looking at Special Forces, you know, small units, guys coming in to do operations and help you and help your army and coordinate between your forces and the U.S. forces that are going to come and attack the Taliban army. We need to coordinate this."

Great, Arif said.

AT THE WHITE HOUSE, the president and Rice talked privately about when military action might begin.

"I have to have a good sense of this timing of when we really are going to be ready to go," Bush told her. "Because I have to keep preparing the American people. They've been through a terrible shock. They can't just cease to hear from us. I have to know when something's going to get started."

Did she think they would be ready early next week—Monday or Tuesday?

"I really don't know," she replied carefully. Her private thought was that it was unlikely they would be ready in five or six days. But she didn't feel it was her place to tell the president that this wasn't likely or possible. She was a coordinator. If pressed hard after the president had heard the views of the others, she would give her opinion, but only then. It was premature for her to speak, and there was no telling what Rumsfeld and Franks might say. Rumsfeld, in particular, was often full of surprises. "It's a question you should put before the group," Rice suggested.

In an interview, the president recalled this day. "One of my jobs is to be provocative," he said, "seriously, to provoke people into—to force decisions, and to make sure it's clear in everybody's mind where we're headed. There was a certain rhythm and flow to this, and I was beginning to get a little frustrated. . . . It was just not coming together as quickly as we had hoped. And I was trying to force the issue without compromising safety."

At this point he understood how cautious the military is. "It's very important to realize how do you balance the military's desire to cover all contingencies at least once, maybe sometimes twice—

they're relatively risk-adverse and they should be, after all they're dealing with people's lives—versus the need to, for whatever reason, to show action."

He had a number of thoughts that caused him to want to be provocative with his war cabinet. "The idea of attacking an enemy, a command I had never given before, is and still is a significant decision by a president. And I wanted to make sure that the people understood that we were getting ready to attack and that I wanted a clarification of their points of view." He said he wanted to ask, "Does anybody doubt?"

"I can only just go by my instincts. Listen, I am a product of the Vietnam world. There is a very fine line between micromanaging combat and setting the tactics" on one hand, which he didn't want to do, and "to kind of make sure there is a sense of, not urgency, but sense of purpose and forward movement." He worried that the United States had lost its edge. "My job is to make sure that that blade is sharp.

"My instincts were beginning to tell me that there was kind of an anxiety beginning to build. And I wanted to make sure that our coalition knew we were tough." Some allies were praising him for showing initial restraint, and he added sarcastically, "We've got a coalition of people who—they *love* the idea that the United States hasn't immediately rushed into action."

His visit to Ground Zero in New York City was still on his mind. "These people looking at you in the eye, these tired faces, 'You go get 'em.' And we're going to get 'em, there's no question about that." He didn't feel public pressure at that point. "On the other hand, my body, my clock is just—or however you want to—instincts . . . I am pushing.

"The president and the war council have got to obviously be decisive, but not be hasty."

So provocation was going to be one tool. Did he explain or warn Rice or the other war cabinet members that he was testing, planning on being provocative?

"Of course not. I'm the commander—see, I don't need to explain—I do not need to explain why I say things. That's the interesting thing about being the president. Maybe somebody needs to explain to me why they say something, but I don't feel like I owe anybody an explanation."

A NUMBER OF pressing matters were coming to a head the morning of Wednesday, September 26, when the NSC met.

Tenet turned to some of the secret operations. The CIA had been able to work some renditions abroad—capturing or snatching suspected terrorists in other countries. Various foreign intelligence services were either cooperating or were being bought off to take suspected terrorists into custody.

In most cases, the suspects were turned over to the local police or law enforcement agencies. It was an effective way to put suspected al Qaeda operatives on ice indefinitely and to question them. Tenet had big ambitions for the rendition program, hoping to take hundreds of suspected terrorists, if not more, out of circulation. Most CIA stations abroad had lists and information on the al Qaeda suspects in their countries. In countries such as Egypt, Jordan or certain African states where civil liberties and due process were not significant issues, the intelligence services were more than willing to accommodate CIA requests. The free ride for terrorists abroad was going to cease.

"We're looking at something going on in Sudan," Tenet said. "We're looking at something going in Bulgaria, we're looking at something that involves the Iraqis and we're looking at something involving Hezbollah," the Iranian-supported terrorist organization, "and South America."

Tenet made it clear the rendition program was not only global but broad. Targets would include terrorist groups other than al Qaeda.

The president, obviously pleased, asked, "At what point are we going to feel comfortable talking about these things?" It was another potential scorecard that could be announced publicly.

The operations were sensitive and most countries were opposed, passionately, even violently, to any publicity that would show they were in bed or in the pay of the American CIA. When there were dozens or even hundreds of successful renditions, the aggregate numbers might be able to be released.

The CIA's first paramilitary team had entered Afghanistan, Tenet said. "We're deploying some small UAVs," meaning the aerial Predator drones that were armed. "We've established some contacts. We're urging the local forces to go after some small targets. We've got some real-time intelligence now to provide targeting information, and we've got our search and rescue in place so we can get some people out if we get in trouble.

"We're in contact with three leaders in the north. We've got 100 targets we're going to work." Focusing on the southern region, he said, "In the south we've got contacts with the southern tribes—we're beginning to get some access. We're using similar messages as we did in the north about what we're about." That meant firm declarations would be made about the U.S. having no territorial ambitions or desire for a permanent presence in Afghanistan.

"The British, as you know, have some sources in the south," Tenet continued. "We're paired up with them. And we're going to add some of our people to their people. We're going to try and work to encourage some defections and surrender from Taliban folks in the south." By sharing with the British, he said they would make sure the two countries' operations or operatives didn't run over each other. "We have sources, contacts in the south, we're going to try and see if we can integrate them and run it as a single operation effectively.

"And then, of course, we need to understand and coordinate the relations between what we're doing in the north and what we're doing in the south," Tenet said. That was a big question, one of many large uncertainties.

Powell said he was working access through Uzbekistan and Tajikistan. "We've had contact now with the president of Tajikistan," Powell said, "and he's given us basically everything we want. He wants to work with us directly, not through any intermediary, and wants us to keep it confidential."

He turned to Oman. "A message is going in today," he said, a request for basing rights, "and I'm pessimistic."

Part of the problem was an ongoing British military exercise in Oman that was crowding out space, such as parking places on airfields and the like, Powell said. "The question in some sense is this a reason or an excuse for being slow to respond to our request? But we're working it." The Omanis had shown no outward signs that they were uninterested in cooperating, but accommodating British war games didn't seem like a particularly good rationale for keeping the U.S. out—especially since the British had pledged support in the real war getting underway in Afghanistan. Maybe they were missing something, or doing too much extrapolating of the Omani position.

Rice had called David Manning, Blair's foreign affairs adviser. Manning had assured her they weren't going to allow an exercise to stand in the way of getting U.S. forces on the ground.

Powell said they were working Qatar, one of the smallest Gulf States, as a potential intermediate stop for U.S. military forces, which then could jump to U.S. Navy aircraft carriers acting as lily pads on their way to Afghanistan. Cheney was going to make a phone call to Qatar, where he had relationships stemming from the 1991 Gulf War.

Powell said that Sudan, a notorious haven for terrorists, seemed to be cooperating with the CIA. "We got a good reaction from them on the financing terrorism EO," the Executive Order on freezing terrorist assets.

"We expect to get a good resolution on terrorism out of the OIC," Powell added, referring to the Organization of the Islamic Conference, a group representing the interests of 57 Muslim nations.

"I'm a little worried about our people in the embassies in Indonesia and Malaysia," Tenet said. There had been threats. Al Qaeda presence in those countries was formidable.

"I'll take that one on," Powell said. The State Department had already issued a general warning on Indonesia that extremist elements might be planning to target U.S. facilities there. Recently, anti-American sentiment had begun spilling over from the militant Islamic minority into the general public and government. The former president, Abdurrahman Wahid, had publicly called the U.S. a "terrorist nation." The current vice president had said the 9/11 attacks could help America "cleanse its sins."

"I want to talk more about humanitarian assistance to Afghanistan," the president said, "and I want to hear about options for getting things going in the south."

Defense announced it was working the assistance issue, and Tenet said he was pushing hard on the options for the south.

"I want to make sure we've got our declaratory policy right," Bush said. Were they saying what they were doing and planned on doing? Clearly, many in the war cabinet, including Tenet, thought the Taliban were so tight with al Qaeda that for practical purposes they were inseparable. But Bush's ultimatum to the Taliban was still on the table.

"Look," Rice said, "we're going to stick to what you asked from the Taliban in your speech the other night. If the Afghan people want to overthrow the Taliban, that's fine. But what we've asked from the Taliban are the things we asked in the president's speech about al Qaeda."

"Yep," the president said, "we've got to stick to what we've asked."

"We've got to emphasize what the president demanded," Powell said. "If we make overthrowing the Taliban government the goal, then we'd need a new campaign plan and there'll be an issue about how the Pakistanis will react." The secretary of state, uncomfortable with wanton regime change, added, "So the president's statement was, Fine, that's where we ought to stay."

"If they reject our demands and they harbor al Qaeda—as they're doing—and we don't respond, then it suggests we're not serious," Rumsfeld interjected. The "as they're doing" was pointed. Rumsfeld wanted a hard line. How long could an ultimatum remain on the table? He didn't want the Taliban hiding behind some fiction. They were harboring bin Laden and his network. The president had said those who harbored terrorists would pay.

"That's right, Don," Rice said. "But we're not there yet."

She reminded the group where they stood. "Our message at this point is still comply with what the president asked for or you will share the al Qaeda fate."

The problem was that bin Laden and the network were virtually untouched in their sanctuary 15 days after the attacks.

For many days the war cabinet had been dancing around the basic question: How long could they wait after September 11 before the U.S. started going "kinetic," as they often termed it, against al Qaeda in a visible way? The public was patient, at least it seemed patient, but everyone wanted action. A full military operation—air and boots—would be the essential demonstration of seriousness— to bin Laden, America and the world. The president took the floor.

"Anybody doubt that we should start this Monday or Tuesday of next week?" he inquired. This was what he would later maintain was intentional provocation.

His words lingered in the room. Monday? Tuesday? He was pushing hard, almost growling Ggrrrhhh!

Powell was a little surprised. He as well as anybody knew how long it took to move forces and get fully prepared for a large-scale military operation. The buildup of forces in 1990–91 before the Gulf War had taken five and a half months before the bombing commenced. Armitage believed that Defense was remarkably ill prepared now. He had gone so far as to express the view privately that Rumsfeld was selling the Old Man—his term for the president—a bill of goods about when they would be ready and how much they could actually deliver.

"If the military is ready," Powell told the president and the others, "then we ought to go." He stressed the "if."

Tenet wanted more time—to get more teams in, work with the tribals, spread some more of the covert action cash around, more fully assess the needs of the tribals, develop a system of shipping in weapons, start the Special Forces teams in. Now with the prospect of military action only five or six days away, Tenet told the president, "The more time I have, the better for me, but I'm ready if it's next week."

Powell said, "Whenever we go we've got to let people know— got to have a notification plan about world leaders and others so that they don't read about it in the newspapers." He didn't want another set of diplomatic messes to clean up on top of the war.

Rice, Hadley, Powell and Armitage agreed to work out a notification plan for calling key foreign leaders at various stages, in some cases only hours before a military strike would begin.

"We need an assessment of how locked down we are," Tenet said, "because once we start there's liable to be a response and we've got to be ready." U.S. military action might unleash a retaliatory terrorist attack.

"I agree, George," the president said, "you're exactly right. We need that assessment. And we need it in the next several days." Bush added that the targets in Afghanistan were going to be the air defense systems, military airfields, runways and other fixed military targets. "And what comes next will require an assessment of our folks, both what's happening on the ground and what we see. Defense and CIA need to continue to develop targets." Then he threw out another idea he had not even shared with Rice, another provocation. "And boots on the ground may or may not be simultaneous."

That was a potentially significant change, because the implied promise in the president's decision on the military strike was that the air action and ground troops would be at the same time—no Clinton-like cruise missiles into tents.

But it was becoming clear that they had a problem about the necessary basing structure for simultaneous action.

"Are we ready to begin next week?" Bush pressed.

"The CINC will be ready by then," Shelton said. "But the issue is CSAR." He was referring to Combat Search and Rescue, the helicopter teams that were supposed to be in the vicinity of combat operations, standing by to rescue downed pilots and crews. The CSAR for bombing runs in the south could possibly be based secretly in Pakistan or the Gulf States. None of the "Stans" to the north—Turkmenistan, Uzbekistan or Tajikistan—had yet agreed to allow the CSAR necessary for bombing the north.

It was bedrock doctrine with Shelton and most military officers that combat operations could not commence without full search and rescue. The CSAR was the lifeline for those who flew combat missions and there was a presumption that the military brass would go all out to ensure it was in place. This was not only because of the lives of the pilots and crew. Any downed airman behind enemy lines is a potential hostage. Anyone who had lived through hostage crises, from the 52 Americans held in Tehran during 1979–80 to those held in Lebanon in the mid-1980s, knew the potential impact of American hostages on foreign policy.

The political impact of hostages could be even greater. The Iranian hostage crisis had crippled the presidency of Jimmy Carter and certainly was a factor in his defeat for a second term. The pictures of the wreckage in the Iranian desert had become symbols of Carter's impotence. In the mid-1980s, President Reagan's overemotional engagement with the fate of half a dozen American citizens held hostage in Lebanon had launched the dubious scheme to trade U.S. military arms for the American hostages, and the Iran-Contra scandal.

Shelton said he and others were still working the Combat Search and Rescue.

"Let me know on Friday," the president said. The Pentagon had two days.

Rumsfeld had not directly answered the president's question

about starting military action next week. Instead he went at it obliquely, raising one of his favorite issues, worrying that the focus of the war was too narrow still and might be perceived to be too Afghanistan-driven. "You know," he said, "some special operations somewhere else in the world at the same time would be important. We should do something on the ground—Special Forces in Afghanistan—but if it's not available you know, we can do it somewhere else." His teams might go into any number of terrorist havens to disrupt or sabotage terrorist groups.

Some of the others thought he was eager to get the military into the action someplace.

"I agree," the president said comfortingly. "We can't wait forever, but we also can't rush. We can manage if there are not boots on the ground." Bush said they would be showing their will because the first air strike would be followed by a second and a third. It was going to be a continuous bombardment.

"Well," Rumsfeld said, "if we don't get new targets, the second strike, the following strikes, will be small."

Rice understood Rumsfeld's frustration. It wasn't as if they had big electrical power grids to go after. Afghanistan was in the 15th century. Wipe out the first target set and they'd be left pounding sand.

"Look," the president countered, "our strategy is to create chaos, to create a vacuum, to get the bad guys moving. We get 'em moving, we can see them, we can hit them."

"Well you know," Rumsfeld replied, "our military buildup has already had that effect." The al Qaeda camps were empty, the terrorists scattered.

They turned to homeland defense and the vulnerabilities of pipelines and harbors. The deeper they went into the issue of defending the country, the more the number of soft spots grew. Nothing was safe.

"There's no question that we need to be concerned about homeland defense," Bush said, "but we can't let our concerns about that prevent us from taking action.

"We've got then basically the same strategy we had before," the president said in summary. "Let's not have any blinking. At Friday's [NSC meeting] give me your final assessment and let me know where we are. I want a briefing Friday on making sure we're buttoned up." He wanted them all thinking about what to do "in the event that there are strikes here."

Cheney had spent time at the CIA trying to figure out how substantial the agency's contacts were in the south. For the moment, the strategy was built around winning over some southern tribals. But the deeper he dug and the more questions he asked, the thinner it looked. The contacts were not that good and were not with the key tribes. The CIA was using information from British maps which were decades old.

Since the Northern Alliance was the more powerful ally, with real fighters on the ground, perhaps they needed to tilt the strategy to the north, not the south. That would mean going after the Taliban in a serious way, rather than attempting to divide them. Maybe they should just try to decapitate the Taliban leadership, he said.

11

ABOUT 3 A.M. Washington time on September 27—noon in the Panjshir Valley in Afghanistan—Jawbreaker team leader Gary sat down with General Mohammed Fahim, commander of the Northern Alliance forces, and Dr. Abdullah Abdullah, the Alliance foreign minister. He put $1 million on the table, explaining that they could use it as they saw fit. Fahim said he had some 10,000 fighters, though many were poorly equipped.

"The president is interested in our mission," Gary said. "He wants you to know the U.S. forces are coming and we want your cooperation and he's taking a personal interest in this." He had secure communications set up with Washington, and exaggerating, he said, "Everything that I write back home [the president] sees. So this is important." Without exaggerating, he added, "This is the world stage."

"We welcome you guys," Fahim said. "We'll do whatever we can." But he had questions. "When does the war start? When do you guys come? When is the U.S. really going to start to attack?"

"I don't know," Gary said. "But it will be soon. We have to be ready. Forces have to be deployed. We have to get things together. You're going to be impressed. You have never seen anything like what we're going to deliver onto the enemy."

• • •

IN WASHINGTON, RICE began September 27, Thursday, with deep
concerns, not only about what they might be able to deliver onto
the enemy, but when. From her soundings of some of the principals
it was clear that there was queasiness. When the president had said
he wanted a decision on Friday, tomorrow, everyone had seemed to
salute, Yes, sir. But she knew there were doubts.

Rice had arranged to go with Cheney to Langley later that day
for a briefing at CIA headquarters on the Northern Alliance. Much
was riding on the Alliance.

Tenet and some of his experts showed them TOP SECRET
maps of Afghanistan with little colored pins designating Alliance
positions and forces. The Alliance had between 10,000 and 30,000
fighters. Rice thought that was a huge range, and not the 20,000
number that had been floated.

There were gaps, significant gaps, the CIA experts acknowledged. But Jawbreaker was now on the ground with the Alliance,
and more teams would be going in to answer their questions. There
was no reliable way to determine the hard-core fighters without an
on-the-ground look by the CIA paramilitary and operations experts.
They would be able to tell quickly. Reports from the first team
would be coming in soon.

Rice could see that the CIA was organized, and the years of
covert work and funding had obviously paid off.

The south, the Taliban stronghold, was another story. The CIA
had only about 12 sources. There was little evidence of opposition
fighters.

Cheney and Rice went up to tour the new center that was
being set up to track terrorism operations.

"The president's on the phone for you," Rice was told.

"Where are you?" Bush asked.

"I'm out at the agency," she said. She was getting briefed on
the Northern Alliance.

"When will you be back?" he asked with some urgency.

"As soon as you would like me to be," she laughed.

"What am I going to hear tomorrow?"

Rice said she wasn't sure, but she would find out. There were people all around in the operations center. "Let me call you when I get in the car."

It was about 6:45 P.M., still rush hour, when Rice reached the president by secure phone from her car.

Am I going to hear what I think I'm going to hear tomorrow? he asked.

You know, Mr. President, they are doing what they can to get ready, she said. But you have to remember that this is hard.

"Why? That's not acceptable," Bush roared.

Rice began to explain that they faced a circular problem. Without intelligence, they couldn't identify targets effectively and precisely. Getting intelligence was a problem because they had not been able to get enough people on the ground. Their conversation was cut off when the secure phone went dead.

They hooked up again but it was a bad connection.

"I'm coming to the White House," Rice said. "I'll come see you as soon as I get there."

The president wanted to talk.

What is the story? What is going on?

Mr. President, she said, your time expectations and those of the military probably are not in sync. They might not be quite ready.

The phone was in and out.

"Mr. President, I'm at E Street. I'll call you."

When she got to the White House, Rice sprinted to her office. The telephone stalker was already on the secure phone. She repeated what she had told him from the car, that the military was not fully ready.

"That's unacceptable!" Bush said again. "Why is that?"

Rice said she would come up to the residence and explain in more detail. She went up and laid out the multiple problems. It was a tough nut for the Pentagon—no infrastructure in the region to speak of, no bases, weak on-the-ground intelligence at this point, scarce targets, the weather starting to get bad. Another problem, as Bush knew, was that the Combat Search and Rescue for the pilots was not in place. I think the key on Friday is to try to figure out the way forward, not to try to make a decision, Rice advised.

The president later recalled this sequence of events. "I'm ready to go," he said. "Sometimes that's the way I am—fiery. On the other hand [Rice's] job is to bear the brunt of some of the fire, so that it—take the edge off a little bit. And she's good at that." It was just in his nature to be fiery, he said.

"I was growing a little impatient. I can be an impatient person. Plus, I feel comfortable being—one of the things, I can be totally unscripted or unrehearsed with Condi. That's the nature of her job, is to absorb my—is to help, you know, kind of say, well, Mr. President I appreciate that point of view, and I think you probably ought to think this way a little bit."

After she returned from the residence, Rice called Rumsfeld. "Don," she carefully warned, "I think tomorrow you need to be able to tell the president what the real timeline looks like, because I think his expectations are not in line with what you're going to be able to say. I think he will be all right with that, but it is important that he really now have a clear view of how long we're talking about."

"I'll be ready to do that," Rumsfeld replied.

THE PRINCIPALS MET without the president later that evening. Cheney said he had talked to the emir in Qatar.

"I've been active," Powell said. "I've demarched him twice." That meant it was a diplomatic warning. "We're working that issue."

Cheney said, "The president wants to avoid putting any artificial constraints or timelines on our military action. Let's do it right. Let's not do something stupid for PR purposes."

Rice agreed.

"You know," Cheney said, "air operations without boots on the ground could look weak." At the same time, they didn't want to force "our guys" to do something for the public relations impact. "Do it because it's smart."

"We talked about seeing if there are any plans for special operations outside of Afghanistan," Powell said.

"Yeah," Rumsfeld replied, "I'm looking at that."

With all of Rumsfeld's pressing, he had nothing from Defense to show in the way of plans.

Powell said his people had had a second meeting with the Uzbeks to get permission to use their territory. They had a question: "What do we do if your action puts us at risk?"

It was a good question, but it went unanswered.

Powell also said they were about to get agreement on a United Nations Security Council resolution that would essentially adopt the president's Executive Order on freezing terrorist assets worldwide. It would be very good to go global with the war on financial assets.

Powell also reported that there was going to be a meeting the next day in Germany of those countries donating money for the reconstruction of Afghanistan. This had to be a visible part of the coalition's strategy, an incentive for the Afghan people to liberate themselves. They had to know there was a pot of money to help rebuild their country if they were prepared to do what needed to be done.

Rumsfeld said General Franks was willing to accept liaison officers from coalition governments at his headquarters in Tampa, Florida.

The others seemed to agree that it was a first step in getting coalition members to contribute forces. Franks could see what was being offered and what really might be useful.

Shelton said, "We're going to have a couple of C-17s after next week ready to air-drop rations, radios, blankets, and we're going to do it in conjunction with our military campaign."

"A major humanitarian effort is required," Rice said. "We need to develop a humanitarian campaign and get in the swing next week." She seemed frustrated. The principals, other than Powell, seemed more interested in war than the humanitarian assistance the president had emphasized. "We need to clarify out of our president's mouth that there is going to be a major effort to help the Afghan people."

"I'm still worried about the CSAR piece," Shelton said, referring to the search and rescue. "Franks says special operations will be ready within 10 days from go." But without basing rights in the region, the special ops teams could not go anywhere. It looked like boots on the ground was going to have to wait.

"Look," Rice said, "we need to close on Special Operations Forces and CSAR. What have we got? What are we going to do?" She went on for some time.

They turned to another headache. Al-Jazeera, the Arab television station based in Qatar, had opened the floodgates to bin Laden propaganda, broadcasting his full statements, which were being picked up by the American television networks, if only in part.

They were conflicted because they wanted some things from Qatar, but at the same time, they didn't like the freedom being granted Al-Jazeera.

"On the Uzbeks," Cheney said impatiently, "our delegation isn't senior enough. We need a swing through the area with a high-level person." John R. Bolton, the undersecretary of state for arms control and international security, was dealing with the Uzbeks. "The president can call, we need a presidential call to Karimov. We need someone to go in and settle it."

It was a shot at Powell, who was in charge of the Uzbek account.

FRIDAY, SEPTEMBER 28, was the day the president had set for the decision on whether to commence bombing early the next week.

John McLaughlin was slated to deliver the President's Daily Brief of intelligence to Bush, taking Tenet's place for a day. McLaughlin had an incredible memory and was famous for being able to digest a lot of material and present the high points.

A year earlier when Governor Bush was the Republican presidential nominee, McLaughlin had been dispatched to Texas to give the routine hour-long briefing to the candidate. He had asked to start with a joke. "Only if it's good," Bush had replied.

McLaughlin told of visiting Russia undercover, going out as a tourist and stopping where the first shot had been fired in the Russian Revolution. The guide had said, "That one shot was the most powerful shot ever fired. It went off and went for 70 years of straight destruction."

Bush had chuckled. McLaughlin had hardly begun his briefing when Bush started asking questions. The briefing lasted four hours. McLaughlin found Bush a good listener and unintimidating. Back at the agency he told them, "If this guy is elected, the briefer better be ready to be interactive."

In the Oval Office Friday morning, McLaughlin reviewed the threats. There seemed to be many plots afoot; al Qaeda had bigger attacks in mind.

"Why do you think nothing's happened?" Bush asked. There was all this chatter, SIGINT, warnings.

"Security matters," McLaughlin replied. "What we are doing matters." Pulling people off the streets, freezing the money, so the guy who was going to buy the forged passports for the team couldn't get them. Also, McLaughlin said, the president's decision authorizing the CIA to go on the offensive—to shift the balance of their efforts from defense to offense—was already making a difference.

"When do you think we should start military action?" Bush asked, instinctively lowering his voice.

"Mr. President," McLaughlin said, "that's your call. I can only give you my personal opinion."

"That's all I'm looking for."

"Well, based on what I see now and where we are, I would give us a couple more weeks to work with these tribals to get assessment of their needs, a system of getting weaponry to them, start bringing in Special Forces. I'd give us another couple of weeks."

"Thank you," said the president.

WHEN THE NSC gathered later that morning Rice was worried that it was not going to be a happy meeting.

"We need to reassess the timing and strategy for military operations," the president said right off. "Wednesday, I said a decision would be made on Friday"—that day. "We may need more time," he said.

Rice was a bit surprised that he was taking some of the pressure off.

"I'm prepared to talk about that," Rumsfeld said, but he waited for his turn.

Tenet offered a view somewhat different from his deputy McLaughlin's. "Next week we need to do something," he said. "People in the region are on the fence. Action next week would help." He cited the divisions in the Pakistan intelligence service, the ISI. "Some favor UBL, some oppose UBL." The head of the service was clearly a fan of Mullah Omar and the Taliban. "An attack next week makes sense. I'd want to hear the button-down plan because there will be retaliation, there's a lot of threat warnings coming in from overseas." They were systematically checking the Taliban military capabilities with overhead satellites.

"There was a letter bomb to our embassy in Chile," Powell said. The large package, addressed to the U.S. ambassador and delivered by a Chilean letter carrier, had contained enough explosives to injure seriously whoever opened it. Guards at the heavily fortified embassy compound, considered one of the world's safest, had notified the police and a bomb squad moved in. "We got an intelligence tip and we detonated it," reported Powell. No one had claimed responsibility, and it didn't appear to be linked to September 11.

They turned to the terrorist problems in Indonesia and the Philippines where there were substantial al Qaeda pockets. What was the ability of the U.S. to encourage the governments there to do more and better counterterrorism? The picture was unclear.

"We've put together an announcement for the president in connection with the humanitarian effort that would accompany our operations. We've also got an AID map which we've given to the Pentagon about where there is the greatest need for humanitarian airdrops," Powell offered. AID is the Agency for International Development, which coordinates U.S. government aid programs abroad.

Hundreds of lives could be on the line, and the potential suffering of tens of thousands could be alleviated if the airdrops got through.

Uzbekistan had decided to accept a 15-man assessment team from the U.S. military that would come in to look at the possibility and feasibility of running the Combat Search and Rescue out of its territory. There was some thought also of getting the Uzbeks to allow Special Forces teams to operate there. The Uzbeks wanted security guarantees. They were worried about defending their border.

The secretary said he needed a clear statement of what others, including the diplomatic posts, could say about what we were going to do.

"And what people can do to help," the president interjected.

Hadley said they were already working it and would have a draft out that day.

Rumsfeld said he would check with Franks that afternoon to see where they were. "There's an Uzbek airport eight to 10 miles from the main airport. We're going to send in our assessment team, we're going to see if the airstrip can accommodate C-5s," the giant transport airplanes. "Our guys will be on the ground in 24 hours and assess whether the field is adequate for our needs. If the runways are okay, we can bring in the CSAR. If the runways are not, we need to look and see if we can get them to let us use the main air-port. So we're into an operational phase with the Uzbeks."

"If the Uzbeks say no," the president inquired, "what's the plan?"

"If we have no CSAR in the north you can't have air operations in the north," Rumsfeld replied, "just in the south." He was holding to the military's demand that operations could not run without search and rescue in place in the general vicinity of air strikes.

Tenet's main action was in the north. He had little to none in the south. Now it looked like the bombing was going to have the exact opposite emphasis—none in the north, only in the south. It would be a total mismatch.

"What about CSAR by Russia?" the president asked. Putin had made the offer.

"We need some coordination there," Rumsfeld said.

"How about CSAR from Tajikistan?" Rice asked.

"We'll talk to Franks about that," Rumsfeld said. "If we get this working, we can have CSAR in four to five days."

Bombing in the north was hanging on that thread.

Rumsfeld summed up, "The CSAR is prepositioned at Ram-stein"—the U.S. air base in Germany. "The Uzbeks have not okayed the Special Forces. Oman is going to give us CSAR in the south, and we're looking at Special Forces options in the south. The three we're looking at now are high-risk."

The defense secretary finally gave his answer: "If we get our assessment done in Uzbekistan in 24 hours and the airfield's okay, then in five days we could be ready to go, so that would make it Thursday at the earliest. Saturday would be more likely."

"You could start in the south and do the north later," Bush said. "Are we ready to go in the south?"

Rumsfeld turned to the target list—a total of 700 overall.

"How many of those are in the south?" Bush asked.

"We'll find out today," Rumsfeld said, deflecting. They were not broken down by north and south.

Rumsfeld then raised one of the president's favorite topics. He said they had two C-17s ready to go that would provide 37,000 meal rations for Afghans. "It'll be close proximity with the strike, maybe one day later."

Shelton said, "We'll be prepared by Monday to do it concurrent with the strike," meaning they could have bombs and rations dropping at the same time.

"We're going to have PSYOP drops," Rumsfeld said. He was referring to so-called psychological operations. Leaflets would be dropped explaining that the United States was there to liberate the Afghan people from the invading bin Laden and al Qaeda, that this was not a war against Islam. On special operations in the north, he reminded them, "We don't have any basing."

The best target that was developing was in the north around Kabul. From intelligence it looked like a place where al Qaeda could be making chemical or biological weapons. (Later U.S. intelligence discovered it was a plant that made agricultural fertilizer.)

Special operations early were not possible, Rumsfeld said. "Can't do it in the north, haven't really got good targets yet in the south." Boots on the ground early was not going to happen.

"Look," the president said, indicating that he was resigned to the military judgment, "we can do special operations later. Are there any coordination problems?"

"We're working with State on the clearances that we need and that cooperation's been good. Our linkage with the intelligence community is good," Rumsfeld replied.

Cheney was looking concerned. "I worry about the connections between what we're doing here and the defense of the U.S. homeland." The vice president was seized with the possibility of another attack and the possibility of retaliation when they unleashed the military.

"Dick," Bush said, "I couldn't agree more."

"We're getting a briefing on that today," Rice said.

"I'm worried about the BW threat," Cheney said, biological warfare.

Several of those present wondered if the vice president knew something, or if he had connected things they had missed. He was a thorough reader of intelligence reports and connector of dots. But there seemed to be nothing specific.

Turning back to Afghanistan, General Myers said, "We're ready to put Special Forces on the ground with CIA forces."

"This is the first time we've ever done it?" Bush asked.

"We haven't done this for some time," Myers replied. In the Balkans, the military and the CIA had conducted secret operations to apprehend Persons Indicted for War Crimes (PIFWC). In those operations, the CIA would gather the intelligence and the military Special Operations Forces would act. Now the plan was for the CIA and the Special Forces to work hand in hand. That would be breaking a lot of new ground. "We're not really experienced at it," Myers admitted. "We're going to start small and get larger."

They turned to rules of engagement—the specific instructions that would be given to the U.S. forces describing the circumstances under which they would be allowed to attack, drop bombs or shoot. How much freedom of action should the forces be given? What efforts should they make to prevent attacks on noncombatants?

In the end they agreed on rules that would allow only low collateral damage. General Franks would have to come back for permission to strike a target if moderate or high collateral damage was expected. The exception, however, was that if the CIA had bin Laden or al Qaeda leadership in its crosshairs, they could shoot the Predator without seeking approval. Tenet had that authority in the new intelligence order that Bush had signed, but Tenet had indicated he would go through Franks.

Myers reminded them that they were 10 days from having the necessary basing for Special Forces.

The group then examined the possibility of using an aircraft carrier, stationed off Pakistan, as a stepping-stone.

"This meeting this afternoon is very important," Bush said, referring to a homeland security meeting that would include others. "We're going to have to ask, Are we doing everything we can do?"

"Have to have no signals out of the meetings on timing," Rumsfeld said. There could be no leaks about when the military action might start. "If you want to button up," he added, "button up now so that it doesn't become a signal."

The president was a jumble of emotions as he attempted a summary. "I don't want any politics into this," he said. "I don't want public affairs to drive military operations. But the angst will build up in the country. We'll try to handle it next week. We'll use figures on what we've done on the war on terror. We're not going to rush into military operations, but press Tommy hard to get ready. We'll have to do something. We'll learn about the Uzbeks over the weekend. We'll assess it on Monday, and the targets have to conform to our objectives. Military, air defense, self-defense, al Qaeda targets."

"When we hit, we'll assume something's coming back at us," Powell said, "and the country will get concerned again."

"We will be meeting like this for some time," Bush said. "It's best if everyone else goes back to normal." He reminded them that they, the war cabinet, were still on alert, had to be ready to meet or act at any time. "What we do in Afghanistan is an important part of our effort. It's important to be serious and that'll be a signal to other countries about how serious we are on terror." He mentioned Syria and Iran—longtime sponsors of terrorism.

"Many believe Saddam is involved," he said. "That's not an issue for now. If we catch him being involved, we'll act. He probably was behind this in the end."

With that the president left the meeting. Rice walked back up to the Oval Office with him.

"I thought that was a really good meeting," she said. "I wasn't sure it was going to be such a good meeting."

The president laughed. "They'll get to work," he said, "and we can take the temperature again on Monday."

The president commented later on why he had backed off. "That's the Rice influence there, you know. Who says she isn't powerful? I'm a realistic person, and again, there is a balance between pushing people and then forcing an operation." He also said he knew then that they could start within a week to 10 days.

"One of the interesting things about being the president is you don't see much mail, curiously enough. The only thing I can tell you is that I rely on my instincts. I just knew that at some point in time, the American people were going to say, Where is he? What are you doing? Where's your leadership? Where is the United States? You're all-powerful, do something." He felt it was his job to educate the public about the nature of the war. "I guess that, plus my instincts about angst, is a reaction to watching the people get disassociated from the commander in chief in Vietnam."

The former Texas Air National Guard F-102 pilot said, "My feeling was that it was a war that was never properly explained, and that the government micromanaged the war. I remember my pilot friends telling me that over Thud Ridge"—the notorious path that American fighter jets took to Hanoi—"they could only fly a certain time, and the enemy knew when they were coming."

IN THE LATE morning the president met with King Abdullah of Jordan. Jordan was providing fantastic intelligence cooperation and receiving millions in CIA covert action funds to assist in the roundup of suspected terrorists. Bush's private comments to the king reflected his dual impulses.

"Our nation is still somewhat sad," the president told the king, "but we're angry. There's a certain level of blood lust, but we won't let it drive our reaction." He noted that the Pakistani intelligence service, the ISI, would soon have to start purging its pro-Taliban elements. "We're steady, clear-eyed and patient," Bush said, "but pretty soon we'll have to start displaying scalps."

At 1:05 P.M. the expanded NSC met again.

"The purpose is to focus on what we're doing to prepare for a further attack," Bush said.

Ashcroft said, "We're thinking about a national neighborhood watch system." Citizens would call in or report strange behavior or suspected terrorists.

"Make sure you don't launch an anti-Arab backlash in this country," the president said. Three Arab men talking might trigger reports.

"We want to convey the message that you're likely to be detected if you're doing something wrong," Ashcroft said.

"Disruption is our goal," Tenet said. "We want to change the profile of what we do to provide security at critical points. To throw them off, to frustrate their planning, show a different security profile. Something they haven't seen before, haven't planned against, can't count on. Because the goal is disruption."

Searching everyone from clergymen to elderly ladies at airport security could send a message to terrorists—no matter how you dress or how unlikely a suspect you may appear, no one is immune from scrutiny.

12

THE BUSHES HAD invited some of their East Texas friends to the White House for the September 29–30 weekend. Mrs. Bush was going to take the women to the Kennedy Center and the men were going to play poker at the White House. But the threats to the White House were too numerous, and Bush called to cancel. "The president has hundreds of threats a month," President Bush said later, "and it ratcheted way up" after September 11. The weekend get-together was postponed to late October.

They had several ways of dealing with threats, and one was denial. The president said his wife never created a second front at home and never complained. "She knew about the threats," he said, but never asked questions like "How can you stay here?" or "How can you ask me to stay here in the midst of this threat?" She had also never asked, "Why did you get me into this mess?" according to the president. "She understands that she has got a function—her job is to help assure the American people."

During my interview with the president in Crawford in August 2002, however, it became apparent that the war had taken more of an emotional toll on the Bushes than they had let on.

When Mrs. Bush joined us late in the interview, the president turned to her and explained how he had told me, "You never pan-

1. President George W. Bush looks out at the damaged Pentagon from a helicopter on September 14, 2001.

2

3

2. Bush and his chief of staff, Andrew Card, talk on Air Force One on the morning of September 11.

3. Vice President Dick Cheney in the White House bunker on September 11.

4. CIA Director George Tenet watches the president address the nation.

5. Defense Secretary Donald Rumsfeld appears with the president at the Pentagon crash site one day after the attacks.

6

6. Bush convenes the full National Security Council in the White House Cabinet Room on Wednesday, September 12. Seated at the table, from left: Tenet, Attorney General John Ashcroft, Rumsfeld, Secretary of State Colin Powell, Bush, Cheney, Chairman of the Joint Chiefs of Staff Hugh Shelton and national security adviser Condoleezza Rice. Seated along the wall: Deputy Secretary of Defense Paul Wolfowitz, Deputy Secretary of State Richard Armitage, presidential counselor Karen Hughes, Vice Chairman of the Joint Chiefs Richard Myers and White House Press Secretary Ari Fleischer.

7. Bush confers with Powell and Rice in the Oval Office.

8. Bush with retired firefighter Bob Beckwith at Ground Zero. "I can hear you, the rest of the world hears you, and the people who knocked these buildings down will hear all of us soon!"

9. At Camp David on Saturday, September 15, for an all-day war-planning session.

10. White House communications director Dan Bartlett, Fleischer, Hughes and Rice meet with Bush in the Treaty Room.

11. Armitage (left) and Wolfowitz (right) with Senator Jay Rockefeller, Democrat of West Virginia.

10

11

12

13

14

12. The president with Tenet, Card and Rice at Camp David in late September, just after the first CIA paramilitary team mated up with Northern Alliance leaders in Afghanistan.

13. The CIA put a "No bin Laden" sign on each page of its TOP SECRET briefing booklet, "Going to War," that was presented at the Camp David meeting on September 15, 2001.

14. Treasury Secretary Paul O'Neill, seated to Cheney's right, joins the war cabinet in the White House Situation Room to discuss the financial side of the war on terror.

1s

1

17

15. Deputy national security adviser Steve Hadley saw the war-planning process for Afghanistan as inevitably makeshift, "Come as you are."

16. Hughes with senior White House adviser Karl Rove in the West Wing. Bush told his longtime friend and top adviser Hughes, "You're in charge of how we communicate this war."

17. Powell and Rumsfeld engage in a heated discussion in the White House Rose Garden—one of the few times the tension flared in public. Rice and Hadley look on.

20

18. Rumsfeld in an afternoon press briefing. "We're not running out of targets, Afghanistan is," Rumsfeld joked a few days into the bombing campaign.

19. Card, Rice and Powell share a light moment. By late October though, the mood in the war cabinet was grim. Winter was approaching and the U.S. bombing was cmboldening Taliban forces, not destroying them. The dreaded "quagmire" word was being tossed around by the press.

20. General Tommy Franks, commander in chief of U.S. Central Command, with Rumsfeld at a press briefing.

21. Myers, who took over as chairman of the Joint Chiefs on October 1, 2001, with Rumsfeld at a Pentagon press briefing.

21

22

22. Deputy CIA Director John McLaughlin answered Tenet's call in late September to draw up a list of likely terrorist targets in the United States.

23. Cofer Black, the head of the CIA's Counterterrorism Center, told the president in a briefing on proposed covert operations, "You've got to understand, people are going to die."

24. Northern Alliance commander Mohammed Fahim greets Rumsfeld.

25. President Bush meets with Afghan leader Hamid Karzai (center) and Foreign Minister Abdullah Abdullah (left). A U.N.-brokered conference in December 2001 selected the moderate, pro-Western Karzai as interim leader as the U.S. fully engaged in nation building.

23

26. The seven principal members of Bush's war cabinet in a meeting in the White House Situation Room, joined by Hadley and Lewis "Scooter" Libby, the vice president's chief of staff. By September 2002, the Bush administration was actively moving toward military intervention in Iraq as part of its new policy of preemption.

icked, you never questioned about why we never left the White House. You never were worried."

Mrs. Bush had a substantially different version. "I was just very apprehensive," she said, grasping her hands tightly in her lap. "There was just so much uncertainty associated with everything that happened, every step, every—you know, obviously, starting with September 11th and the way people felt. You know, I worried, I'm sure, that there would be some sort of strike back immediately. I think that was the scary part. Certainly, that was, I guess, what was showing up in the threat assessments enough then.

"I was nervous, I was anxious," she added carefully.

"Well, I never knew it," the president said. "I think I was paying attention to you then," he added, laughing.

"I didn't ever talk about it that much," Mrs. Bush said. "I woke up in the middle of the night. I know you did. I mean, I'd wake up in the middle of the night and know he was awake."

"I don't remember that. Was I some?" he inquired, looking at her.

She nodded a strong affirmative.

"Yes," the president conceded.

"You had to," I interjected.

"Yes," he said. "Right after the attacks, I mean, I was emotional."

How many nights?

"It wasn't a lot," the president replied.

Of course he was waking up at night. A significant portion of Washington was waking as the Combat Air Patrol could be heard droning overhead all night with a distinctive, distant roar. I was waking up and I didn't live at Ground Zero. Bush turned to his wife, "If you were nervous . . ."

"Well," she said, "I didn't say that to you."

"That's true, you didn't," he said.

"I mean, I wouldn't have said that," she replied, knowing part of her job was to reassure.

The Bushes had another way of dealing with the threat environment. "I guess in some ways there was sort of a fatalism about it, and if it happened, it happened," Mrs. Bush said, and the president added, "If it's meant to be, it's going to happen. And therefore there's no need to try to hide from a terrorist."

ON THAT SATURDAY, September 29, the president and his wife were at Camp David. He met in the morning with the NSC by secure video.

"We need to focus on the overseas threat," Tenet said as the meeting got underway. Al Qaeda wasn't just after the American homeland. They wanted to hit military bases or embassies abroad. There were hundreds of good targets, and the U.S. needed to lock them down.

Powell said, "We've got the U.N. resolution. That's a good thing." The United Nations Security Council had passed a U.S.-proposed resolution that called for member countries to cut financial, political and military ties with terrorist groups and freeze assets. He said the Spanish were now willing to commit troops, and some African nations were agreeing to take steps.

Powell said that Jesse Jackson, black leader and perennial presidential candidate who had involved himself in hostage and peace negotiations in Syria, Kuwait and Yugoslavia, had announced that he would not go to Afghanistan, which was a break, given what they were planning to do there.

Powell was still working Uzbekistan, but whatever he offered, it was dismissed as not enough, not in the ballpark. The Uzbeks wanted immediate membership in NATO for starters—something the U.S. could not grant and a sensitive issue with the Russians to say the least. As Powell put it, the Uzbeks wanted a bilateral treaty of mutual defense, love, cooperation and economic support. They wanted some proof that the love would be permanent, a kind of

"Will You Be There Tomorrow?" declaration. He was drafting an agreement.

Powell would deal with the Uzbek foreign minister and the military, and then the matter would go to Karimov, who would sit on it, if only to prove he was the sole decision-maker.

Why would the Uzbeks go along? They had bad relations with the Russians and their attitude seemed to be anything-but-the-Russians, though at the same time they seemed to fear alienating the Russians. They wanted bragging rights that they were permanent friends of the United States. Americans were rich and the Uzbeks wanted things like $50 million in loans from the U.S. Export-Import Bank. Lastly, they had their own fundamentalist rebellion with the Islamic Movement of Uzbekistan, which wanted to overthrow Karimov. The IMU had a safe operating haven in Afghanistan, so Karimov would be delighted to have the Taliban deposed. Though the dance would continue, Powell said the Uzbeks were now fine on the CSAR.

On Pakistan, his other major account, the secretary said, "Musharraf has the situation under control." Anti-U.S. protests had been drawing smaller crowds than expected, but a government-declared "Solidarity Day," designed to stir up nationalist sentiments, had also attracted meager crowds.

There was major concern about the U.S. Embassy in Indonesia, fear of a backlash to any U.S. military action in Afghanistan.

Hadley said, "We got through the anniversary of the Intifada 2 but it wasn't pretty." Six Palestinians had been killed and dozens wounded during weekend protests marking the anniversary of the latest chapter in the Israeli-Palestinian conflict.

"We need to identify what the Pentagon wants from countries," Powell said. Rumsfeld had insisted he be involved in or approve all discussions with the State Department on such issues.

"How do we warn Americans not to go to Afghanistan right now?" Bush asked.

"We got the warnings out," Powell said.

Rumsfeld reported that a U.S. team had arrived in Uzbekistan to evaluate their airfields. "The CSAR in the south is okay. We're not able to use Special Forces in the north. We're going to more fully develop the idea in the south."

"We may be able to have an option to do it in the north later," Powell interjected.

"Let's push hard," Bush told them. He was frustrated. The attack plan was looking Clintonesque. "Let's not give up on the northern piece, let's develop an option for Special Forces in the north. Let's not give it up!"

Rumsfeld had some dreary news. "The target list cannot impose much damage on the people we want to impose it on."

Most of the targets, he said, were Taliban military—early warning radar, airfields, their few aircraft. They were going to hit the mostly empty al Qaeda camps. Of the hundreds of targets, 50 or 60 might include different aim points in just one camp, such as the large Tarnak Farms complex south of Kandahar. They were static targets. "We still need to work targets. We might want to emphasize that our first action is heavily intelligence gathering and humanitarian aid," Rumsfeld said. He worried about inflated expectations. But then he corrected himself, "We want to avoid discussing our military action." Maybe silence was best.

General Myers reinforced the point. During the Cold War and even the 1991 Gulf War, the military had geared itself to attack fixed targets such as communications centers, early warning radar, the command and control, the military assets—aircraft, tanks, storage and weapons depots, even the economic infrastructure such as power plants and bridges. "We've got a military that does great against fixed targets. We don't do so well against mobile targets. You're not going to topple a regime with this target list," he said.

Rice thought, It is true they weren't going to topple the regime without ground troops. That was the real problem, but she was confident they would find a way.

Eighteen days after September 11, they were developing a response, an action, but not a strategy. It was Powell's worst night-mare—bomb and hope. Vietnam kept flooding back.

"We've got to manage our expectations," the president said. "We've got to think through it on Monday. We need to be able to define success after the first round of action." They could not look weak.

"We might be able to do that on the talk shows tomorrow," Rumsfeld said.

"We need to," Bush interjected. "It's part of the credibility of our overall effort. Conventional warfare is not going to win this, this is a guerrilla struggle."

That was the problem. The United States had never figured out how to win a guerrilla war. The discussion was almost exclusively about aerial bombing. There was one team of 10 CIA people on the ground, Jawbreaker, and no prospects of getting Special Forces in anytime soon.

Myers turned to some things that were working. "AID is coordinating the humanitarian assistance with Franks. We've got CAPs up, we've got AWACS up." Combat Air Patrol and Airborne Warning and Control System planes were being deployed for reconnaissance and potential intercepts. "Deputies need to push it country by country, what we want from various countries."

The president said that since the Africans wanted to help, "Maybe we should ask them to help defend our embassies."

The emphasis on such a side issue revealed how far they were from solving the main ones.

ANDY CARD AND Bush had regular private side conversations about the progress of the war planning.

"You're a little too interested in the tactics," Card teased at one point. Bush seemed too interested in what types of planes were doing what, whether Special Forces could get into the north, etc. "That's interesting but that's not the mission," Card cautioned.

He was just 10 months younger than Bush, and they both knew about the 1960s and 1970s—Vietnam. Both had somewhat the same experience. "Don't be a general, be a president," Card told Bush.

Yes, Bush said, there was a fine line between micromanaging combat and setting the broad goals. But so much hinged on the small issues.

"You have to win," Card said, "but you have to let the generals win. If you put constraints on the generals that impact their ability to win the war—"

Oh, no, Bush promised, he was not going to do that. "I am not going to be a general."

Yet Card saw that it was a balancing act. The president had to be familiar enough with the details, sufficiently immersed in the tactics, so that he never appeared ignorant in public. That would be a true disaster. At the same time, both Bush and Card had to avoid getting overly involved in the details of military tactics.

THE PRINCIPALS MET on Sunday, September 30, without the president.

After a brief discussion of the NATO resolution invoking Article 5, declaring that the attacks on the United States on September 11 were an attack on all NATO countries, Rumsfeld turned to the idea of a white paper. Powell had floated the idea three days earlier when he had told National Public Radio, "The information will be coming out."

"I think the precedent is bad of having to go out and make your case publicly," Rumsfeld said, "because we may not have enough information to make our case next time, and it may impair our ability to preempt against the threat that may be coming at us." Preemption was going to be necessary, and probably sooner rather than later. It was one of the first mentions of the concept, which would grow in importance over the year.

Rumsfeld continued with the white paper. One of his favorite lines was that first reports are always wrong. "If we use the paper we've got to take out all the excess verbiage. If it's put out, it shouldn't be the president, the secretary of state. Bump it down," he added with disdain, "someplace down to the FBI or CIA. Treat it as an early report. Have a frontispiece on it that urges caution. Are we going to have to make our case every time?"

"It's not much of a precedent," Powell countered. "There's a lot of evidence. Most of it's factual. You can say up front it's preliminary. We've been asked by some of our closest allies for some of this information. We've been working on it for a while, this isn't a rush job." Being conciliatory, Powell added, "Everything you suggest is acceptable. We ought to be able to do it. The allies expect it, it enhances our case and it's going to be to our benefit."

Rumsfeld and Powell went back and forth at each other in a way they would not have if Bush were present. Rumsfeld's real worry was that they might release a white paper and face a negative reaction—the pundits and foreign affairs experts declaring that it wasn't a very good or convincing case. What would they do then? Not attack?

"It's largely a historical case," Rice said. "It's pretty well established in what has happened in prior actions that al Qaeda has taken. There were people indicted after all, you've got bills of particulars. I'm not so concerned about this."

Undeterred, Rumsfeld asked, "Why not use the briefing that Paul Wolfowitz used?" His deputy had gone to Europe to brief NATO defense ministers on some evidence pointing to bin Laden.

"Paul's briefing was part of the problem," Powell said. "It didn't give enough detail."

"Look," Card said, "add a caveat up front that says we don't think we really need to do this. That'll help you counter the precedent."

"Push it into my channel," Tenet said. "People need more detail."

Myers reported that search and rescue out of Uzbekistan

would take longer than the initial estimate of four days. The assessment team had sent word that the airstrip could only accommodate the smaller, more maneuverable C-17 transport planes, not the large C-5 transports. Presently, the airfield could handle only one C-17 at a time, pushing the estimate of CSAR capability to 12 days. Basing out of Tajikistan above northeastern Afghanistan was an alternative, but that too presented problems—high mountains would have to be navigated to enter Afghan territory. The Soviets had lost a lot of force coming down that way.

"I'm concerned about going through the Russians to the Tajiks," Rumsfeld said.

"We're not doing that," Rice replied. "I'm less concerned. All we need is for the Russians to say yes and they've said they'll say yes. We'll deal with them directly." They could not allow the northern strategy to fall apart, because they didn't have a southern strategy. It was the northern strategy or nothing.

"The Tajiks have offered anything we need, and they haven't asked for a thing," Myers said. Franks's Central Command was sending a liaison team to go up to talk to the Russians about CSAR from Russia. Putin had told the president they would allow CSAR. "They're going to go up and talk to them tomorrow," Myers said. "We got small numbers of U.S. military to go in with the CIA and with the Northern Alliance. We don't have any ability to do special operations in the north at this point even if we got some permission to do some Special Forces in the north. Of course we couldn't start anything until the CSAR was in place, so let's talk about getting the CSAR in place."

"It won't be until mid-month," Rumsfeld said, at least two weeks away.

"Why do we need the CSAR?" Powell asked.

"For the bombers and TAC air," Myers replied, referring to both higher-flying bombers and lower-flying tactical aircraft.

Rice believed that there were only a few ways to make a really big mistake in this operation. A captured pilot was one of them. It wasn't just Carter's hostages in Iran or Reagan's in Lebanon, it was that bin Laden or al Qaeda with hostages would change the terms of the debate, give them immense leverage.

Rumsfeld was unhappy with the targets. "For this value of targets," he said, "I wouldn't go in without CSAR." To lose a pilot for these low-value fixed and mud-hut-type targets made no sense. For a really high-value target, yes, he might consider the risk. Not these.

"CSAR may delay air operations up to 12 days if we can't mitigate this in some sense," Rice said. She knew that was not going to be acceptable to the president.

"We're trying to see if we can get into working 24 hours a day to fly airplanes into Uzbekistan. We're also looking at Dushanbe [in Tajikistan], but that's uncomfortable," Myers said.

"How about the south?" Rice asked.

"The CSAR is okay," Myers said. "It's going to go out of Oman, either airborne or on call. Also we're looking for a forward refueling point over Pakistan. We want to be unobtrusive." He added what they wanted to hear, "We'll solve it."

"It's going to be in place by when?" Rice asked. The president wanted the strikes in six days, Saturday.

It would not inhibit our Saturday strikes, Myers said. But that meant air operations only in the south and no Special Forces in either the north or south. It was a quarter loaf. He said they were going to move the USS *Kitty Hawk* aircraft carrier without its regular strike aircraft but with Special Operations Forces on board to take up station off the coast of Pakistan. "That will give us some capability," Myers said, meaning Special Forces in the south.

The *Kitty Hawk* was in Japan. Powell, who knew how long it took to move an aircraft carrier, elicited from Myers that it would not be on station until October 11, nearly two weeks away.

Rice turned to the allies who were clamoring to participate. Getting as many of them invested with military forces in the war was essential. The coalition had to have teeth. She did not want to leave them all dressed up with no place to go. "The Aussies, the French, the Canadians, the Germans want to help," she said. "Anything they can do to help. The Aussies have Special Forces in Tampa," Franks's headquarters. "We ought to try and use them."

"We'll prepare a paper on this," Rumsfeld said, stalling.

Powell smiled at Rice as if to say, See what I have to deal with.

Rumsfeld recovered. "We want to include them if we can."

But Rumsfeld didn't want other forces included for cosmetic purposes. Some German battalion or a French frigate could get in the way of his operation. The coalition had to fit the conflict and not the other way around. They could not invent roles. Maybe they didn't need a French frigate.

Tenet turned to Germany. It was now apparent that the September 11 plot, at least parts of it, had been hatched in Hamburg cells that included the lead hijacker, Mohamed Atta. "The best thing the Germans can do is to get their act together on their own internal terrorist problems and the groups that we know are there," he said. He was worried about more German-based plots.

Responding to Rice and showing more sympathy, Myers said, "We'll put together a paper on what we plan to ask them to do. We'll prepare it—we're going to try to be forward-leaning. We understand it's a political issue."

For Card, it didn't add up. "I still worry that the president's timeline expectations are off from what I'm hearing here," he said.

"I know," General Myers said.

"We need to explain to the president that it's going to be eight to 10 days before air operations can go in the north," Rice said. Did it make sense then to go to just the south?

"We could bomb Tuesday without CSAR," Powell said. "When would CSAR be ready?"

Myers said they planned to be ready by Thursday and therefore they could bomb in the north on Saturday, October 6. That was six days away, better than Rice's various estimates.

The president had to understand that if they started now in the south, there would be a large time gap before they could begin bombing in the north, Rice said. "We need some clarity."

Hadley asked if they wanted to go in with a major delegation to the Uzbeks.

"Not now," said Powell. If the issue was Special Forces on the ground, they still had to wait. "We can't do Special Forces operations out of Uzbekistan until we get CSAR. Once we get the CSAR in, then let's look, really look at the whole situation. Let's not go in heavy now."

"Let's look again at [the] Tajiks because that may be the only way we can get it done," Rice said. "We may, at the end of the day, not be able to rely on the Uzbeks." It wasn't at all clear the Uzbeks would allow Special Forces operations out of their territory. It was one thing to allow search and rescue. It was another to allow Special Operations Forces, clear offensive operations.

Rice thought back to when she had been the Stanford University provost, and the Army Corps of Engineers had given a briefing on earthquake preparedness. During a disaster, the briefer had said, the first thing you have to do is determine "the enabling condition"—the thing on which progress hinged the most. It might be clearing the roads or providing medical assistance. Well, the principals had finally figured out that their "enabling condition" was Uzbekistan. Without it, no bombing in the north. Bombing in the south, where there was no significant opposition ground force, made no sense.

Powell attempted to summarize. It was a remarkable statement, focusing on his own role and denigrating the military, whether intentionally or not.

"Phase 1 is diplomacy.

"Phase 2A is getting Tenet on the ground"—the CIA paramilitary teams.

"Phase 2B is some military operations. We may have to do it without CSAR. Go after some targets that won't get us in trouble with either the Arabs or the Europeans. Do it in the south, it helps George get some things.

"Phase 3 do an audible," meaning change signals at the last

second like a quarterback at the line of scrimmage. "Go for targets of opportunity. And Special Forces may not get in place for a while. That's just the way we are."

In Powell's analysis, military operations were only a part of the three phases—2B—and the operations had to be designed to avoid diplomatic problems with the Arabs or Europeans.

Rumsfeld could have exploded. He said nothing.

Whether the others agreed with Powell's framework, what he said had a certain realism to it. Hadley saw the process as makeshift, "Come as you are." They were making it up as they went.

Tenet said, "We have to avoid looking like a U.S. invasion. That message is even more important in the south, to get the Pashtuns to rise. The northerners are getting a lot already—they're getting a lot of money." He knew the critical importance of money.

"Do we have enough weapons in the north?" Rice asked.

"We got an assessment from the field," Tenet replied. "We have to look at it."

"How do we deal with actions by al Qaeda? We need to think about the unconventional, how they will respond to what we are doing," Card said.

None of them really had any idea, neither conventional nor unconventional. They were underprepared for what had happened on September 11, and uncertain about the path ahead.

Rice said that the president needed more information. He was also hanging out there, just like they were. "What's the first 24, 48, 72 hours of this operation going to look like? We need to get back to the president on that. It needs to be briefed to this group." The military plan needed to be briefed. But first they had to figure out what it was going to be.

After the meeting, Rice spoke to Powell.

Is it not, she asked smiling, the secretary of state's concern to arrange for the allies to assist? I'm just doing your job.

Powell laughed.

• • •

RICE BRIEFED THE president. It's coming along, she told him, but we aren't there.

What's the problem?

She summarized, focusing especially on the Combat Search and Rescue. "You might want to press about that on Monday."

Rice was sympathetic to Rumsfeld and the Pentagon. It was a tough nut. The military could not just show up and start bombing. They had to have bases. After September 11, all the necessary countries had given permission for overflight rights. That was the easy part. When it got down to can we run elite commando Special Operations Forces out of your territory, it got hard. There was also the absence of good targets, and a president who was determined that bombing not just be for show faced a bit of a catch-22. The Pentagon could not say what the first 24 or 48 hours would look like until they had the basing rights lined up. It didn't just *look* dreary, Rice thought, it *was* dreary.

13

In the northeastern corner of Afghanistan, CIA team leader Gary dispatched several of his men to the Takar region, the front between the Northern Alliance and the Taliban forces. They went north, a good 60 miles to the east of Konduz. They found the Northern Alliance forces disciplined, their clothing and weapons clean. But the safeties were on the rifles, a signal that this was not a hot combat zone. The troops lined up in formations and conducted drills. There was a command structure. But there were not enough troops or heavy weapons to move against the Taliban, who were dug in on the other side. Like World War I trench warfare, the military situation was static.

Gary knew that CIA headquarters believed that the Taliban would be a tenacious enemy in a fight and that any U.S. strike would bring out its sympathizers in Afghanistan and in the region, especially Pakistan. They would rally around Mullah Omar.

Gary saw it differently. He believed that massive, heavy bombing of the Taliban front lines—"really good stuff," as he called it— would cause the Taliban to break and would change the picture. On October 1, he sent a SECRET appraisal to headquarters. "In this case," he wrote, "a Taliban collapse could be rapid, with the enemy shrinking to a small number of hard-core Mullah Omar supporters in the early days or weeks of a military campaign."

"That's horseshit!" could almost be heard off the Directorate of Operations walls as the old hands and experts openly disparaged the appraisal. But Tenet took the cable to Bush.

"I want more of this," said the president.

AT 9:30 A.M., Monday, October 1, Bush met with the NSC.

Tenet reported that Jawbreaker was on the ground with the Northern Alliance and he hoped to have a second team in soon. "In the south they're not going well, they're not doing that much." The south was still a bridge too far. The Afghan strategy was still in limbo.

It was General Myers's first day as chairman of the Joint Chiefs. He gave a detailed status report on the airfield in Uzbekistan. "They can do five flights a day, only in daylight, only in C-17s. Think they can handle two aircraft at once but they can't do C-5s. It'll be 12 days before we're fully ready up there in Uzbekistan. It would be six to eight days if we could go 12 hours a day. But you'd get further if we go 24 hours a day. And we're taking in a deployable staff to try and make it 24-hour-capable. We need 67 flights in order to have enough flights giving us a CSAR capability."

It would take 67 deliveries from the C-17s to ferry in the personnel, equipment and helicopters to get up and fully ready with the search and rescue.

"So that's going to delay our special operations?" the president asked.

Yes, and it could delay bombing in the north because they would have no search and rescue.

"In the south we're ready to go with bombers and cruise missiles," Myers said. "We'll do special operations later in the month. We'll do lily pads with carriers as our operating base, but we need Oman as a base to load up the carrier."

The British exercise in Oman was still crowding out U.S. basing. Powell said he would see if they could encourage Oman to rearrange things. Maybe the British would be willing to cut short their exercise and allow us to get in there earlier, he said.

The president said he would talk to Tony Blair.

"But if we get the British exercise out of the way, we still need Omani approval," Powell noted. That did not figure to be a major hurdle, since the U.S. military had staged activities from Oman for over two decades, going back to the aborted 1980 hostage rescue attempt in Iran. But each extra step took precious time.

"Look," Bush said, "we need to look at alternative ways to do this thing. Couldn't we load up a carrier with our Special Operations Forces someplace else? Why does it have to be Oman?"

"We'll look at that," Myers promised.

"Your people think we need to do something militarily at this point?" Bush asked Tenet.

"Yes. We can work the south, look at B-52s heading up to the north. It would complement the guerrilla war."

"We're going to review it every day," the president said. "I think we need something by the weekend or shortly thereafter. The targets in the north could be a second phase." There was a discussion of how far up north into Afghanistan they could bomb without the CSAR. The answer was that some targets would not be covered.

"It's not perfect," he said, "but it's time to get moving. Are we going to talk to Tommy today?"

Rice said General Franks would be coming Wednesday afternoon.

"We're going to do it by video on Wednesday," Rumsfeld corrected her.

"It is impossible in war to get everything perfect," the president later recalled, "and therefore you try to get as much perfect as possible." He felt they should have been bombing already. "The moment had been there as far as I was concerned. I was fully prepared to tell the nation through body language, and if need be, word, that our troops will be as protected as they can be, but it is time to take the action to the enemy."

• • •

THAT AFTERNOON TENET and his special operations chief for counterterrorism, Hank, went to the Pentagon to meet with Rumsfeld, Wolfowitz and Myers. Tenet's chief of station in Islamabad, Bob, was going to come up on the secure video.

Bob said he expected that the shock and awe of bombing would open up negotiations with moderate Taliban. A bombing pause might be desirable for such negotiations. He was concerned about civil war between the north and south. Hard bombing in the north might allow the Northern Alliance, General Fahim and the others, the ethnic Tajiks and Uzbeks, to make a lot of progress. In the south, the Pashtuns would look on this unfavorably. The Pashtuns would eventually see progress in the north as an attack against them. Again, a bombing pause might give the Pashtun tribes in the south some time to gain traction on the ground.

Rumsfeld said that as far as he was concerned there were not going to be any bombing pauses—especially for some kind of negotiations. Period. Bombing pauses smacked of Vietnam. No way.

"GOT ANYTHING YOU'RE doing today?" Rumsfeld said to Pentagon spokesperson Torie Clarke in a phone call to her home at about 6 A.M., Tuesday, October 2. Later that day, he said, they—she included—were going to the Middle East and South Asia to visit Saudi Arabia, Oman, Uzbekistan, the United Arab Emirates, Bahrain and Qatar. They would be back Friday night or Saturday morning.

That morning at the NSC meeting, Rumsfeld said, "I want to give the final briefing at 2:30 P.M. today, and then I want to button it up." He meant it literally. No one else was supposed to speak publicly.

The president asked, "Is CSAR going to be ready in the south?"

"It will be ready," Myers answered.

Rumsfeld said they had a solution to bomb in the north. "We can hit targets in the north without CSAR using B-2s and cruise missiles." The B-2s are Stealth bombers that cannot be picked up by any Taliban radar so they could not be attacked. The pilots and crew would only be in jeopardy if their bombers had an accident or malfunctioned—a risk he was willing to take. The unmanned cruise missiles were not a problem.

"It's going after it without the optimal weapon," he said, "but if we do that we can get all the targets over the first five days."

Tactical bombers would be the optimal weapons because they flew lower and could visually sight targets. Without laser target designators from Special Forces on the ground, the high-flying bombers would be at a disadvantage.

The plan had just ever so much a ring of how Clinton might do it—safe, less than optimal, a compromise. No one raised the point, but there was some discomfort.

"We'll use the cruise missiles, B-1s, B-2s, B-52s, TAC Air in the south," Rumsfeld said. And, just to be clear, he added, "All targets will get the preferred weapons in the south. North, we'll get all targets but without the preferred weapons.

"We're not going to be able to do Special Forces in the north. In the south it's a question mark on special operations. The issue is with Oman, and we'll have to work it out."

The president liked the idea of using the USS *Kitty Hawk* as a platform for special operations. "Psychologically it shows it's a different kind of war, and we're going to be doing things differently."

"Once we get an okay on Oman for the special operations," Rumsfeld told them, "it'll still take 10 days. But you know the targets are not impressive for special ops at this point. But it's still unfortunate that we can't be doing special operations contemporaneous with the air operations."

He planned to keep such a clamp on operational details that the press and the public would not have to know what was less than optimal, not preferred, even unfortunate.

Tenet said the CIA was expanding in the north and looking for ways in the south.

"We have sent Special Forces in from the north, they'll arrive today. We're looking for ways to get them into the south," Rumsfeld said. His Special Forces teams were at staging areas outside Afghanistan, not yet in-country. It was a source of mounting frustration.

"The first targets will be air defense, some military targets and camps. We'll hope to have emerging targets in the days after the first couple of days. The first day there'll be humanitarian airdrops, all of them in the south, C-17s. They'll be from about 18,000 feet." That could put them out of the reach of any Taliban air defense that survived the first strike, though there seemed to remain some worry a plane could be shot down.

The president, focused as always on the public relations component, asked Defense to work with Hughes on the "themes" that were going to be used in the announcement of military action.

RUMSFELD DISPATCHED A 15-page TOP SECRET order that day to the service chiefs, the combatant commands and the undersecretaries: "Campaign Against Terrorism: Strategic Guidance for the U.S. Department of Defense."

If there was waffling in other departments about what the president wanted, he was going to make sure there was none in his. The guidance paper, which had the force of an order, said that the president had ordered a global war on terrorism. That meant just that, not only the al Qaeda network or Afghanistan. In a section on "means," Rumsfeld said "All tools of national power" would be utilized in the war on global terrorism. The department should anticipate multiple military operations in multiple theaters.

The focus was terrorist organizations, state sponsors of terrorism and nonstate sponsors including terrorist funding organizations. Another focus was directed at weapons of mass destruction.

It said specifically that the department would be targeting "organizations, states that harbor, sponsor, finance, sanction, or otherwise support those organizations or their state supporters to acquire or produce weapons of mass destruction."

ARMITAGE, POWELL'S DEPUTY, had little interest in appearing on television talk shows. When the White House called early that week asking him to make the rounds, he politely declined. They pressed.

The White House wanted to counter charges that the U.S. was not getting everything it wanted from Saudi Arabia and Pakistan because of political pressures in those countries.

Armitage went to Powell and explained about the White House request. "Look, that's not my deal," he told his boss.

"Nah, I'm in the icebox again," Powell replied. Maybe because he was pushing to release a white paper detailing evidence against bin Laden. "We've got to get the story out, so go do it," he told Armitage.

On October 3, Armitage appeared on ABC's *Good Morning America* and CNN's *Live This Morning*. Asked on CNN if there was a degree of disagreement between the United States and Saudi Arabia, he said, "Well, every nation has a home political audience, but I'm unaware of any major difficulties with the kingdom of Saudi Arabia." He told ABC that the administration was "quite heartened that the anti-American activity in Pakistan has been relatively low."

The message had been dutifully delivered: the Saudis were cooperating, Pakistan was under control.

ON WEDNESDAY, OCTOBER 3, inside Afghanistan, Gary went in search of an airfield to bring supplies into Northern Alliance territory. The team found one airfield in an area called Golbahar that had been used by the British in 1919. He asked the Alliance's intelligence chief Arif to grade out an area and turn it into an airstrip, and handed out another $200,000. He bought three jeeps for $19,000 and forked over another $22,000 for a tanker truck and helicopter fuel. Arif promised they would buy the truck in Dushanbe and drive it over the mountains to the CIA team, but it never arrived.

Gary's team did front line surveys of the Taliban and al Qaeda forces, getting exact geographic coordinates—precise GPS (Global Positioning System) readings. Many Pakistani fundamentalists had come over and joined the Taliban. Gary got exact GPS readings on their locations.

U.S. bombing with precision weapons would be coming. He was confident, but he had lived through the five-and-a-half-month buildup for the Gulf War, and he knew careful preparation took a long time. Bombing seemed a long way off, maybe months, and no advance warning had come in on their secure communications system from CIA headquarters. So his cables began asking for humanitarian supplies for the Afghan people—food, blankets, medicine.

THE PRINCIPALS MET at 9:30 A.M. on Wednesday.

Wolfowitz, sitting in for Rumsfeld, said, "We've got permission to do CSAR, search and rescue, from the Uzbeks today and it could be up in time."

General Myers reported that they were still trying to find a role for the key allies.

Powell said there had to be leadership in Kabul after a Taliban defeat that represented all the Afghan people. Richard Haass, his policy planning director, would go to Rome to visit with the former king, who said he would help the transition to a post-Taliban government but wanted no formal role in a new regime.

"Even Musharraf wants to talk about post-Taliban Afghanistan," Rice said. "We need to exploit that."

"In the short term it would be useful to be obscure on the future of the Taliban," Cheney suggested, "to exploit fissures in the Taliban." There was, at this point, still hope of winning over some moderate Taliban. "But the long term—we need the Taliban to be gone."

Tenet was pleased. Since September 11 he had held that the Taliban and al Qaeda were bound together, that they had to be treated as one enemy and eliminated. The United States was embarked on regime change in Afghanistan. The transition to that policy—or their realization of it—had occurred at this meeting. Lashing the leadership in the north to the south would be essential to future stability. The problem was that he hadn't yet figured out how to do it.

"The president won't want to use troops to rebuild Afghanistan," Card cautioned. Bush had said repeatedly during the presidential campaign: No combat troops for nation building, the American military did not exist for that purpose. In the second of the three presidential debates, he had declared, "Absolutely not. Our military is meant to fight and win war." He had eased off slightly in the third debate, "There may be some moments when we use our troops as peacekeepers, but not often."

Everyone in the room knew they were entering a phase of peacekeeping and nation building. The overriding lesson from the 1990s in Afghanistan was: Don't leave a vacuum. The abandonment of Afghanistan after the Soviets were ousted in 1989 had created the conditions for the rise of the Taliban and the virtual takeover of the country by bin Laden and al Qaeda.

Now it looked like the main U.S. presence in Afghanistan if and when the Taliban was ousted was going to be thousands of combat troops, perhaps most of them American. Rumsfeld knew it. Powell knew it. On this issue, they had at times been almost glaring at each other across the table. Rumsfeld wanted to minimize it, Powell wanted them to face the reality of it.

• • •

THE DEPUTIES MET later that day. The focus was post-Taliban reconstruction. They agreed that the United States should lead the efforts to stabilize post-Taliban Afghanistan, including helping with food production, health, education for women, small-scale infrastructure projects and clearing the country of land mines. What about the political structure? What about a security plan? What about a plan to explain it to the public?

Hadley's to-do list included: action plan for the G-7 world economic powers, the World Bank and other international financial groups; find some countries to make multibillion-dollar commitments and announce them publicly; need to announce publicly an international conference on the political future; find some donors to pony up to the United Nations for Afghanistan; cables to be sent out making the requests of allies; find key allies who will quietly agree to help with post-Taliban security.

In other words, nation building on a huge scale.

THAT DAY, HANK, the counterterrorism special operations chief, met with General Franks in Tampa, Florida, for the first time. Using maps of Afghanistan, Hank laid out how CIA paramilitary teams working with the various opposition forces could get them moving. The opposition forces, chiefly the Northern Alliance, would do most of the ground fighting. If the U.S. repeated the mistakes of the Soviets by invading with a large land force, they would be doomed.

Franks's Special Forces teams could follow on into Afghanistan and pinpoint targets that could be hit hard in U.S. bombing runs. On-the-ground human intelligence designating targets would allow extraordinarily specific and exact information for the precision bombs.

Hank, under instructions from Tenet, made it clear that the paramilitary teams would be working for Franks, and in that spirit and somewhat contrary to recent practice, the CIA would give Franks and his Special Forces commanders the identities of all CIA

assets in Afghanistan, their capabilities, their locations and the
CIA's assessment of them. The military and the CIA were to work
as partners.

Franks basically agreed with the plan. He disclosed that the
bombing campaign was scheduled to begin any time from October
6 on—three days away.

Money talked in Afghanistan, Hank said, and they had millions
in covert action money. On one level, the CIA could supply money
to buy food, blankets, cold weather gear and medicine that could be
air-dropped. The fighters on both sides, and their families who
often traveled with the fighters, would be cold and starving. The
humanitarian aid would work to the U.S. advantage.

Warlords or sub-commanders with dozens or hundreds of
fighters could be bought off for as little as $50,000 in cash, Hank
said. If we do this right, we can buy off a lot more of the Taliban
than we have to kill.

Good, the general said.

BUSH WENT TO New York City that morning for a rally near
Ground Zero and a private meeting with business leaders about rebuilding the city. "I truly believe," he told the executives, "that out
of this will come more order in the world—real progress to peace in
the Middle East, stability with oil-producing regions."

He was less optimistic about the threat of more attacks. "I
can't tell you whether the bastards will strike again."

14

At the NSC meeting on Thursday, October 4, General Myers had some good news. "CSAR in the north will be stood up by Monday in Uzbekistan"—meaning ready to go. "Special Forces are beginning to flow into Oman. The *Kitty Hawk* will be in place October 13, which will allow things to go forward in the south. I wouldn't preclude SOF in the north." Within days of the initial bombing, ground operations by the Special Operations Forces would be possible.

As for post-Taliban Afghanistan, Wolfowitz and Rice talked about getting other countries to put up money for rebuilding.

"Who will run the country?" Bush asked.

We should have addressed that, Rice thought. Her most awful moments were when the president thought of something that the principals, particularly she, should have anticipated.

No one had a real answer, but Rice was beginning to understand that that was the critical question. Where were they headed?

LATER IN THE morning the president went to the State Department to thank the staff members. Near the end of his remarks he teared up. Why today? Ari Fleischer wondered from the front row.

Back at the White House, Bush motioned Fleischer to the Oval Office. "We got a report this morning of a case of anthrax in Florida," he said. "We don't know how widespread it is. We don't know if it's more than one. We don't know a whole lot."

It was the first time Fleischer had seen worry in his eyes.

Bob Stevens, a 63-year-old photo editor for *The Sun* tabloid in Florida, was very ill with inhalation anthrax, a deadly disease long associated with possible biological warfare. The first announcements said it was an isolated case and probably arose from natural causes, and the news stories ran in the middle pages of the newspaper.

The news about anthrax was about to build.

In a private meeting with the emir of Qatar, Bush showed how much he was following the signals intelligence, especially on bin Laden. "We know Osama bin Laden called his mother," Bush told the emir. "One of these days, he'll make the mistake, and we'll get him."

APPEARING BEFORE PARLIAMENT on Thursday, Prime Minister Blair presented evidence that Osama bin Laden's al Qaeda network was responsible for the September 11 attacks. His office released a 16-page unclassified document on the Internet which laid out the most detailed case yet but did not disclose extremely specific and sensitive intelligence.

The release of the British report came 12 days after Secretary of State Powell had promised a public presentation of evidence amid calls from allies and foreign leaders. Also on Thursday, Pakistan's Foreign Ministry announced that the U.S. had supplied sufficient evidence of bin Laden's complicity in September 11 that they could bring an indictment in court. The clear endorsement of the American case by a Muslim state was a boon.

In a day, the issue of a white paper that had put Powell and Rumsfeld at loggerheads had floated away.

• • •

ON PAGE SEVEN of the 11-page TOP SECRET/CODEWORD Threat Matrix for Friday, October 5, was a report from a Defense Intelligence Agency source with the codename "Dragonfire," who had said terrorists might have obtained a 10-kiloton nuclear weapon from the former Soviet Union stockpile. It might be headed for New York City, the source had alleged. Detonation of even a small nuclear device in a city could kill tens of thousands and create unimaginable panic. It was the nightmare scenario everyone worried about most.

The Threat Matrix, however, deemed Dragonfire's report "noncredible" because it had technical details wrong. It turned out the source was a U.S. citizen who said he had overheard some unidentified people discussing the possibility of a nuclear weapon in a Las Vegas casino. It was totally bogus, but the atmosphere was such that reports like the Dragonfire claim regularly filled the Threat Matrix. No one wanted to leave any threat unmentioned.

THE PRESIDENT WAS in the Oval Office later that day reviewing a speech by Israeli Prime Minister Ariel Sharon. Sharon had suggested that the United States was on the road to repeating the mistakes of Munich in 1938 when British Prime Minister Neville Chamberlain had abandoned Czechoslovakia to Hitler.

"Do not try to appease the Arabs at our expense," Sharon said, addressing the American president. "Israel will not be Czechoslovakia."

"We're going to respond to that, yes?" Rice asked Bush.

"Of course I'm going to respond to that."

They discussed a forceful blast back. Someone cautioned, "You're going to get a headline that says: 'BUSH RAPS SHARON.' "

"Mr. President," Rice said, "he just called you Neville Chamberlain. I think it's time to say something pretty strong."

Fleischer later called Sharon's comment "unacceptable," as Israeli tanks, helicopter gunships, bulldozers and ground troops
moved into Palestinian-controlled West Bank territory.

BUSH CALLED NICK Calio, the White House chief of congressional
liaison, to the Oval Office.

"Nicky," Bush said, "you take this, you get this up to them
now. We're not . . ."

Calio had a perplexed look on his face.

"Do you know about this?" Bush asked. He was furious about
leaks to the news media.

"Can I see it?" Calio asked, as Bush handed him a single sheet
of paper. Calio read quickly. It was a memo to Powell, O'Neill,
Rumsfeld, Ashcroft, Tenet and FBI Director Mueller. Subject: "Dis-
closures to Congress." The order, signed by Bush, said that only the
so-called Big Eight—the Republican and Democratic leaders of both
Senate and House, and the chairmen and ranking members of the
two intelligence committees—could receive classified information
or sensitive law enforcement information.

"No," Calio said, saying that he had not seen it.

"Well, they were supposed to tell you," the president said, referring to Andy Card or the White House counsel.

(That morning The Washington Post had run a front page story
headlined "FBI, CIA Warn Congress of More Attacks" that I had
coauthored with Susan Schmidt. The story focused on a classified
briefing that CIA and FBI officials had given on the Hill earlier in
the week. We reported the high probability of another terrorist attack, and said one intelligence official had told Congress there was
a "100 percent" chance of an attack if the United States retaliated
with military force in Afghanistan.)

Calio tried to explain to the president that such a restriction
would be a disaster. It would be like cutting off oxygen to 527 of the
535 members of Congress.

"I don't care. Get it up there. This is what's going to happen," Bush ordered.

"Okay," said Calio, "but I just want to tell you that you can expect—"

"I'm not defending it," Bush said. "Do you get the picture here?"

Calio nodded.

"Get it up there to them, okay?"

"Fine," Calio said.

"It's tough shit," the president said.

Bush later talked with Senator Bob Graham, the Florida Democrat who chaired the Senate Intelligence Committee. It was the longest conversation Graham had ever had with Bush, and he heard a real stream of Texas profanity.

Calio then undertook what was basically an intense Middle East–style shuttle diplomacy between Bush and the Congress trying to bring both toward the middle. Finally Bush agreed to lift the order. He had sent the message that he could cut them off if he wanted.

SECRETARY RUMSFELD APPEARED at a press conference in Tashkent, Uzbekistan, on Friday with President Karimov. Karimov said that Uzbekistan would grant the U.S. use of its airspace and one of its airfields for humanitarian and search and rescue operations, and was ready to step up cooperation for the exchange of intelligence.

A reporter asked what the United States had offered in exchange. "There have been no specific quid pro quos if that is what you are looking for," Rumsfeld replied.

Karimov quickly added, "I would like to emphasize that there has been no talk of quid pro quos so far."

Rumsfeld, his eye down the road, said what Karimov wanted to hear. "The interest of the United States is of a long-standing relationship with this country," he assured all, "and not something that is focused on the immediate problem alone."

• • •

AT THE NSC meeting that morning, General Franks joined in on the secure video from CENTCOM headquarters in Tampa.

"Tommy, are we ready to go?" Bush asked.

"Yes, sir, we're ready to go."

"We need a summary of the targets," the president said.

The first day's strike was going to be somewhat small—only about 31 targets overall. They were going to use about 50 cruise missiles, 15 land-based bombers and about 25 strike aircraft from aircraft carriers. They would attack bin Laden training camps, the Taliban air defense system and any concentrations of al Qaeda if there were any that could be located.

Defense was also rescrubbing the so-called no strike list, targets that were not supposed to be hit—power plants, schools, hospitals and especially mosques—to show it was not an attack against the Afghan population. The list was to be updated each day.

"We need to discuss rules of engagement," Myers said, proposing that they do it the next day by secure video.

The president said he had told Senate Majority Leader Tom Daschle, House Speaker J. Dennis Hastert and Senate Minority Leader Trent Lott of the coming strikes. He said he would inform House Democratic Leader Richard Gephardt.

When they turned to freezing terrorist assets, one of Bush's favorite instruments, Powell said, "Hezbollah and Hamas will go on the list of organizations subject to the financial war on terror."

The president bristled. "We have a long-term campaign against terrorism," he said, "but first things first. We'll get to the others in due course." The wait and delay was getting to him. Al Qaeda and Afghanistan had to receive all the energy now. After he got his latest feeling of frustration off his chest he reminded them, yes, he was not backing off. "I'm committed to an overall effort in the war on terror."

Powell said that some of the international relief organizations were worried about dropping food to the Taliban and were trying to identify which villages were not controlled by them.

Wolfowitz said there was good flow into Uzbekistan. Already nine of the necessary 67 planeloads had arrived and they would now be ready by October 7 when they hoped bombing would begin. He said, "We have 33,000 people in the theater. We had 21,000 in the theater September 10." So 12,000 had been recently deployed, though no U.S. military were yet inside Afghanistan.

AT CIA HEADQUARTERS, Hank had hung a sign outside his office door taken from a recruiting poster used by British explorer Ernest Shackleton for his 1914 Antarctica expedition.

It read, "Officers wanted for hazardous journey. Small Wages. Bitter cold. Long months of complete darkness. Constant danger. Safe return doubtful. Honour and recognition in case of success."

Inside, Hank was about to dispatch the most important message of his career to the field. Approved by Tenet and Cofer Black, it was addressed to about a dozen stations and bases in Pakistan, Tajikistan and Uzbekistan which were running secret assets and sources inside Afghanistan. This included the tribal allies and the Northern Alliance. The message also went to Gary's Jawbreaker team on the ground and to several other CIA paramilitary teams that were preparing to go in-country.

The three-page message, headed "Military Strategy," listed these points:

1. Instruct all tribal allies to ground and identify all their aircraft immediately.
2. Instruct the tribals to cease all significant military movement—basically to stand down and hold in place.
3. The future plan was to have the opposition forces drive to isolate enemy forces, but to wait before moving.

4. Instruct all assets throughout Afghanistan to begin sabotage operations immediately everywhere. This would include tossing hand grenades through Taliban offices, disrupting Taliban convoys, pinning down those moving Taliban supplies and ammunition, and generally making pests of themselves. (This would be the first employment of concerted lethal force in Bush's war on terrorism.)

5. Informing all of them that paramilitary insertions would go forward in the south and be combined with more specific air strikes.

6. All would have to define no strike zones—hospitals, schools.

7. All tribal factions and leaders should identify and locate primary targets.

8. Assets should try to identify possible escape routes out of Afghanistan for bin Laden and his al Qaeda leadership—and then try to set up reconnaissance of the routes for interdiction.

9. Be prepared to interrogate and exploit prisoners.

10. Assess humanitarian needs.

They were instructed to share the full text with General Franks to make sure of complete transparency with the military commander.

Hank closed the message, "We are fighting for the CT [counterterrorist] objectives in the Afghan theater and although this sets high goals in very uncertain, shifting terrain, we are also fighting for the future of CIA/DOD integrated counterterrorism warfare around the globe. While we will make mistakes as we chart new territory and new methodology, our objectives are clear, and our concept of partnership is sound."

Leaflets to be dropped into Afghanistan were prepared with a crude drawing of a military tank wedged between two small Afghan-style buildings.

In Pashto, Dari and English, the leaflet read, "The Taliban are using civilian areas to hide their equipment, endangering everyone in the area. Flee any area where military equipment or personnel are located."

ON SATURDAY MORNING, October 6, at 8:30 A.M., the president was at Camp David for the secure video NSC meeting. Tensions over the disputed province of Kashmir were flaring.

"We're watching India," Powell said. "We're waiting for a read-out of Blair conversations."

The British prime minister had promised to make calls to defuse the intensifying situation with Pakistan over Kashmir. "We've instructed our ambassadors to go into capitals—then we'll decide whether the president needs to call." By way of understatement, he added, "Want to head this thing off."

On Israel, Powell referred to Sharon's statement that Israel would not allow itself to become Czechoslovakia. "Sharon's behavior in the last few days borders on the irrational," Powell said, thinking he might say that about the Israeli leader on a regular basis.

Rumsfeld, back from his whirlwind trip, reported that he had been rather successful as a diplomat. The Saudis, he said, were gracious and warm, even complimentary. The only negative was their worry that the United States was unhappy, and he believed he had "tamped down" that idea. But the Saudis definitely need senior-level attention regularly.

In Uzbekistan, they had closed the deal on access. "The Uzbeks were friendlier at the end of the meeting than the beginning."

Rumsfeld said that he needed an increase on the ceiling for reserves, up to 300,000 from the current level of 50,000. "We need more headroom."

"You want to do it on Monday?" Bush asked.

"Yes," Rumsfeld said.

Though some 80 countries had made offers to help, only the British would participate in the first wave of strikes.

"The bombers that need to leave Missouri are about to leave," Rumsfeld continued. "And that will be noticed." The radar-evading B-2 Stealth bombers that were participating in the initial strikes in Afghanistan were being deployed directly from Whiteman Air Force Base in Missouri, and would have to leave 15 or more hours in advance, potentially tipping off the start of operations.

"Let them go," the president said. "Try some disinformation."

"We'll tell people they are full of food," Rumsfeld said.

"When is the humanitarian drop?" Rice asked.

"From 2:30 to 3:30 D.C. time," Myers said, "about two hours after the start of military action. And the threat to the aircraft will be gone by then." The meager air defense system of the Taliban was, they hoped, going to be pulverized in the first strikes.

The president said he would announce the attacks in a brief appearance on national television on Sunday. "We'll certainly have a statement. We'll circulate to the principals for review."

"We need a 'go' for the operation," Rumsfeld said.

"Go," Bush said. "It's well thought through. It's the right thing to do."

15

_____

THE MORNING OF Sunday, October 7, Karl Rove was at his home in Northwest Washington. The days since the terrorist attacks had not been Rove's happiest. Though he had known Bush for 28 years and been his strategic adviser, Rove had been excluded from the war cabinet and NSC meetings. Bush and Cheney had deemed it impossible to have the controversial political guy in on the war discussions. It would send the wrong message.

Rove could see their point, but at the same time, politics was a continuing element of the presidency even during war, not to be ignored. Bush and Rove both believed that the Bush presidency would be judged largely on his performance dealing with September 11.

On one of the days shortly after the attacks, Rove was in the Oval Office and Bush had told him, Just like my father's generation was called in World War II, now our generation is being called. His father had signed up for the Navy, sworn in as a seaman second class in 1942 on his 18th birthday. They were being called to serve when they were in their 50s.

"I'm here for a reason," Bush said, "and this is going to be how we're going to be judged."

Rove, 50, had been hailed by many, including Bush himself, as the architect of the 2000 victory. Just before September 11, _The_

Weekly Standard, a plugged-in conservative magazine, had run a cover story, "The Impresario, Karl Rove, Orchestrator of the Bush White House." A large, respectful drawing of Rove, intellectual, learned and carrying a presidential folder, graced the cover. A miniature, clownish-looking Bush was in the breast pocket of Rove's jacket.

That Monday, the White House Office of Strategic Initiatives, which Rove headed, had sent around a two-page analysis of the latest polling data.

This was Rove's *Racing Form*, which he studied methodically.

"The president's job approval is stronger than ever." The numbers were 84 to 90 percent.

"The president's recent job approval increase is unprecedented even for a time of crisis." Bush's job approval had been around 55 percent before September 11 and the jump to 90 percent in the ABC News/*Washington Post* poll "is unparalleled in modern polling." Sudden crises had in the past triggered an immediate increase in a president's job approval. "The durability of such increases is usually only seven to ten months," meaning presidents sink back to normal approval averages rather quickly.

Bush's father had an approval rating of 59 percent before the Gulf War began, but it jumped to 82 percent at the height of the crisis. Forty-one weeks later, it was back to 59 percent.

Rove took the polling information to Bush, and explained that if history was a guide, they had about 30 to 40 weeks before the polls returned to the norm.

"Don't waste my time with it," Bush told Rove, pretending to have no interest but looking at the data. Later Bush recalled their discussion of the poll numbers, which he said are a snapshot that might be inaccurate 24 hours later. "My job is not to worry about the political consequences, and I don't," the president maintained. It was Rove's job, and Bush knew that Rove managed the account with an unparalleled intensity and devotion to mission. This was definitely one thing that somebody else could handle better.

At the same time, the president carefully monitored his political standing. On this, like all matters, there was a scorecard.

Rove also kept in touch with the party apparatus and leading conservatives. One important-looking confidential communication came in to Rove from one of Bush senior's friends, so Rove took it to the Oval Office.

Roger Ailes, former media guru for Bush's father, had a message, Rove told the president. It had to be confidential because Ailes, a flamboyant and irreverent media executive, was currently the head of FOX News, the conservative-leaning television cable network that was enjoying high ratings. In that position, Ailes was not supposed to be giving political advice. His back-channel message: The American public would tolerate waiting and would be patient, but only as long as they were convinced that Bush was using the harshest measures possible. Support would dissipate if the public did not see Bush acting harshly.

ABOUT 8:30 A.M. Rove's phone rang.

"I suggest you be at the office at about 11 o'clock," the most recognizable voice said from Camp David. Things are going to happen. Get my drift? Bush asked over the nonsecure phone line. "I'm going to speak to the country this afternoon. And, so be there."

Rove arrived at the White House about 11 A.M. A serious amateur historian, he hung out with his notebook.

Rove walked up to the White House Treaty Room on the second floor where Bush was to give his televised announcement. He looked around. On the right was the painting that gave the room its name: President McKinley supervising the signing of the treaty ending the Spanish-American War in that room. The painting included the corner of the room where the chair and cameras were set up for Bush.

At 12:30 P.M., the president was in his chair ready to address the nation. Someone came in to apply the president's makeup. Five minutes later someone announced that there was a leak, one of the networks had said this was the beginning of the war.

"They don't get it," Bush said in a loud voice. "The war already began. It began on September 11th."

Card and Rice were conferring off to the side, and the president seemed irritated that he was not in on the discussion. "What is it?" he called out.

Card told him it was the Pentagon. "They're asking for more authority."

"I've told them they have whatever authority they need," Bush said, "as long as it abides by the rule of low collateral." Commanders and pilots had discretion to hit targets as long as they expected it would only cause minimal damage to civilians. Anything that could cause high collateral damage or make it look or feel like a war against civilians had first to come to Rumsfeld and then him for approval.

At 12:40, the staff began clearing the Treaty Room.

Where are the cards with the text as a backup for the Tele-PrompTer? Bush asked. Someone brought him the cards. He did a dry run of the speech.

"You've got the paragraphing wrong," he said, and requested changes so the pauses would be more natural. Someone brought him a glass of water.

"We've done this before," Bush said impatiently to one of the crew members he recognized. "Let's get doing it."

The awkward moments of the countdown continued and Bush looked around.

"Big Al!" he said to a Secret Service agent he had run with. He asked where the agent had been on a recent run.

Silence.

One agent said he had done a five-minute mile.

"I'm impressed," Bush said, adding that he had recently had an excellent run, 21 minutes, 6 seconds for three miles. The second mile had been the slowest, the first and third were the good ones, he added.

Silence.

"Where's the pool?" Bush asked. The networks had just received notice and a camera and sound crew was on its way that would feed video and sound for all. Finally, at 12:50 the pool showed up. They were late and frantic, rushing to get set up in time. One pool member couldn't get fully hooked up.

"Plug it in," Bush said, motioning to the location.

"Good afternoon," Bush said at 1 P.M. "On my orders the United States military has begun strikes against al Qaeda terrorist training camps and military installations of the Taliban regime in Afghanistan."

The Taliban had not met his demands. "And now the Taliban will pay a price." He didn't mention ground forces, but he came close. "Our military action is also designed to clear the way for sustained, comprehensive and relentless operations to drive them [the terrorists] out and bring them to justice."

The president promised food and medicine to the people of Afghanistan. "We will win this conflict by the patient accumulation of successes.

"I know many Americans feel fear today," he acknowledged, pledging that strong precautions were being taken by all of the government. To the men and women of the military, he said in effect this would not be Vietnam. "Your mission is defined; your objectives are clear; your goal is just; you have my full confidence; and you will have every tool you need to carry out your duty."

He read a letter he had received from a fourth grade girl whose father was in the military. She had written, "As much as I don't want my dad to fight, I'm willing to give him to you."

AT 2:45 P.M. Secretary Rumsfeld and General Myers appeared in the Pentagon press room. In a long introductory statement, Rumsfeld presented the military strikes as a "complement" to the diplomatic, financial and other pressure. He laid out six goals—sending a

message to the Taliban, acquiring intelligence, developing relationships with the anti-Taliban groups such as the Northern Alliance,
making it increasingly difficult for the terrorists, altering the military balance over time, and providing humanitarian relief. He gave
no numbers or timetables.

General Myers offered some details—15 land-based bombers,
25 strike aircraft from carriers and 50 Tomahawk cruise missiles
from U.S. and British ships and submarines. What he did not say
was that they had only 31 targets on their strike list, all very low
collateral damage targets in remote areas. The targets were the al
Qaeda brigade, early warning radar, some command facilities used
by al Qaeda and the Taliban, Taliban military aircraft, Taliban military airports and runways, the terrorist training camps, which were
largely empty, and several surface-to-air missile sites.

"Was Osama bin Laden targeted in the raid?" a reporter asked.

"The answer is no with respect to him," Rumsfeld replied,
though he noted that command facilities in Afghanistan had been
targeted.

Rumsfeld lowered expectations; he called it "this so-called
war."

Asked how many targets had been hit, he replied, "There is no
way to discuss the outcome of this operation." There was a way, but
he was not going to do it publicly. The vagueness was a protection
from later contradiction, revealing the smallness of the operation
and his own frustrations.

Another reporter asked, "Are you running the risk of being
characterized as attacking the Afghan people rather than military
targets?"

"You know," Rumsfeld replied, "in this world of ours if you get
up in the morning you're running a risk of having someone lie and
someone mischaracterize what it is you're doing. What the United
States of America is doing is exactly what I said." It was defense
against those who killed thousands of Americans and now threaten,
intimidate and terrorize the world. "Thank you very much."

Bin Laden issued his own threat through a videotape that was released by Al-Jazeera. Sitting in an unidentified rocky site, wearing his military fatigue jacket, holding a microphone like a lounge singer, he said, "Here is America struck by God Almighty in one of its vital organs, so that its greatest buildings are destroyed.

"God has blessed a group of vanguard Muslims, the forefront of Islam, to destroy America."

BEGINNING BEFORE 7 A.M. on Monday, October 8, Rumsfeld made brief appearances on all five television network morning shows to offer a low-keyed and hedged assessment. Of the targets he said to ABC television, "We know they were successfully hit in many respects."

At 9:30 A.M., at the NSC meeting, Tenet said, "The picture is of the Afghans against al Qaeda in the north." The CIA was trying to help with the targeting up north. "The picture in the south is still unresolved. The Predator is flying in the north."

General Myers turned to the target problem. They didn't know what to hit. "Our TAC air are loitering, waiting for emerging targets identified by the Predator." It was an incredible moment, barely imaginable in the annals of modern warfare. After a day of strikes, the airborne might of the United States had been a somewhat helpless giant lumbering around the sky—"loitering," in the words of the nation's top military man, waiting for targets of opportunity.

Rumsfeld had some good news: "All aircraft are back safely," he said, "including the humanitarian aircraft."

Myers had harder news, the Bomb Damage Assessment, the key after-action analysis about what damage had been inflicted from bombs and cruise missiles. He said lots of targets were not destroyed sufficiently. "We're going to go back today to those things we missed."

The BDA was going to be treated as highly classified and the press and the public would not be told much.

Bush said that the latest communications intercepts and other intelligence showed that some major al Qaeda lieutenants, even possibly including bin Laden, were in Tora Bora, a region of natural and man-made caves in the White Mountains along the Pakistan border near Jalalabad. As the mujaheddin did during the Soviet occupation, al Qaeda and Taliban fighters were using the Tora Bora cave bunkers, accessible only by mule, as hideaways and depots.

"What ordnance do we put in Tora Bora?" he asked.

Myers's answer grabbed everyone's attention—32 individual 2,000-pound bombs.

"We're not hitting a number of Taliban military targets," Rumsfeld said, because of potential high collateral damage. The question for tomorrow, he asked, was whether and when to go after more Taliban military targets.

"Look," Bush said, "we're going to have a series of strikes. We're going to then slow down, we're going to do our intelligence, see what the picture is, then we're going to restrike." At the moment, he seemed to be exhibiting some patience, glad finally to be bombing. But in an interview later, the president said he realized they weren't doing much of consequence militarily. "We're bombing sand. We're pounding sand," he said.

He was still on edge about anthrax. The first victim in Florida had died and a co-worker from the same building was infected. The FBI had launched a massive investigation, and anthrax was now front page news.

THE PRINCIPALS MET later that day. Tenet was happy. Musharraf had dismissed his intelligence chief, Mahmoud, and several of his key lieutenants, a dramatic signal. The bad witch was dead. The Pakistani intelligence service had been the Taliban's sugar daddy, and the removal of Mahmoud meant that Musharraf was increasingly serious.

The French had 30 aircraft they wanted to move into the theater, and wanted U.S. support diplomatically with the Tajiks and Uzbeks to find a place to put them.

Rice said, "We'll check with Franks as to the need for those aircraft. And then we can discuss how we can facilitate it diplomatically. I'm grateful that Tommy is allowing the coalition partners to participate in different ways."

Rumsfeld turned to the sensitive subject of the Bomb Damage Assessment for the second day's strikes. "We destroyed 11 of 12 SA-3 radars. We hit seven of eight airfields. We've hit one half of the long-range radars, we'll go after the rest with our aircraft. We pounded Tora Bora. We don't know what effect. We got three radio towers, we made humanitarian drops. We used 70 attack aircraft doing 166 sorties."

The group turned to one of the most challenging problems they faced. How might the U.S. deter bin Laden and his network from using weapons of mass destruction?

No one had any great ideas.

"They may not be deterrable," Rice said, "but we can discourage others who would support him in it and incentivize them to turn on him."

But bin Laden was already pretty isolated. He seemed to have little support other than the Taliban, and the U.S. had failed to get them to turn on him.

DURING A MEETING in the Oval Office that day it was suggested to the president that he visit the Pentagon.

"I'm not going over there to say the planes all returned safely," Bush said, "because some day all the planes aren't going to return safely."

TENET BEGAN THE 9:30 A.M. NSC meeting on Tuesday, October 9, addressing the No. 1 problem—the lack of military targets in Afghanistan three days into the bombing campaign. "Today we're focused on working with the CINC to provide new targets, especially in the north," he said. His CIA paramilitary men on the ground in the north, Jawbreaker, might help identify "emerging targets" by flushing out new information on installations and troop concentrations. The Predator drones, the unmanned aerial vehicles, were also providing excellent reconnaissance video. "We're using the UAV to look at Tora Bora, to validate the maps provided by the Northern Alliance.

"Tribal groups in the south are not yet moving. We're holding the Northern Alliance in place and there's a question of when we release them."

So the ground situation remained static, partly at the U.S. military's behest, as everyone waited to see what effect the bombing campaign would have.

"In the south they're still on the fence. There are folks in Paktia—that's the most active group in the south," said Tenet, referring to the province due south of Kabul that includes the cities of Gardez and Khowst.

One promising development he could tell the president was the change in leadership of the ISI, the Pakistani intelligence service. The new chief was cleaning out the agency's pro-Taliban members. This was a big deal for the CIA and a gutsy move by Musharraf. "We'll then ask them for more information," he said. He still distrusted ISI and wasn't sharing all his intelligence with them, and CIA source development in the south was being done independent of the Pakistanis.

Tenet also reported that switching of sides among the less militant Taliban had begun. It was something the agency had anticipated. "We're getting some defections of Taliban commanders in the north." Thirty-five to 40 Taliban commanders and about 1,200 men had defected Monday, handing the Northern Alliance control of a key Taliban resupply route northwest of Kabul. The commanders had been bought with CIA money.

"Weather is going to limit the Northern Alliance," said Cheney. "After a month they'll be locked in, so if we're serious

about unleashing the Northern Alliance, we need to do it soon."
Given the time constraints, Cheney wasn't convinced that holding
the Northern Alliance back was the most expedient strategy. They
had to do more than slowly grind down the enemy through bombing and defections. "Is Franks focusing on the targets that will
make it easier for the Northern Alliance to move?

"We should encourage the Northern Alliance to take Kabul,"
Cheney said. "We as a superpower should not be stalemated." He
was worried that they had a weak defense at home and a weak offense in Afghanistan.

"We need a victory," Bush said.

"The only victory to the world might be taking the capital,"
Cheney replied.

"We're going to release the Northern Alliance on Thursday or
Friday," Tenet said, "and Franks is going to strike targets in the
north to facilitate their move." The CIA director was almost speaking for the CINC—a blurring of operational lines between CIA and
Defense that made Rumsfeld uneasy.

Tenet continued, "We can't stop them from trying to take
Kabul—the only issue is whether they can do it or not."

How does taking Kabul help us against al Qaeda? someone
asked. All agreed that the Afghan capital city could be a symbolic
step forward. Since Afghanistan was factionalized, perhaps the capital did not have the political importance it did in other countries.

They discussed how important it was for the U.S. to be mindful of the wishes of Pakistan, which feared the influence of Russia
and Iran on a Kabul that would be controlled by the Northern Alliance. Still it would be hard to claim success if the Taliban retained
control of the capital through the winter.

Rice asked whether the Northern Alliance was getting uniform
advice. Were they hearing one thing from the U.S., another from
the Russians and yet another from the other players in the region?
No one answered. The group moved on to the Middle East, Indonesia and a timeline to expand the terrorist list beyond al Qaeda to
freeze finances of other terrorist groups.

Rumsfeld again raised the question of anti-terrorist actions in a theater beyond Afghanistan. No one seemed interested.

He announced more bad news. "We're unlikely to go with Special Forces in the north," at least in the short term.

Myers said, "In the south we could get boots on the ground on the 16th, 17th or 18th." That was a week away, but it was something.

"We need the American people to understand we're being successful without bragging," the president said.

"We can be more positive now," Rumsfeld said. Most of the Taliban airfields had been damaged and the military could now carry out strikes more or less around the clock.

"I think I'm going to say that the guys have done exactly what we asked them to do and we're well satisfied with the progress," said Bush.

Myers gave the day's Bomb Damage Assessment, the top secret scorecard. "We're doing 70 sorties over Afghanistan. Sixteen of the 35 targets on the second day need to be evaluated." That meant that they may have failed to destroy nearly 50 percent of the targets. Monday's Pentagon press conference had not disclosed this. "Need to go after the transport aircraft. They've got one SA-3 that's still up but it doesn't threaten our forces." The U.S. had wiped out two of the three surface-to-air missile sites that comprised the Taliban's air defenses. They also dropped leaflets and 37,500 humanitarian daily rations into famine-stricken areas.

"We're going to hit low collateral damage Taliban military targets tomorrow," Rumsfeld said.

"There'll be pressure to step up the targets with higher collateral damage," the president said. "We've been successful so far because we've focused on the military, demonstrably important targets. It's important to maintain this focus."

Bush asked about caves and hitting camps in the south. He said he was going to give an evening press conference in two nights. "We need to think about how to describe the military campaign, what we're trying to achieve." Testing some concepts, he said the next phase of the conventional military operation would be ongoing, but sporadic. "You may not see bombing for a while, and we're not going to tell you when we will resume bombing."

"You're right," said Rumsfeld.

"We're going to strike at the time of our choosing, when it's required for our mission," Bush continued. "UBL may not be caught, but it's still useful to do what we're doing."

The president said he would be asking children to contribute $1 each to an Afghan Children's Fund. "The Department of Education is going to try and sponsor elementary school to elementary school exchanges, and we want to make a pitch to Muslim women and reach out to Muslim women." The Taliban's oppressive treatment of women was one of the most visible affronts of the strict fundamentalist regime, and Bush wanted to show that overthrowing it would liberate women.

Cheney returned to the hard questions they were skirting. "Where will we be in December and January when UBL has not been hit, the weather has gotten bad and the operations have slowed?"

"We're trying to get something going in other parts of the world against al Qaeda," said Rumsfeld again. He still thought that if the anti-terrorism campaign stalled in Afghanistan, they could always do something elsewhere. It would be in keeping with the global nature of the president's war on terror. At the top of the list for expanding anti-terror actions were the Philippines, Yemen and Indonesia. In the Philippines, a predominantly Catholic island nation of 83 million people, Muslim insurgents had rooted in the south, most notably the terrorist group Abu Sayyaf, which had suspected ties to al Qaeda. Yemen continued to sprout a large al Qaeda presence after the October 2000 terrorist attack on the USS *Cole*, and the country was also home to representatives of Hamas, Palestinian Islamic Jihad and other terrorist organizations. In Indonesia, Muslim extremists were everywhere.

But he was sounding like a lone drummer.

"I'm thinking a lot about endgames," said Bush, taking them back to Afghanistan. "And if we're stalled by the weather, are we where we want to be?"

"Look, pressure works," Rumsfeld said, trying to steer the discussion back to terrorist groups worldwide. "Let's get something started against them elsewhere in the world. The focus cannot only be Afghanistan."

Cheney snapped back, "If UBL is in a cave and we get a hit, people won't care what's going on elsewhere."

Rumsfeld launched into a discussion of what should be said publicly about the possible use of U.S. weapons of mass destruction if the other side used them. It was a frightening prospect, but it had to be addressed.

Look, Cheney retorted, we just need to say we reserve the right to use any means at our disposal to respond to any use of weapons of mass destruction. That's the Gulf War formula—what had been said in the 1991 war on Iraq—and that's what we ought to do. Ultimately, the use of such weapons was a decision that the president would make.

The current and former secretaries of defense, both deeply concerned about nuclear, biological and chemical warfare, stuck with the topic for a while. The U.S. was at war with an unconventional foe and they had to examine the possibility that bin Laden might have weapons of mass destruction.

"UBL might not be deterrable," said Cheney.

"Well," the president said, "sponsoring nations of UBL, those that support him, might have some influence with him. Should we send some messages, private or public?"

We need to think some more about this, said Rumsfeld.

The question of al Qaeda's weapons of mass destruction capability was what Rumsfeld often called a "known unknown"—something they knew they didn't know, something both possible and important but on which they had no definitive intelligence. It was chilling in itself. But it was in some ways less of a concern than the "unknown unknowns," the things that the U.S. didn't know it didn't know, the potential ugly surprises.

Bush returned the discussion to known problems. "We need to think through how we're going to get some victory before the snow falls. And we need to think through Kabul."

"Do we want to take it?" asked Powell. "Do we want to hold it? If we want to hold it, what are we going to do with it?"

"You know, the Russians never took Kabul," Rice said. That almost suggested it was a good reason to try to take the capital, since the Soviets seemed to have done nearly everything wrong.

"Maybe the U.N. should handle Kabul," the president said.

"Yeah, the U.N. is the best way to handle it," Powell agreed. "If the Northern Alliance take it first, though, they won't give it up." The slain Alliance commander Massoud had said he would never occupy Kabul single-handedly, but Powell did not think his successor, Fahim Khan, was as disciplined or diplomatically inclined.

Rumsfeld said the weather was still good in the south. Playing off that, the president ended the meeting on an optimistic note. "The weaker troops are in the north so the Northern Alliance can take over the north," he said.

AT 1:15 P.M., Rumsfeld and Myers appeared in the Pentagon briefing room. Rumsfeld announced that the U.S. had struck several al Qaeda terrorist training camps and damaged most of the Taliban's airfields and antiaircraft radars and launchers. "We believe we are now able to carry out strikes more or less around the clock, as we wish."

Myers did not give the same report that he had given to the NSC—that 16 of the 35 targets needed to be evaluated. He said, "U.S. forces struck 13 targets yesterday."

He showed slides of Afghanistan revealing the Day One and Day Two targets. "We did well in our initial strikes, damaging or destroying about 85 percent of the first set of 31 targets." He was being vague. In military terms, the difference between "damaging" and "destroying" is night and day, much as a car damaged in an automobile accident might still function.

"You say you're running out of targets though, Mr. Secretary," said one reporter. "What are you going to continue to hit?"

"Well, for one thing, we're finding that some of the targets we hit need to be rehit," answered Rumsfeld. It was more revealing than what Myers had said.

"Second," he said, "we're not running out of targets, Afghanistan is."

There was laughter. This was vintage Rumsfeld. Yet it left open the question: How do you win a war if the enemy can't be hit?

Other reporters pressed on issues of bombing troop concentrations, providing close air support and otherwise directly supporting the ready-to-advance forces of the Northern Alliance. Both Rumsfeld and Myers responded cautiously, refusing to comment on when or if U.S. ground forces might be deployed, or how they would support anti-Taliban groups. At one point, Myers delivered his view of this new war.

"You know, if you try to quantify what we're doing today in terms of previous conventional wars, you're making a huge mistake," he said. "That is 'old think' and that will not help you analyze what we're doing. . . . And that's what we've been trying to tell you for three days. It's a different kind of conflict."

Replying to a question about what responsibility the U.S. might have if the Taliban were overthrown, Rumsfeld demurred. "I don't think [it] leaves us with a responsibility to try to figure out what kind of government that country ought to have," he said, adding, "I don't know people who are smart enough from other countries to tell other countries the kind of arrangements they ought to have to govern themselves."

He didn't want the United States committed to nation building.

• • •

WEDNESDAY, OCTOBER 10, the NSC convened in the White House Situation Room at 9:30 A.M.

The president raised the issue of how much classified and sensitive intelligence to share with Congress. "It's important for Don and Colin to brief their respective committees," he said. "We're giving the Congress colonel-level operational briefings. We need to do it at a higher level."

They would appease lawmakers by sending Rumsfeld and Powell, both of whom knew how to speak candidly without giving out anything critical. "I want to accommodate Congress without giving up classified information," Bush said. In a practical sense this was impossible. Classified information tells the story of what is happening, which is what Congress wanted.

The meeting turned to Syria, well documented as a state supporter of Hezbollah. Syria had condemned the September 11 attacks.

"Syria needs to be against all terrorism," Powell said.

The others agreed, and Rumsfeld added, "We can't let Syria help us with al Qaeda and then us feel constrained about pursuing them with respect to their support for other terrorists."

"We need to get some of our people on Al-Jazeera," Bush said. "Let's get a daily schedule of appearances, let's get press briefings. We need people to feed some information to them."

Rumsfeld gave his somewhat formulaic daily operational briefing on the war.

"We did 65 flights," he said, although 70 had been planned. "Low collateral military targets. We're getting some emerging targets. We have not gotten all the helos, transports or the jets." Both Rumsfeld and Myers had said the day before that the U.S. owned the skies over Afghanistan and that the Taliban had only a few meager air assets left.

"Let's make sure we don't hit any mosques," Bush said.

"We got some additional caves and we're working Tora Bora," the hard-to-reach cave complex in the east, Rumsfeld said.

Franks said he had a 12-man Special Forces A-team waiting to deploy into Afghanistan.

"We'll work with the DCI to get them in," said Rumsfeld. He was seething about the slow progress of getting the Special Forces teams in. Weather was now one more excuse. He had sold the president on the concept of getting boots on the ground, and he wasn't delivering.

"Given the weather," the president said, "now is the time to move in the north. We still have later options in the south, but we've got to move in the north."

Rumsfeld made a general comment about U.S. policy on the Asian subcontinent. "We've got to avoid the image of a shift to Pakistan," he said. The anti-terror alliance with Pakistan was worrying rival India.

Powell agreed. "Whenever we talk about the Paks, we have to talk about the Indians as well."

Rumsfeld said, "DOD is linked well to AID"—the humanitarian assistance agency. "We want to make sure we're feeding the right people."

"We're doing $170 million a year," Powell said.

"Only refugee camps?" Bush asked.

"Both on the border and in Afghanistan," Powell replied. More than 2 million Afghans had fled their homes during the last two decades and many were living in refugee camps in the border areas of Pakistan and Iran. Still more were flowing across the border every day since the start of the bombing.

Rumsfeld put forth one of his trademark aphorisms: "Do no good and no harm will come of it." Doing good is risky. They should expect difficulties and criticism over their humanitarian assistance. Critics would say it wasn't enough, that it was feeding the wrong people, but they shouldn't let it deter them.

"There's a point where we're going to need to do something visible elsewhere in the world," Rumsfeld said for about the fifth or sixth time. It was a point he had been trying to discuss for days now, but the others were not inclined.

As they turned to finding new targets, the president warned again, "Just make sure we don't start hitting a mosque.

"Why can't we fly more than one Predator at a time?" he asked. He had been impressed with the raw intelligence provided by the Predator. It was a useful, low-risk tool—and at a cost of only $1 million apiece, a bargain as far as military hardware went.

"We're going to try to get two simultaneously," Tenet said.

"We ought to have 50 of these things," Bush said.

Powell then turned back to the overall military strategy. "We ought to try and consolidate the north and east before winter," he said. "Seize Mazar-e Sharif, control the border and the valleys."

"I asked people to look at this," Tenet said. The CIA was indicating that Kabul too could fall before winter, and Tenet knew this posed a much tougher political challenge than the takeover of Mazar. "The Northern Alliance will want to take Kabul, and it would be hard to control," he warned again. "We need a non-Taliban Pashtun to cooperate with the Northern Alliance on Kabul. And we should tie humanitarian assistance to it." Tenet said the food would "incentivize" someone to cooperate. But using food as leverage was not in the spirit of widespread humanitarian assistance the president was envisioning.

Cheney seemed uneasy and indicated that he wanted to get the president away from such discussions, almost give him deniability. "The broad question of strategy needs to be decided by the president," Cheney said. "We will be judged by whether we get concrete results in Afghanistan. We need the PC to address the issue and then come to the president." The principals' committee was the proper place for this sort of tactical issue, and not in front of the president.

The president later said his worry was that they would not keep their focus. "I believe we need to be a first-things-first administration." Afghanistan was first and foremost.

At the meeting, Rumsfeld said about Afghanistan, "We need to lock things down so that Omar and UBL do not leave. We want to keep people bottled up."

"Bottled up?" Powell almost sneered. "They can get out in a Land Rover."

Powell had learned that bitter lesson years earlier when he was chairman of the Joint Chiefs during the United States's invasion of Panama in December 1989. The U.S. had spent days chasing after Panamanian strongman General Manuel Noriega. Afghanistan was eight times the size of Panama and its border regions were remote and lawless—to think the U.S. could keep anyone bottled up was folly.

The president disagreed with Rumsfeld's view. "Part of our strategy is to get UBL moving, get him moving," he said. If bin Laden was on the run, he couldn't be plotting and planning. "We didn't expect to get him on the first day. We want to unsettle his safe haven. That's why he's on the run."

FOLLOWING THE NSC meeting, Bush made the short trip down Pennsylvania Avenue to FBI headquarters. Appearing with Powell, Ashcroft and Mueller, he unveiled a list of 22 "Most Wanted Terrorists" to supplement the bureau's popular and successful "Ten Most Wanted" list. "Now is the time to draw the line in the sand against the evil ones," he said as head shots of the named figures were displayed. At the top of the list were Osama bin Laden and two of his key lieutenants, Egyptians Dr. Ayman Zawahiri and Mohammed Atef.

Bush took a classified version for himself that had photos, brief biographies and personality sketches of the 22 men. When he returned to his desk in the Oval Office, he slipped the list of names and faces into a drawer, ready at hand, his own personal scorecard for the war.

16

S TEVE HADLEY EXPRESSED his concern to Rice about the situation in Afghanistan. "I don't think we're really on top of this. At least I'm not on top of it the way I want to be. I've got it laid on. The deputies and I are going to go out to the CIA and sit down with George and his people."

Rice went with them to Langley later that Thursday. Tenet and some of his people tossed out a number of observations:

Iran and Russia had both supported the Northern Alliance with millions of dollars over the years. Iran was probably the biggest contributor, providing money to support thousands of Alliance troops. Both countries were still active with the Alliance. They seemed okay with the U.S. and CIA dealing with the Alliance, but there was no coordinated message.

Iran has a big influence on Ismail Khan—the Shiite Tajik warlord who controlled territory around Herat in western Afghanistan, near the border with Iran.

The tribes all wanted U.S. air support, ammunition and food if they were going to move against the Taliban and al Qaeda, but the tribes wanted to move by themselves.

Afghanistan is stable only in a decentralized structure. It was not a modern state with a strong central government and might not have one in the future.

Everybody, each tribe and warlord, has to have a seat at the table in Kabul in a future government.

Because the situation was so fluid and many of the tribal leaders in southern Afghanistan maintained ties to the Taliban, Tenet still was not prepared to send paramilitary teams into the south. It simply was not secure. Nor was there a definable front line as there was in the north.

Intelligence and an introduction to some Pashtuns had been requested from the new Pakistani intelligence chief, according to one of the CIA briefers.

"We need to run special operations in the south, we need to strip Taliban of their fighting force. We need to get the Pashtuns to play with us, and we need to calm the Paks down," Tenet summed up.

A new government or administration of Kabul had to be even-handed with all factions and tribes, the agency experts stressed and stressed again. The symbolism of ethnic Tajiks and Uzbeks—the bulk of the Northern Alliance—in Kabul would be a real problem for the Pakistanis and the Pashtuns.

"Do you have to defeat the Taliban?" Rice asked.

Yes, otherwise it would remain a rallying point for the terrorist elements.

"We had a counterterrorism strategy, now we need a political strategy," Tenet said. "We need to tell the southern tribes what the political scenario is. We need the vision. We need to make it clear that we're there for the long term."

As to what might be achieved by winter, Tenet and his experts offered a four-part answer: 1. Take over the north. 2. Get resupplied from Uzbekistan. 3. Have Kabul under the structure they discussed. 4. Create a safe passage for supplies into the south via Paktia, which shares a 150-mile border with Pakistan.

The U.S. could have the Pakistanis communicate the political strategy to the Pashtuns. Anti-Taliban forces could drive south, pin the enemy down, encircle and hit them. Continue to strike targets, the CIA analysts recommended. It would be easier to find some targets in winter given the high-tech advantage U.S. forces had. By cutting down the mobility of the enemy and localizing them, they might even be able to induce some more defections.

The CIA briefers repeated how important it would be to offer incentives to the Pashtuns to withdraw support from the Taliban. What would the message be? "Withdraw and get fed. If you don't withdraw, you don't get fed," one said. It was a highly questionable proposition. If the situation in the south turned dire, the U.S. could be accused of abetting famine—the use of organized starvation as a political tool, compromising the American moral high ground.

It would eventually become clear this would not be necessary. The south had adequate food. The serious food shortages were in and around Northern Alliance–controlled areas.

AT 5 P.M. the deputies' committee focused on the kinds of threats the U.S. faced, and what they could do now to deal with them. A mounting concern was the possibility of a radiological weapon, but the more they talked the more it was clear it wasn't really something they could prepare for. The likelihood, the impact—psychologically and physically—were big unknowns, in part because to their knowledge no such device had ever been detonated. It was only a concept, as worrying as that might be. Of course, hijacking a passenger airliner and using it as a missile had, until recently, seemed improbable.

"I'M DOING A press conference tonight," Bush reminded at the start of the Thursday, October 11, morning NSC meeting. "I'm going to reframe the conflict, set the expectations at the right level." He was brimming with confidence. "It's going to be a long conflict, we've got to have a deliberate, intense and well-thought-out strategy. I'm going to call on the patience of the American people. We're going to go after the hosts and the parasites. It's a broader war. If we don't get UBL, it doesn't mean it's a failure."

Powell said the Organization of the Islamic Conference had released a strong statement condemning the terrorist acts against the U.S. The OIC communiqué, released the day before, said the acts were in direct contravention of the teachings of the divine religions and of all moral and human values. The president said he was going to use some language from the OIC statement in his answers that night.

"The OIC statement suggests that the coalition is holding together," Powell said.

On humanitarian aid, he continued, "We're getting some trucks in from Turkmenistan, Tajikistan and Iran. Remember that most of the food is distributed by NGOs. That's the distribution network. We need to get them coordinated, and coordinated with CENTCOM." With Afghanistan a combat zone, military oversight was important to keeping the aid program orderly and safe.

Rumsfeld gave his daily report on operations. "We did 75 strikes in Afghanistan yesterday. We're looking for emerging targets. We got 31 of their 68 aircraft; we can't find their helos; we got nine of their 15 transports. We looked at their drug labs and heroin storage and we didn't hit it because of collateral damage."

These were the detailed damage assessments that were guarded in most cases with TOP SECRET/CODEWORD classification—the highest possible. An authoritative leak would be a major setback. They could imagine the headlines: "U.S. Destroys Only 31 of 68 Taliban Aircraft; Can't Find Helos; Spares Drug Labs, Fearing Collateral Damage."

AFTER THE NSC meeting, the president's motorcade made the short drive across the Potomac to the Pentagon for a memorial service on the one-month anniversary. Bush addressed a crowd of 15,000 that had assembled on a grassy parade ground by the building's River entrance, which was shrouded in black.

"We have come here to pay our respects to 125 men and women who died in the service of America," the president said. "We also remember passengers on a hijacked plane—those men and women, boys and girls who fell into the hands of evildoers."

Rumsfeld spoke about the friends, family and co-workers they had lost. "They died because—in words of justification offered by their attackers—they were Americans," Rumsfeld said.

Likening the terrorists to the vanquished totalitarian regimes of the 20th century which sought to rule and oppress, Rumsfeld said, "The will to power, the urge to dominion over others . . . makes the terrorist a believer not in the theology of God, but the theology of self and in the whispered words of temptation: 'Ye shall be as gods.'

"In targeting this place, then, and those who worked here, the attackers, the evildoers correctly sensed that the opposite of all they were, and stood for, resided here."

After the speeches, oversized television screens scrolled the names of the dead as "Amazing Grace" was played. Rumsfeld was finally overtaken, tears in his eyes.

AT 3:30 P.M., the principals gathered in the White House Situation Room.

The anniversary was on everyone's mind. Tenet posed the question, "What are our objectives?" and then commenced a lengthy answer.

"We'd like the Taliban to collapse as a military entity." Second, they wanted the Northern Alliance in control of the territory in the north, linking up to the Tajik and Uzbek borders.

"UBL killed, captured or on the run," he added, stating the objective so loosely that it had already been achieved. "But we need to raise all boats at once. The north is a little farther along, no reason to go south of Kabul."

The earlier CIA briefing was still on Rice's mind: even if they had wanted to work the south, there wasn't much they could do. Much of Tenet's summary was a rehash. It showed how little was really moving.

"The Pashtuns are anti–Northern Alliance—they could be anti-Taliban. They're not anti-U.S.," Tenet said. In other words their allegiances were negotiable—just like everybody else's in Afghanistan. "They only want to control their shura," referring to an Islamic principle of self-governance. "We need to give something more than 'Go kill Arabs.' Have to incentivize them.

"The Northern Alliance is not monolithic. They could easily fragment. They could go against each other, you know, fall apart, fall to fighting. We need to be evenhanded in our aid.

"We have an Iranian dimension in the west and a Russian influence in the north," Tenet said of the Northern Alliance. The American CIA, formerly a junior partner among the Alliance's outside supporters, was now trying to buy the entire operation and control it as senior partner.

He said they had put their fate in the hands of the Afghan tribals, who were going to act at a time, place and pace of their own choosing. They had their own issues, endgames, ambitions and internal power plays. It was a mercenary force—not under U.S. command. That was the price of admission when it was decided at the front end that the tribals were going to do the bulk of the ground fighting and not the U.S. military.

As for the Northern Alliance factions who were holding fast to U.S. requests, Tenet said, "When the CINC releases them, we want them to take Taloqan, cut off al Qaeda, take Mazar-e Sharif, close the gap in Baghlan"—a key city on the road from Kabul north to Konduz—"and trap al Qaeda in the north."

Jawbreaker had been inside Afghanistan for two weeks. The next CIA paramilitary team would come in from Uzbekistan with

Special Forces and would join the Northern Alliance leader General Abdurrashid Dostum south of Mazar. There was a team of U.S. military Special Forces in Uzbekistan now, ready to deploy in the next couple of days to Ismail Khan, who was holding near Herat, 80 miles from the Iranian border.

"The CINC and CIA are joined at the hip. The people on the ground are working targets for the CINC," Rumsfeld said.

"Are they armed adequately?" Rice asked, referring to the Northern Alliance. Someone responded that they had small arms in the theater.

"We don't want to take Kabul. Our priority ought to be Mazar-e Sharif," Powell said. If Mazar were taken, it was only 40 miles from Uzbekistan. That would make it possible to open a land bridge between Afghanistan and Uzbekistan, a continuous overland route by which military and humanitarian supplies could flow. Air-dropping humanitarian aid was expensive and inefficient. The diplomatic challenge of ameliorating all the factions was going to require more thought, more time. "Do the bridge. Don't take Kabul."

On Kabul, "Let the U.N. administer it or maybe the OIC administer it. Make a center for humanitarian assistance, and make it the site for the loya jirga"—the traditional meeting of Afghan tribal leaders from across the country. Powell had a grand, even extravagant vision for the city's future. "This is Kabul, the international city, symbol of a united Afghanistan," he said. "Have a U.N. mandate plus third country forces ruling Kabul." Powell knew that Bush was loath to use U.S. troops for nation building.

"How would the Northern Alliance feel if you turn Kabul over to the Pashtuns?" Cheney asked.

"We'll turn it over to Brahimi and the U.N.," Powell responded. Lakhdar Brahimi was the U.N. special representative for Afghanistan.

"Can we show enough of this plan that we've outlined here before the Northern Alliance are in Kabul and alienate the Pashtuns?" someone asked. It was a critical question.

A CIA operations specialist who was attending, and still worked undercover, suggested, "If we can get the Pashtuns to sign on to this plan, Russia will go along."

How about Iran?

They would want some kind of role, he said.

There was the matter of the king. Should they use him, and how? The CIA man said that having him as a nominal head of government would not work, but he could convene the loya jirga and act as figurehead.

There was discussion of how much they needed someone in Afghanistan with the stature of the assassinated Massoud. He could have reined in any Alliance move to take Kabul. He could have been a great asset as they tried to work out a post-Taliban solution.

Powell was still skeptical. "Can they take Kabul?"

Yes, the CIA man said. "We're pretty confident they can get to Kabul in the near term." He reported positively on two southern provinces where there were CIA-paid assets. "We're working with them out of Islamabad. It's an administrative break with the Taliban. We don't know if they'll let us put people in there.

"We've got active assets in Logar and Nangahar Provinces." Nangahar Province, which hugged the Pakistani border, was the location of the Khyber Pass, a strategic gateway on the road from Jalalabad to Peshawar, Pakistan.

"We need to accelerate this move toward autonomy," Tenet said. "We need to offer humanitarian aid. Even if they don't want to fight, we need them to break with the Taliban. We need to offer a vision to those southern tribes.

"Some of them are into vision and some of them are into money," he said bluntly. "We need to administer to both." A vision about the greater good of Afghanistan was too abstract, heady and distant a prize for some tribesmen—but they understood and would gladly accept cash. The CIA was continuing to dispense millions. Tenet said the agency was arming many. Afghans responded to "weapons and a sense they're on the winning side."

Card repeated Powell's question. "Can they take Kabul?"

"They can at least get to the city," Tenet said.

The CIA man added, "When the Northern Alliance gets to the outskirts of Kabul, the Taliban will go to the hills to the south." That was good news and a warning. No one asked if they had a plan to deal with fleeing thousands.

"We need a vision of Kabul," Rice reiterated. "The vision for Kabul is important to avoid alienating the Pashtuns." Again they lamented the absence of Massoud, who had said he would have ruled Kabul from the outside with various tribes, including from the south. Fahim, the nominal replacement as head of the Northern Alliance, did not have his former commander's political skills.

"Look, we don't have to take Kabul to show results by December 1st. We need to figure out Kabul, the Pashtuns, the Northern Alliance," Cheney said.

"But the priority is in the north," Powell replied. "We need to talk about Kabul, tell them what the solution is, stop at the border, internationalize it, don't alienate the south, give the south a role in Kabul. That's more valuable that way than taking it. It gives me something to talk to the Paks about."

With all the talk of taking or not taking Kabul, they were overlooking the important matter of how vulnerable the CIA and Special Forces teams were in the field without support. "It's dangerous, the teams may be betrayed," said Wayne Downing, a retired four-star general who had been commander of U.S. Special Operations and was now a deputy on the National Security Council staff. The whole situation could turn with the death or capture of 10 to 12 men.

It was an uncomfortable truth and no one responded to it.

"We need a rebuilding package," Powell said.

"We need a political vision now," said Tenet.

"This is about the Taliban," Cheney said, trying to steer the conversation back. "Do we have an equally vigorous program against al Qaeda?"

There was some discussion of what might constitute victories, but Rice quickly came back to political problems. "We need a strategy for Kandahar." Kandahar, population 225,000, was the spiritual home of the Taliban.

The CIA man described the Taliban. "If they're hunkered down in Kandahar while the Northern Alliance is making progress in Kabul, that will incentivize the tribes to defect. And remember, in the higher elevations they may shut down, but in the lower levels we can still have activity."

The CIA had received a cable from the chief of station in Islamabad that day. Based on multiple sources, including the new Pakistani intelligence chief, the cable said that the bombings had so far been a big political disappointment and were not dividing the Taliban. "Taliban leadership remains united and defiant around Mullah Omar, while tribal commanders sit firmly on the fence waiting to see who will prevail before committing themselves." In other words, splitting the Taliban was a fantasy. It was very sobering. Maybe the enemy was stronger than they had imagined.

THE REPORTS OF threats were so intense that Tenet recommended that the FBI take the unusual step of issuing a national warning of possible terrorist attacks "over the next several days." He did it so forcefully that FBI Director Mueller had little choice but to act. The warning went out in the late afternoon: "Certain information, while not specific as to target, gives the government reason to believe that there may be additional terrorist attacks within the United States and against U.S. interests overseas over the next several days."

If Mueller had failed to comply, and there had been a terrorist attack, he might never have been forgiven. But the warning lacked details because none of the credible intelligence had specifics such as time, place or method of attack. It was more the high number of intercepts and other intelligence reporting that triggered Tenet's reaction. Given what had happened on September 11, better to overreact than underreact.

Cheney worried the intelligence agencies might be trying to cover their asses but he didn't voice any objection.

The president said later, "National alerts are very interesting issues, if you think about it. First of all, we never had had a national alert." He worried, "How many national alerts does it take to numb the American psyche?" The threats were serious. "Tenet is not a person who scares easy," he said, but he also disclosed that there was a mind game of sorts being played with bin Laden and his terrorists.

"We came to the conclusion at this point in time that a national alert was important to let the enemy know that we were on to them," the president said. In other words if something was planned and the other side saw the FBI announcing a national alert, there was a chance, perhaps remote, they might be delayed or even deterred. Bush said that the alert was "trying to get in their mind as much as anything else."

The alert was big national news as Americans attempted to figure out what it meant.

That evening, President Bush held a televised press conference, his first in prime time since taking office. He delivered a short opening statement before taking questions. He said little that was new, though he did offer the Taliban another opportunity to turn over bin Laden.

"I will say it again: If you cough him up and his people today that we'll reconsider what we're doing to your country," Bush said. "You still have a second chance. Just bring him in, and bring his leaders and lieutenants and other thugs and criminals with him."

Ann Compton of ABC News asked a question that stuck with the president 10 months later. "What are Americans supposed to look for and report to the police or the FBI?"

"Well, Ann, you know if you find a person that you've never seen before getting in a crop duster"—one of the suspected methods for terrorists to deliver chemical or biological agents—"that doesn't belong to you, report it."

The room erupted in laughter.

• • •

AT THE NSC on Friday, October 12, Rumsfeld said no strikes were planned for that day, the first Friday of the bombing campaign. Friday was the Muslim Sabbath. The pause would emphasize that the U.S. was not at war with Muslims.

Hank, the CIA special operations chief, gave a ground report. "CIA is integrating the CINC's air plus the Northern Alliance ground. They have an order to hold fast. The CINC will hit targets over the next three or four days. Then he's going to release the Northern Alliance. They will then have three and a half weeks of movement until snows in the mountains and they'll be able to work the lower elevations until December."

"Baghlan is going to defect," Hank continued, "and it will link up." Baghlan was a province and city about 100 miles north of Kabul between the Northern Alliance forces in the northeast and General Dostum's forces, which were to the west. "We'll link up the Northern Alliance forces, we'll open the land bridge from Uzbekistan to Dostum via Mazar-e Sharif. They'll take Herat and then we'll have an air base and we'll make an air base in the south.

"The Northern Alliance think they can get to Kabul. They have no intention or capability to go south of Kabul."

Bush asked Tenet, "How do you get the Northern Alliance to accept the Pashtun tribes?"

"The U.N. administration."

"It's okay by me," Bush said. "No problem with the U.N. doing Kabul."

"We've got to work on the Shamali Plains north of Kabul," Hank said.

"Look," said Rice, "we need not just a solution for Kabul, we also need to start thinking about the Afghan government."

"They'll cross the Shamali Plains and we will have some influence as to the process of entering Kabul," Tenet said, referring to the Northern Alliance forces.

"Do we want to free them to move south with impunity?" asked Bush.

Cheney answered, "It's not as strong a case to take Kabul as there was last week. Outskirts is enough given the other things that we are doing."

"We're in Logar and Nangahar Provinces," Hank said of his CIA team. "We're looking for al Qaeda targets there."

They discussed intelligence that indicated 100 or so people per day were going from Pakistan into Afghanistan to join the Taliban. There was some talk of sealing the border. It seemed an impossible idea, not practical given the hundreds of miles of mountainous and rough terrain, some of the most formidable in the world. There were few roads. Getting from one point to another could only be done on foot, with mules, or on horseback.

They talked about trying to encourage defections in Paktia and Paktika Provinces.

"Even if they are not going to fight," Tenet said, "we want to help them exercise control of their province. This will deny territory to the Taliban and squeeze them."

The vexing problem of getting the Special Forces teams into Afghanistan was addressed. The Russians had intervened to help get the CIA team in through Tajikistan. Maybe they could help again.

"Look," said the president, "I oppose using the military for nation building. Once the job is done, our forces are not peacekeepers. We ought to put in place a U.N. protection and leave, but if fighting resumes and the Taliban come back from the hills, who has to stabilize the situation?"

"Well, the new entity has to have a capacity to defend itself," Powell replied.

"Well, our covert action network will remain," Tenet added.

The CIA might have to continue to use its suitcases of cash.

17

JAWBREAKER, STILL THE only American on-the-ground, in-country presence, was trying to find bombing targets. Calls from the U.S. military were coming in at night, Can you verify this target? Get the coordinates? Do you have U.S. eyes on target? The team was not that night-capable and was using Russian maps. The Russian coordinates had to be translated to English maps with pencils and rulers. The team did not have the laser equipment to designate a target appropriately for the precision bombs. They also did not have direct communications with the U.S. bombers. They were supposed to provide intelligence, not act as spotters. They tried at times, and resisted at times.

This is not the way to do this, Gary concluded.

"Just hit the front lines for me," General Fahim told him. Bomb the Taliban and al Qaeda on the other side. "I can take Kabul, I can take Konduz if you break the line for me. My guys are ready." Fahim was short and stocky, looked like a thug, seemed to have had his nose broken about three times. His forces were decked out in new uniforms, supposedly waiting for the carpet bombing to begin so they could attack.

One night General Franks's headquarters sent a message to Gary saying essentially: You have provided intelligence that says there's an enemy position at the following coordinates. Is that really the enemy there? Are there any friendly forces around?

We can't verify, Gary answered. We are not going to say where the targets are good. We don't have the wherewithal.

He tried to keep focused on the intelligence mission.

Arif, the Alliance intelligence chief, was expanding contacts on the other side of the battle line—Taliban, al Qaeda and their sympathizers. Information came in that Dr. Zawahiri, bin Laden's No. 2, was in the Kabul area.

There's big money to be made if you can ambush Zawahiri, Gary said, promising millions in cash. He visited Fahim's general who was in charge on the Shamali Plains. The general was even more bullish, saying the Alliance could take Kabul in a day if the front lines were broken with U.S. bombing. The bombing around the country wasn't accomplishing anything, the general said. His men were intercepting some Taliban radio communications showing that the Taliban were unimpressed. The general was disappointed. He pointed at the Taliban lines, Look, there is where the enemy is. Blowing up some depot in Kandahar wasn't doing anything for them.

Gary concluded that the bombing might be making the chain of command back in Washington feel good, but it wasn't working.

THE NSC MET at 9:30 A.M., Monday, October 15. John McLaughlin was sitting in for Tenet. "We have the right to fly over Tajikistan without restriction," he announced. "The second CIA team is going to join up with Dostum." The CIA team, designated "Alpha," was going in on Wednesday near Mazar. They were hoping to get some Special Forces A-teams in for target spotting very soon. "Once released," he said, "the Northern Alliance will need guidance—we'll need to give guidance to the Northern Alliance about whether they should take over Kabul."

"Do they have enough troops in the north to go both west and south?" the president asked. South was to Kabul and west was toward Konduz.

"The Northern Alliance believes they have enough troops to do both at once," replied McLaughlin. "Winter will slow us down in the Panjshir Valley, but we'll still be able to fight on the Shamali Plains."

Armitage was representing the State Department since Powell was on a trip to Pakistan and India. "In 1996," he said, "Tajik-Uzbek control of Afghanistan helped spark the Taliban. It could now create a civil war. We should ask the Northern Alliance to stop at the frontier of Kabul."

Bin Laden "could be hiding in Kabul or in the Jalalabad area," Cheney said. "We need to get into that area and clean it out."

The president said again, "Before we give them the green light to go into Kabul, let's get them on the outskirts and then decide how it looks."

"That'll suggest to the Northern Alliance that we only want our objectives," Cheney said. It was important to show we were interested in *their* agenda too.

"Why not let them base on the outskirts of the city," Bush retorted, "and they can conduct the missions that they want on the inside."

"Let's see if we can carry out this arrangement by basing them on the outside of the city, bringing in Pashtuns. And we'll arrange for control of Kabul and use it for humanitarian assistance," McLaughlin offered.

"Well, you know, the land bridge and squeezing the Taliban out of the north was an initial objective. Now we think we can put pressure on Kabul too," Bush said.

"We've hit most of what we think they have," Rumsfeld said. "On targets, we're working on Mazar and Konduz. We're not working on the Shamali Plains yet. The reason is we cannot find the forces deployed there. When we have the people on the ground, then we may be able to find them." He then gave a rundown of when his Special Forces teams were getting in. Twelve more people were to go in with the CIA's existing Northern Alliance team, and over the next four days more were expected: a 12-man Special Forces team, another CIA team just south of Mazar, then a second and third Special Forces team.

"There's anecdotal evidence that we're beginning to affect morale," General Franks said. "We did 110 to 120 sorties, some on the Shamali Plains," correcting Rumsfeld, who had just told them they were not working the Shamali Plains. They had found very few targets of opportunity. "We hit two camps, we think. We made the first use of the AC-130 gunships." The slow-flying planes, equipped with a 105mm howitzer and a Gatling gun, could spray 1,800 rounds per minute, laying down a withering carpet of fire so intense that Afghans said they "breathed fire."

"The AC-130 gunship, the old Puff the Magic Dragon during Vietnam, was way more effective than a Northern Alliance cavalry," the president would later recall. "It is a lethal weapon. My reaction was, if you've got a shot at the enemy, take it in any way you can."

"Will there be movement next week on both the north and Kabul?" Bush asked.

"I think that it's likely to be the case," McLaughlin replied.

Rice and Armitage said they had asked the Uzbeks for a base where they could leave perhaps up to 1,000 U.S. troops over the winter.

"I don't want to nation-build with troops," Bush said yet again.

"We need to focus on getting UBL," said Cheney yet again.

"We need to keep digging on the timetable," the president said. "If they can move south we want them to do it before winter, but we need to try to work on accommodation." They were losing their focus, he said. "There's been too much discussion of post-conflict Afghanistan. We've been only at it for a week. We've made a lot of progress, we've got time. It may take a while. A rush to a conclusion on Afghanistan after just one week is too premature. This is a different kind of a deal. We're making progress, we're isolating, we've got him on the run."

Cheney asked about reports of defections. "We validate some, but mostly in the south," answered McLaughlin. "We'll ask the Northern Alliance to try and validate some of them."

Hadley, taking notes in a steno pad, was thinking that they were having too many meetings that week. Fatigue was starting to show. Full throttle for over a month wasn't good. People were running out of gas. At the principals' meeting that evening without the president, Rice and the others returned to Kabul. They weren't getting anywhere, but they couldn't let the issue go.

Earlier that morning, NBC had announced that an assistant to Tom Brokaw, its anchorman, had tested positive for cutaneous anthrax received in a letter. But the most startling development of the day was the discovery that a letter opened in the offices of Senate Majority Leader Daschle tested for traces of anthrax.

"Anthrax Scare Comes to Capitol Hill," said *The Washington Post* headline the next morning.

TENET WAS IN London for a memorial service for Sir David Spedding, former chief of the British Secret Intelligence Service, MI6. Spedding had been one of Tenet's mentors in the intelligence world. Tenet wanted to pay his respects, but he also had some business with two important players. First was the current chief of the British service, Sir Richard Dearlove. The CIA and MI6 were cooperating on certain counterterrorist operations in the Afghanistan theater and around the world. The second person was King Abdullah of Jordan, also attending the memorial service. The CIA was subsidizing the Jordanian service to the tune of millions of dollars a year.

MCLAUGHLIN STARTED OFF the 9:30 A.M. NSC meeting on October 16 with good news. "The second CIA team gets in tonight. Links up to Dostum."

Rumsfeld and Armitage asked about how to get military hardware to the Northern Alliance. Can the CIA do it, can Defense do it?

Each had an edge to his voice. They had had an unpleasant relationship, 10 months old, that had begun before all the senior positions in the administration had been filled. Powell had been pushing Armitage to become Rumsfeld's deputy, and Rumsfeld had agreed to interview Armitage. Rumsfeld had begun the interview by saying that he understood Armitage was a straight-shooter so he wanted to be direct with him. "You've got less than a 50-50 chance of becoming my deputy," he said.

"Mr. Secretary, I've got zero chance of becoming your deputy," Armitage replied.

That morning, Rumsfeld vented some of his frustration at the delays of getting the Special Forces teams into Afghanistan. "It's important to get our people on the ground," said Rumsfeld. "The CINC and the Northern Alliance are in communication. The CINC says he's ready to stop the bombing when the Northern Alliance says so. We're relying on what the Northern Alliance tells CIA about readiness." The plan was to halt bombing when the Northern Alliance was ready to attack the Taliban. That way the U.S. bombs would not land on friendly Alliance forces. "The CINC has done all he can do until he gets better targeting information and the Northern Alliance moves to generate targets," he said.

Word that the Alliance wanted the U.S. to bomb the Taliban front lines before they moved had apparently not filtered up to the defense secretary.

At one point, Rumsfeld's frustration boiled over. "This is the CIA's strategy," he said. "They developed the strategy. We're just executing the strategy."

McLaughlin disagreed. "Our guys work with the CINC," he said gently, knowing that Tenet's position always was that General Franks was the boss. "We're supporting the CINC. The CINC is in charge."

"No," Rumsfeld argued, "you guys are in charge. You guys

have the contacts. We're just following you in." The secretary of defense was distancing himself. "We're going where you tell us to go."

"I think what I'm hearing is FUBAR," Armitage said.

Why? What do you mean? asked the president. He knew FUBAR means Fucked Up Beyond All Recognition. It was an old military expression, reserved for when things were really haywire.

"I don't know who's in charge," Armitage answered.

Card saw everyone in the room brace. There was a pall.

"I'm in charge," Bush said.

"No, no, no, no, Mr. President," Armitage replied, trying to recover, "that wasn't about you. I know who's in charge here, no question about it, Mr. President.

"I want to know who's in charge *out there*. It's about who's taking responsibility on the ground over there."

"That's the kind of discussion that frustrates me," the president recalled later, "because I like clarity. You can design a system so that nobody is held accountable." He was frustrated to hear the discussion because it looked like Defense and CIA were talking past each other. His concern was, "If there is failure, nobody shows up to—who do you look to to fix it?

"Sometimes things are best left unsaid, and let them kind of hash it out, and kind of get their emotions out. . . . It's hard for a deputy to go against a principal in a debate at an NSC meeting," the president said.

"I looked at Condi Rice and said, 'Get this mess straightened out.' "

Card could see a shotgun wedding between the military and the CIA. He didn't remember anybody saying, Gee, yeah, we're looking forward to this new arrangement.

As the meeting continued, Bush said, "We have to unleash these guys. We cannot have this discussion one week from now."

"We're nowhere in the south and we need to get there," Rumsfeld said.

"In five weeks the snow will not prevent operations on Kabul, but it does matter in the north," interjected Bush. "Therefore, the north should be the priority."

"What are the impediments to troops in the south?" Rice asked.

McLaughlin answered that the CIA did not have its best contacts in the south and it was hard to get to them from Pakistan. There was no Southern Alliance.

"CIA and DOD need to produce on the south in the next two to three days," Rice said firmly.

"It's much more dangerous in the south. There's no enclaves, we have to create enclaves," McLaughlin said.

"The alternative is to create an enclave—build an airfield. I've got a candidate in Helman Province," Rumsfeld said. It was due west of Kandahar. "I have to ask Franks to look at it."

After the meeting, Rice motioned Rumsfeld into the little office used by the Situation Room director.

"Don," she said, "this is now a military operation and you really have to be in charge." Their strategy was a cross between a covert operation and a military operation but there was a point where it moved from being mostly covert to being mostly military. That point was now.

"I know that," Rumsfeld replied, "but I don't want to be seen to be usurping what the CIA is trying to do. It's also George's operation."

"One person's got to be in charge of this, and it's you."

"Got it," he said.

Later in a discussion with the president, Rice explained what she was trying to do with Rumsfeld. The CIA and the military had to be totally integrated on the ground. One person had to be running the show. It was a classic case of unity of command. It wasn't simply a handoff—passing the ball from the CIA to the military—because the CIA was going to stay and increase its presence. She and the president often spoke in sports analogies.

"Mr. President," she said, "you have to have a quarterback for this."

"Am I not the quarterback?" he asked.

"No, I think you're the coach."

SEVERAL DAYS LATER there was a second FUBAR meeting, when it was still not clear who was in charge. Steve Hadley thought that Rumsfeld was too frequently separating his military plan from the CIA operations and operatives on the ground. Rumsfeld did not see the CIA as an available instrument. It was not just a matter of who was in charge, it was critical to have a clear, articulated strategy that incorporated military and CIA functions. Though Hadley was only the deputy national security adviser, Rice encouraged him to speak directly with Rumsfeld.

"Mr. Secretary," Hadley said as the two walked out of a meeting around this time, "somebody needs to pick this up and design a strategy. Quite frankly, it's yours for the taking."

"Then I'll take it," Rumsfeld said.

Powell weighed in later with Rumsfeld. The secretary of state could see that the CIA was buying its way across Afghanistan, at least trying, giving out rice, guns and cash. He told Rumsfeld that the president was expecting something to happen, and Rumsfeld had to figure out how to get his arms around it. Rumsfeld was in charge whether he wanted it or not.

Rumsfeld did not respond directly, but he was stirred up. He went back to the Pentagon and directed his policy shop, headed by Undersecretary Douglas Feith, to draft a paper outlining an overall Afghanistan strategy. He wanted it in six hours. On October 16, the SECRET—CLOSE HOLD papers flying around Feith's office included a six-page "Draft for Discussion" titled "U.S. Strategy on Afghanistan." Another, which reflected both the policy imperative and Rumsfeld's mood, was labeled "How to Get More People into Afghanistan."

• • •

WHEN TENET WAS back he called Hadley for a read.

How does it go? Tenet asked.

"Not real well," Hadley said. "John," he said, referring to McLaughlin, "kind of got pushed around on this issue of who's in control, and the president's confused and this is not good."

Tenet said he had been emphatic that his paramilitary teams worked for the CINC.

Yeah, Hadley agreed, but the only person who seemed not to understand that was Don Rumsfeld. What was not clear was Rumsfeld's motive. Was it his way of inviting the CIA to work with him? Or was it his way to shift blame? It also was not clear that Rumsfeld wanted the CIA part or that he knew how to integrate the forces. In any case, Hadley suggested that Tenet should get it sorted out.

For Rumsfeld, the difficulty illustrated the critical importance of getting boots on the ground—U.S. military boots, his boots. He did not command the CIA paramilitary teams, and he still had none of his own. He increased the pressure on everyone involved in the chain of command. He was relentless as he laid down his own withering carpet of fire. Senior generals put their heads down on their desks in despair. Two attempts to get a Special Forces team into Afghanistan were aborted because of bad weather. Worse than not being there would be a crash.

VICE PRESIDENT CHENEY chaired the NSC on October 17 because Bush was traveling in Asia. The day before, an American F/A-18 Hornet jet had bombed some supply warehouses used by the International Committee of the Red Cross in Kabul. Rumsfeld explained that the U.S. had thought they were Taliban military depots. He said the ICRC had given the wrong coordinates for its own warehouses.

He sped through a briefing on Special Forces teams going into

Afghanistan. Tenet talked about CIA teams already on the ground. His Alpha team had arrived. "Guys met with Dostum this morning and with several of his commanders. We put in a big chunk of money.

"We have 120 tons of ammo in Germany tonight. We're going to deliver 60 tons in the north. We're going to try to get an airfield up and running, up within 48 hours. Dostum said he'll be in Mazar-e Sharif in one week.

"We're trying to get Ismail Khan and Khalili to meet with Dostum." Karim Khalili, leader of the second-strongest opposition party to the Taliban, controlled pockets of territory in central Afghanistan near Bamiyan. The CIA was anxious to get ammo and support in to Dostum, and coordinate among the warlords friendly to the U.S.

"How do we get people into the south?" asked Rumsfeld.

Tenet mentioned a minor Pashtun tribal leader the agency had contact with. His name was Hamid Karzai. Gentle-looking with a salt-and-pepper beard, Karzai, 44, spoke perfect English. "Karzai is operating around Tarin Kowt. It's a beachhead—we can get a CIA team in. We are trying to get food and ammo dumped down there. The U.K. is in no better position than we are."

They turned to the hot topic of anthrax. The powder in the letter mailed to Senator Daschle's office had been found to be potent, prompting officials to suggest its source was likely an expert capable of producing the bacteria in large amounts. Tenet said, "I think it's AQ"—meaning al Qaeda. "I think there's a state sponsor involved. It's too well thought out, the powder's too well refined. It might be Iraq, it might be Russia, it might be a renegade scientist," perhaps from Iraq or Russia.

Scooter Libby, Cheney's chief of staff, said he also thought the anthrax attacks were state-sponsored. "We've got to be careful on what we say." It was important not to lay it on anyone now. "If we say it's al Qaeda, a state sponsor may feel safe and then hit us thinking they will have a bye because we'll blame it on al Qaeda."

"I'm not going to talk about a state sponsor," Tenet assured them.

"It's good that we don't," said Cheney, "because we're not ready to do anything about it."

ON OCTOBER 18, Cheney reported to the NSC that an alarm in the White House had gone off, signaling the presence of radioactive, chemical or biological agents. Everyone who had been there might have been exposed. He seemed worried but no one else knew what to say. Later it was determined to have been a false alarm.

IN AFGHANISTAN ABOUT 10:20 P.M. on Friday, October 19, Gary's Jawbreaker team marked a landing zone on the Shamali Plains. The first U.S. Special Forces A-team, Team 555, "Triple Nickel," was finally on its way in after numerous weather delays. Two MH-53J Pave Low helicopters, the Air Force's largest, missed the target zone and landed far apart from each other. Army Chief Warrant Officer David Diaz, the leader of the 12-member A-team, hopped out, unsure and worried that it might be bad.

Hey guys, how you doing? Gary asked. Welcome to Afghanistan. He introduced himself—yes, CIA. Get your stuff on the truck. We have hot tea, rice and chicken waiting for you. Your room is ready, everything but the phone number for a concierge.

Diaz and his men were surprised. They had expected they would have to live in tents. They were the essential eyes-on-target that the American pilots needed to bomb front lines. Each man was responsible for about 300 pounds of gear and supplies, including equipment needed to laser-designate targets.

At the same time, two teams of Special Forces and Army Rangers were launching assaults on an airfield and a compound near Kandahar that had been used by Mullah Omar. These were largely demonstration raids, orchestrated to show capability and to gather intelligence. U.S. soldiers left behind posters of photographs of New York firefighters hoisting the American flag at the World Trade Center, and workers raising a flag at the destroyed section of the Pentagon.

PRESIDENT BUSH, STILL in the midst of his five-day trip to the APEC summit in Shanghai, kept in touch through an evening secure video teleconference.

The principals met for a little over an hour on Saturday, October 20. Rumsfeld gave a briefing on military operations. Some 90 to 100 sorties were planned, some of which would be directed to support the opposition forces. "We have Special Forces at the front line," he was at last able to report, "and we're beginning to get some good stuff. We have a second team that's 30 miles from the front and a third team that's going to go in with Fahim.

"I'm going to confirm that one or more Special Forces have gone in," said the secretary. It was time to make public that the campaign had moved beyond bombing, that U.S. forces were on the ground. Strikes were also planned for Mazar-e Sharif, he said.

"Are we hitting Taliban defending Kabul on the Shamali Plains?" Cheney asked. He was keeping up with the intelligence which showed reports from Jawbreaker saying that Fahim was waiting for the bombing of the Taliban front lines.

"It's on the agenda," Rumsfeld said, "we'll work it today. The problem with the A-team with Fahim is it's not on the front line, it's 30 to 40 miles back."

Tenet said, "Ismail Khan has IRGC ties but we want to put a team in on Wednesday." Khan's ties to the Iranian Revolutionary Guard Corps were well known, but he had a large following in the western part of Afghanistan and would help rout the Taliban and al Qaeda in the far regions of the country.

At Monday's NSC meeting, October 22, Tenet said with a burst of optimism that they were ready to unleash the tribals.

"They've been unleashed all along," Rumsfeld snapped. "Franks has said they can move." The static situation on the ground was because of Northern Alliance inaction. Franks was not holding them back. Fahim was playing with them—sitting and waiting for U.S. bombers to do his work.

EVEN IN THE midst of uncertainty and tensions about what was or was not happening on the ground, there were still moments of levity. At one point, the president asked General Franks, "Tommy, how are you?"

"Sir," he replied, "I'm finer than the hair on a frog's back." Later during the same meeting, Armitage, who was reporting for State, said, "Mr. President, your diplomats aren't finer than frog's hair, but they're meaner than rust and tougher than woodpecker lips."

But the atmosphere was generally one of deference to authority, especially by Franks to Rumsfeld. In another meeting, Rumsfeld said something, and the president asked Franks, "Tommy, what do you think?"

"Sir, I think exactly what my secretary thinks, what he's ever thought, what he will ever think, or whatever he thought he might think."

Despite the deference, Franks and his staff found ways to circumvent Rumsfeld's rigid control and use the informal old-boy network of current and former military officers to keep Powell and Armitage in the loop on plans that might affect the State Department. Armitage called it "under the blanket." He loved to get the latest intelligence or gossip to pass immediately to Powell, telling his informants, "Feed the beast."

18

On Tuesday, October 23, President Bush gathered with his NSC in the Situation Room. It was the 14th day of bombing.

Hank said that the first Special Forces A-team was now within 500 meters of the Taliban front line. But nothing was moving. The mercurial Fahim was out of Afghanistan, visiting Tajikistan to the north, but he wanted the Special Forces team to direct massive air strikes at the Taliban front lines.

"The lack of air attack on Taliban is emboldening the Taliban," Hank explained in his Southern accent, "and demoralizing the Northern Alliance forces. Nothing is going to happen until Fahim comes back."

What do you mean! thought Rice. What was Fahim doing out of the country? But she didn't interrupt.

Arms and ammunition to Fahim's forces of several thousand were on the way, Hank said. The CIA was continuing to deliver millions of dollars in cash. In contrast, he said, Dostum, who was outnumbered at least three to one, was leading a cavalry charge on Mazar-e Sharif, the northern city of 200,000.

Cavalry in the 21st century? Bush and the others were astounded.

"How do you assess our progress toward our objectives?" Rice asked.

"Well," Hank said, rather plaintively referring to the latest color-coded map called "A Guide to Territorial Control in Afghanistan," which was classified TOP SECRET, "we are getting yellow across the board and it should be green up north and it's not."

Yellow across the board meant no gain of territory.

"We need to see a measure of effectiveness," Rice said, "that degrades 50 percent through bombing and defections." In military terms, a degradation of 50 percent or more means a force or unit is considered ineffective. The yellow cloaked the failure to degrade. The Alliance either controlled territory or it didn't. "We don't see that—we don't see what we're doing up there," Rice said.

The war cabinet had had many discussions of the Afghan culture, and the deadly joke was, "You can't buy an Afghan but you can rent one." It was a world of no permanent, even semipermanent loyalties. The warlords followed money and victory. They were attracted to the winning side, would shift in the blink of an eye. At the moment there was plenty of money, but no measurable sign of victory. To be effective, money and a sense of inevitable victory needed to be mutually reinforcing.

Powell thought the weeks after the beginning of the Afghanistan bombing campaign were a dark and confused period. More than usual, it was unclear what was real, especially on the ground in Afghanistan, a potentially disastrous cash-and-carry undertaking. As the former top military man, he found it best to try to "stay in his lane," as he put it, pay attention to his role as chief diplomat and avoid military second-guessing.

But Powell couldn't resist. What was the objective besides just bombing? he wondered. He had an Army man's distrust of airpower and a belief in the doctrine of massing force on a single objective.

"Should we mass in one place?" he asked, veering out of his lane. "Should we focus on Mazar?" Get that, and then they could do other things.

"Not Mazar," Hank replied, "but focus on the Shamali Plains." The area north of Kabul, the capital, was where the Northern Alliance's Fahim had the biggest, and seemingly best organized, concentration of force.

"Look," interjected General Myers, "we can do both."

"We have to get UBL and their leadership," the president said.

Cheney wanted to address the core issue. "Do we wait for the Northern Alliance, or do we have to go get involved ourselves, which is a wholly different proposition?" He knew that Rumsfeld was secretly working on contingency plans for putting some 50,000 to 55,000 U.S. troops on the ground—if that was the only way to win. Outright Americanization of the ground operation was the most sensitive issue. The stakes in the war were so high that they had to consider all available options.

Later at a principals' meeting that day, they discussed how disappointed they all were in Fahim, who was promising to move but then failing to advance. Hank reported that the Taliban forces opposite Fahim's lines had increased by an astonishing 50 percent. Satellite and other intelligence only weeks ago had shown anywhere from 6,000 to 10,000 Taliban fighters at the front. Now the count was 10,000 to 16,000.

Cheney, Powell and some of the others knew that during the 1991 Gulf War they wanted to degrade the Iraqi ground forces by 50 percent with bombing before launching the ground campaign. Instead of being 50 percent down, the Taliban were up 50 percent! What was going on?

RICE REALIZED SHE was going to have to deal with this. Normally she saw her job as twofold: first, to coordinate what Defense, State, the CIA and other departments or agencies were doing by making sure the president's orders were carried out; and second, to act as counselor—to give her private assessment to the president, certainly when he asked, perhaps if he didn't. In other words, she was to be the president's troubleshooter. This was trouble.

Two days later, on the evening of Thursday, October 25, Rice phoned the president's personal secretary, Ashley Estes.

"I need to talk to the president," she said. Could Ashley ask the president if it was okay for her to come to the residence for a few minutes? Access to the residence was a special privilege, and Bush only granted it to the senior White House staff. It was the end of the normal working day for the president, about 6:30 P.M.

The president had intentionally organized his White House so that Rice and others could come see him on the spur of the moment, he said in an interview. "All power should not go through an individual to the Oval Office." He had learned this from observing his father's presidency, especially during the first three years when Bush senior's White House Chief of Staff John Sununu controlled access with such an iron fist that those with bad news often couldn't get through. "I believe that a president must give people access," Bush also said, "that part of the job satisfaction of being a White House staffer is the capacity to talk to the president one-on-one."

His father's political strategist, Lee Atwater, had told him, "Access is power." Bush said he learned this firsthand in 1988 when his father, the vice president, was running for president. "I can remember going to the vice president's house, and they'd be getting ready to have the campaign team come over. And I would be there about, you know, about 20 minutes before they arrived so they would see me with Dad. They didn't have any idea. We were probably talking about the pennant race or, you know, a brother or sister. They didn't know that. They knew that I had access to him, that it was just me and him alone. It was a very interesting lesson. I watched my stature grow the more that I had access to him."

Cheney, Rice, Card, Hughes, Rove and Fleischer could just stop by and ask Ashley if he had five minutes or whatever might be needed. The president said it worked the other way around too. "It makes my job a heck of a lot easier to be able to have access to a lot of people" to get their feedback or reactions. "It was very likely that a Condi or a Dick Cheney would come in, and I'd say, 'What are you thinking now?' "

Rice in particular was frequently pressing him. "She's a very thorough person, constantly mother-henning me," the president said.

Bush's leadership style bordered on the hurried. He wanted action, solutions. Once on a course, he directed his energy at forging on, rarely looking back, scoffing at—even ridiculing—doubt and anything less than 100 percent commitment. He seemed to harbor few, if any, regrets. His short declarations could seem impulsive.

"I know it is hard for you to believe, but I have not doubted what we're doing," Bush said in a later interview. "I have not doubted. . . . There is no doubt in my mind we're doing the right thing. Not one doubt."

Rice knew this characteristic. Yet doubt could be the handmaiden of sound policy, she thought. Careful reconsideration is a necessary part of any decision-making process. Rice felt it was her job to raise caution flags, even red lights if necessary, to urge the president to rethink.

Sometimes the best decision is to overrule an earlier one. Now events were their own caution flags. The static situation in Afghanistan might signal big trouble. On top of that, the news media was raising questions about progress, strategy, timetables and expectations. *Newsweek* magazine had used the dreaded "Q" word—quagmire—evoking Vietnam. A few days earlier, *The Washington Post* had run an op-ed article entitled "The Wrong Battle Plan," by Robert A. Pape, a University of Chicago expert on airpower. It began, "The initial U.S. air strategy against Afghanistan is not working."

"What's up?" Bush asked as Rice arrived in the Treaty Room. He had finished his daily physical fitness routine and was still in his exercise clothes. He was not dripping sweat but had cooled down—perhaps the right time for such a conversation, if there ever was.

The south was dry, and the north was not moving, she said.

"And we've bombed everything we can think of to bomb, and still nothing is happening."

Bush sat down.

"You know, Mr. President," Rice said, "the mood isn't very good among the principals and people are concerned about what's going on." She said there was some hand-wringing.

The president jerked forward. *Hand-wringing?* He hated, absolutely hated the very idea, especially in tough times. He was getting some reports from Hughes and Rove about media stories, but not much more.

"I want to know if you're concerned about the fact that things are not moving?" Rice asked.

"Of course I'm concerned about the fact that things aren't moving!"

"Do you want to start looking at alternative strategies?"

"What alternative strategies would we be looking at?" he asked, as if the possibility had not crossed his mind.

"There always is the thought that you could use more Americans in this. You could Americanize this up front." That could mean substantial ground forces—several Army or Marine divisions. A division normally has about 15,000 to 20,000.

Bush was aware that in these very rooms some 35 to 40 years earlier, Presidents Kennedy and Johnson had confronted similar decisions. Vietnam was the precedent.

"It hasn't been that long," the president said, referring to when the military action had begun.

"That's right."

"Do you think it's working?"

Rice did not really answer.

"We have a good plan," the president said. "You're confident in it?"

Kind of yes—maybe, Rice replied. He knew as well as she that the progress was yellow, not green.

They went back and forth. Rice was intentionally ducking and unwilling to take a firm position, worried it might tilt further discussion, close off options. Also she was unsure. She felt most comfortable when she knew precisely what the president was thinking, so she was sounding him out. But the president was on his chosen course and he had not really thought of shifting strategies.

The really important thing, she told the president, was for him to take the principals' pulse the next day, and if he was committed to the strategy, he better let people know it because he didn't want people starting to fall off.

Starting to fall off? Who was nervous? Who was concerned? The president wanted to take names.

Everybody is concerned, she confided. Nobody is very sanguine or comfortable. They all have concerns about what they are achieving and might be able to achieve. He had heard some; she had heard more. He was going to have to make some tough decisions pretty soon—about whether they were just going to stay on course or whether they were going to try to make adjustments.

The NSC was going to meet the next morning, she mentioned, and that was the time to affirm the plan or consider changing it. Winter was coming to Afghanistan and the conditions would be brutal, and military gains on the ground could become increasingly difficult.

"I think it would be good if you expressed confidence in this plan. Or if you don't feel that, then we need to do something else." Did they need an alternative strategy? The important thing, she said, was for him to go think about it before the NSC meeting the next morning. Then, at the meeting, he could give his view. "You need to talk about this," she said at the end of their 15- to 20-minute talk.

"I'll take care of it," the president said.

FOR BUSH IT was a memorable discussion. Rice's job was to tell him things. Sometimes he liked to hear them, sometimes he didn't.

He found it an "interesting full circle" that the discussion took place in the Treaty Room where he had just 18 days earlier announced the commencement of military action. But he knew what he wanted to do the next morning.

"First of all," he later recalled, "a president has got to be the calcium in the backbone. If I weaken, the whole team weakens. If I'm doubtful, I can assure you there will be a lot of doubt. If my confidence level in our ability declines, it will send ripples throughout the whole organization. I mean, it's essential that we be confident and determined and united."

The president wanted the same from everyone on the team. "I don't need people around me who are not steady. . . . And if there's kind of a hand-wringing attitude going on when times are tough, I don't like it."

He attributed the concern to the echo chamber in the media. He was paying only peripheral attention to it. "I don't read the editorial pages. I don't—the hyperventilation that tends to take place over these cables, and every expert and every former colonel, and all that, is just background noise." He knew, however, that members of his war cabinet paid attention. "We've got these very strong people on the National Security Council who do get affected by what people say about them in the press.

"If there's going to be a sense of despair," Bush said, "I want to know who it is, and why. I trust the team, and it is a team. And I trust them because I trust their judgment. And if people are having second thoughts about their judgment, I needed to know what they were, and they needed to lay them on the table."

No member of the war cabinet had come to the president privately to express any concern. Before the next morning's NSC meeting, he talked to Vice President Cheney about what Rice had brought to him.

"Dick," he asked, "do you have any—is there any qualms in your mind about this strategy we've developed? We've spent a lot of time on it."

"No, Mr. President," Cheney replied.

• • •

THE NEXT MORNING, Friday, October 26, Bush arrived at the
White House Situation Room for the NSC meeting. None of the
principals, including Andy Card, knew what Rice had raised
with him the evening before. He decided to let the meeting proceed
with its routine presentations. He did, however, report that he
had just spoken by phone with Crown Prince Abdullah of Saudi
Arabia.

"The crown prince said we shouldn't strike during Ramadan."
The Muslim holy month would begin in several weeks. "I'm going
to write him a letter saying we'll continue because al Qaeda contin-
ues to threaten the United States, and they will keep fighting
whether we bomb or not." As if to hint at his mood, he added, "And
that's at the end of the day what is decisive."

"There's concern about the Russians," Tenet said. "Russians
are providing arms to the Northern Alliance. That's good. We want
to make sure the Russians don't play the Tajiks and the Uzbeks
against each other." Russia still wanted to have influence, if not
dominance, in the breakaway republics. There was a lot of regional
positioning going on, and the U.S. had to take this into account.
"The Russians are more focused on the endgame than we are."

Tenet reported that they had CIA paramilitary team Alpha in
Afghanistan with the Northern Alliance leader Dostum and were
about to get one in with Attah Mohammad, another Alliance leader.
Both Dostum and Attah were south of the city of Mazar. "There's a
meeting with leaders in the north without Fahim Khan's approval."
Fahim was still not moving so the CIA was going ahead without
him. Tenet also said he hoped to have a team with Karzai, the leader
in the south of Afghanistan. "I believe the southern piece is beginning to develop."

"There is more than enough food in the region," Powell said.
The problem was that the food was being distributed by Afghan na-
tionals. "That's what is not working."

"We need to do a major meeting to dramatize our humanitarian assistance," Rice said.

Rumsfeld reported they had done only 60 sorties the day before because the weather was bad. It was better today. "We hit yesterday in the Shamali Plains and Mazar"—the two places General Myers had said could be their focus. Some barracks had been hit in the eastern city of Herat. They planned to concentrate the bombing on the front lines in support of the tribes, not the fixed targets such as Taliban aircraft. "One half is on the Shamali Plains and half of it is on Herat and Mazar-e Sharif.

"We've got a third team in, plus some communications with Fahim's people.

"We have five teams in Uzbekistan waiting to get in," he added in some frustration. Two more teams were at Fort Campbell in the United States.

Now it was time for the president to deal with Rice's advice.

"I just want to make sure that all of us did agree on this plan, right?" he said. He looked around the table from face to face.

There is an aspect of baseball-coach, even fraternity-brother urgency in Bush at such moments. He leans his head forward and holds it still, makes eye contact, maintains it, saying in effect, You're on board, you're with me, right?

Are we right? the president was asking. Are we still confident? He wanted a precise affirmation from each one—Cheney, Powell, Rumsfeld, Tenet and Rice—even backbenchers Hadley and Scooter Libby. He was almost demanding they take an oath.

Each affirmed allegiance to the plan and strategy.

"Anybody have any ideas they want to put on the table?"

No's all around.

Rice believed the president would tolerate debate, would listen, but anyone who wanted debate had to have a good argument, and preferably a solution or at least a proposed fix. It was clear that no one at the table had a better idea.

In fact, the president had not really opened the door a crack for anyone to raise concerns or deal with any second thoughts. He was not really listening. He wanted to talk. He knew that he talked too much at times, just blowing off steam. It was not a good habit, he knew.

"You know what? We need to be patient," Bush said. "We've got a good plan.

"Look, we're entering a difficult phase. The press will seek to find divisions among us. They will try and force on us a strategy that is not consistent with victory." In the secrecy of the room, the president had voiced one of his conclusions—the news media, or at least some elements, did not want victory or at least acted as if they did not.

"We've been at this only 19 days. Be steady. Don't let the press panic us." The press would say they needed a new strategy, that the current strategy was a failed strategy. He disagreed. "Resist the second-guessing. Be confident but patient. We are going to continue this thing through Ramadan. We've got to be cool and steady. It's all going to work."

Hadley thought the tension suddenly drained from the room. The president was saying he had confidence and they should have confidence. In their souls, Hadley believed, some of them had to wonder if the president might be losing confidence in them. Presidential confidence, once bestowed, was vital for all of them to function. Any hint of less than full trust would be devastating. They served at his pleasure. They could be gone or sidelined in an instant. Not only had Bush declared confidence in their strategy but more importantly, Hadley believed, he had declared confidence in them.

Tenet wanted to stand up and cheer. He went back to Langley and told his senior leadership what the president had said. What it meant, Tenet said, was simple: Keep going.

Rice believed it was one of the most important moments. If the president had opened up to alternatives, the war cabinet would have lost the focus of trying to make the current strategy work and flitted off to think up alternatives. She hoped that the recommitment would cause everyone to redouble their efforts on the current strategy that he had just then fully blessed.

Rumsfeld reported to some of his senior aides that the president had been particularly strong that day. He didn't provide details.

Powell found the situation in Afghanistan troubling, but he didn't think they were in a quagmire, yet.

Pakistani President Musharraf, their friend, was interviewed that evening by ABC anchorman Peter Jennings, who asked him right off the bat if the United States was facing a quagmire.

"Yes," the Pakistani president declared, "it may be a quagmire."

19

JAWBREAKER TEAM WAS approaching its one-month anniversary on the Shamali Plains. The Special Forces A-team 555 had been with them for a week with its laser target designators. Though the A-team had some initial successes calling in bombing runs, Gary could see they were getting leftovers—U.S. bombers who had been assigned to other fixed targets. If these bombers didn't find their target or for some reason did not expend their munitions, they were available to come to the front lines and attack Taliban fighters there. So there was an increase in bombing. But Gary had witnessed too many occasions when the A-team would spot a convoy of Taliban or al Qaeda trucks—once there were 20 trucks—and they would call and call to get a bomber and couldn't get one. The planes were still focused on predesignated fixed targets.

The battlefield on the Shamali Plains was unusually flat. About 35 miles separated the Alliance force of some 3,000 and the Taliban, Arab and Pakistani volunteer force of about 7,000. They formed battle lines in trenches, bunkers, fortifications and other military hardware placements protected by some minefields. Rain clouds were crossing the mountains which rimmed the plains, a forerunner of winter and the coming snow.

Gary sat down at one of the 10 computers his team had in their dusty quarters and wrote a cable to CIA headquarters. If we don't change the pattern, we're going to lose this thing, he wrote. The Taliban had never been bombed hard; they have not been impressed very much; they think they can survive this. The Northern Alliance is ready; they want to go and they are as ready as they ever will be, but they're losing confidence; they think what they are seeing is all we can do. If we hit these Taliban with sustained bombing for three or four days, the young Taliban are going to break. Most of them were conscripts, joining up because it was the thing to do, believing they were on the winning side. Hit the al Qaeda Arabs here also, and the younger Taliban would see it and crack. Three or four days maximum would be all that was needed. The front lines would collapse.

Most of the Taliban had come from the south, and they would want to leave, return south. But there were only a few roads they could come down, and the Northern Alliance, with bombardment from U.S. airpower, would control those roads. The Taliban would find themselves trapped. Less a few pockets around Mazar and Konduz, the Alliance would soon have the entire north of the country, even Kabul.

Gary sent the cable, which was only two pages long. Tenet decided to take it to the White House the next day.

DURING THE EARLY morning secure phone conversation that Rumsfeld had with General Franks on Saturday, October 27, the secretary wanted to make sure they were planning and thinking way ahead—to the worst case scenario if necessary.

Suppose the Afghan opposition, the Northern Alliance, the mercenary force that was being paid by the CIA, could not do the job? They were going to have to consider the possibility that they would have to Americanize the war, send in large numbers of U.S. ground forces.

Marine General Peter Pace, Joint Chiefs of Staff vice chairman, was taking notes in a white spiral notebook. He wrote, "Be prepared to go in—major land war—either on our own or with coalition partners. . . . Process of organizing for it would be very, very useful. . . . It would become visible and people would know that we're not kidding, we are coming, if you don't change sides now, we are going to continue the process."

Rumsfeld and Franks agreed to step up bombing the Taliban front lines as the Northern Alliance wanted. With the first A-teams now inside Afghanistan, that would be possible. But both the secretary and CINC were skeptical of the Alliance and General Fahim, who seemed slow to move on their own.

PRESIDENT BUSH AND the first lady were supposed to have their friends from East Texas for the rescheduled poker and Kennedy Center weekend that Saturday and Sunday. But the threat assessment was increasing, not abating, so Bush called his best friend in the group, Elton Bomer, who had been Texas insurance commissioner when Bush was governor. "Elton, I just can't let you come," the president told Bomer. "I'm just too worried, the assessments look too bad, and I just don't want to take the chance."

The Bushes instead went to Camp David, and the president joined the secure video-teleconference at 8:30 A.M. Saturday morning.

Tenet reported that he had two more CIA paramilitary teams scheduled to go into Afghanistan in the coming week. He was staking much on his paramilitary teams. Other than two U.S. military Special Forces A-teams inside Afghanistan, there was still no other direct U.S. presence in-country.

Tenet was still scrambling in the south of Afghanistan. One setback in the south was that the Taliban had just captured and killed Abdul Haq, a 43-year-old Pashtun leader who had successfully fought the Soviet invasion from 1979 to 1989. In 1987, Haq, then 29, lost his right foot in a land mine. The Taliban had later killed his wife and son.

He had returned to Afghanistan with a group of 19 to consolidate support among Pashtuns in the south against the Taliban and al Qaeda. Haq was not a CIA asset who took direction but the agency had had contact with him. They had urged him to have a fallback plan and had offered communications gear. Haq said he thought the communications equipment would enable the CIA to spy on him. He refused.

Haq was captured by the Taliban, tortured and executed. At the last minute the CIA had dispatched one of its Predators, which fired on some Taliban forces who were surrounding him, but it was too late. The Taliban intelligence chief was publicly gloating.

Tenet, with a dozen secret paid assets in the south, was still not making headway in the crucial region.

Powell reported that he had talked to Musharraf, who said he needed more economic assistance. The demonstrations in two Pakistani cities were the largest so far. Musharraf was continuing one of the all-time political balancing acts.

On the military operation, Rumsfeld said that "70 percent of our effort today will be in support of the opposition." Rumsfeld said one focus continued to be the Tora Bora area outside Jalalabad, believed to be a refuge for al Qaeda and Taliban fighters.

The secretary also reported that the humanitarian drops and the information drops were continuing.

Tenet said, "We're going to move ahead without waiting for Fahim." It was a dramatic decision since Fahim was the overall leader of the loose affiliation of warlord forces in the Northern Alliance.

No one objected.

"We're sending a message to the Northern Alliance," Rumsfeld said, "that we want them to do more." Bypassing their leader was not a subtle message.

Cheney said there had been press reports that the Northern Alliance might shut down for Ramadan.

Tenet said the agency would have to assess that likelihood.

The news got worse. The Defense Intelligence Agency (DIA),

the sprawling service created by former Secretary of Defense Robert McNamara to integrate Pentagon intelligence efforts, had been asked to come up with an alternative assessment about the prospects on the ground. In a highly classified memo, the DIA suggested that neither Mazar nor Kabul would be taken by winter.

The memo in large part blamed General Fahim, essentially calling him a wimp who would talk and talk, then not show up for battle. Fahim was never quite ready, always declaring his need for more money, more bullets.

It was alarming—a weak Fahim and no prospects for taking a city by winter. With discussion of a quagmire already in the media after three weeks of bombing, it was hard to imagine what would be said after months of apparent stalemate.

Referring to the DIA memo, Cheney said, "It raises two questions. Are we doing everything we can to get something done before Ramadan?" The holiday started in three weeks.

"And secondly," he continued, "what military operations could be done during the winter?" They had to get very concrete, not just to obtain a specific objective for obvious military reasons but for psychological reasons. "We want to create a feeling of inevitability so that people will come over to our side." Alternatively, imagine the Taliban sitting in Afghanistan for months, continuing to provide bin Laden and his terrorists with sanctuary. Cheney didn't have to say anything about the likely impact of that.

He worried also that if they didn't do something before winter, would the Taliban be able to regroup? Would they be emboldened now that they had not been defeated rapidly?

"Is there anything that the U.S. can do between now and winter, such as set up a U.S. operating base in the north?" Cheney asked. At least that would be something up on the board. "I'm worried that we won't have anything concrete to point to by way of accomplishment." When the snow and bitter cold came next month, the Northern Alliance force would be malpositioned, meaning they would not be able to move for months.

"What is our objective for accomplishment before the snow?"

They went through some sensitive, fresh intelligence which was even more depressing. The Northern Alliance was still not moving, further supporting the notion that there was no chance of getting to Mazar or Kabul very soon.

Rice knew the principals didn't like to argue in front of the president, who had said very little. "Principals need to review this on Tuesday," she said, referring to an upcoming meeting without the president when they could thrash it out.

"We need to look at some limited objectives," Tenet said, picking up on Cheney's point, "such as Mazar-e Sharif which are achievable and where we should concentrate our effort."

No one seemed to know for sure.

The next day, October 28, Rumsfeld hit the Sunday talk shows.

"Is the war just not going as well as you had hoped it would at this point?" Cokie Roberts asked him on the ABC television show *This Week.*

"No, quite the contrary," Rumsfeld said. "It's going very much the way we expected when it began. . . . And the progress has been measurable. We feel that the air—air campaign has been effective."

THE TOP SECRET/CODEWORD Threat Matrix for Monday morning, October 29, was filled with dozens of threats, many new and credible, suggesting an attack in the next week. All kinds of signals intelligence, SIGINT, showed that many known al Qaeda lieutenants or operatives were saying that something big would happen soon.

It was quite a list. Some said that good news would be coming, perhaps within a week, or that good news would be bigger and better than September 11. Some of the intercepts revealed discussion of a radiological device—the use of conventional explosives to disperse radioactive material. Other intercepted discussions mentioned *making lots of people sick.*

A nongovernmental organization in Pakistan called Umma Tameer-e-Nau, or UTN, could be putting a structure in place linking senior al Qaeda members and several Pakistani nuclear scientists who had been involved in developing their bomb, according to other intelligence.

Taken together, it was evident that something was going on at least with a radiological device. The intercepts indicated that there was going to be another attack, and since al Qaeda tended to come back to targets it might have missed, Washington and the White House were particularly vulnerable.

The bottom line was a consistent though uncorroborated worry about a radiological weapon, and some concern that it might be headed for Washington or New York. It might be another try to decapitate the government.

All this was presented to the president in the Monday morning intelligence briefing.

"Those bastards are going to find me exactly here," the president said. "And if they get me, they're going to get me right here."

Whoa! Rice thought.

"This isn't about you," Cheney told the president. "This is about our Constitution." He was focused on their responsibility to ensure continuity of government if something happened to Bush. "And that's why I'm going to a secure, undisclosed location," he said. He was not asking permission. He was going.

Card found it sobering. Cheney was right.

"We began to get serious indications that nuclear plans, material and know-how were being moved out of Pakistan," the president would recall. "It was the vibrations coming out of everybody reviewing the evidence."

Rice asked Bush, "Do you think you need to leave too?"

He refused. "Had the president decided he is going too," Bush recalled, "you would have had the vice president going one direction and the president going another, people are going to say, 'What about me?' I wasn't going to leave. I guess I could have, but I wasn't."

The most dramatic action was kept secret. Four special covert monitoring teams who operated out of vehicles capable of detecting the presence of nuclear material were dispatched. Said one of the most senior administration officials, "We had teams roaming around the city"—Washington, D.C. "We had a team in New York. That was a time of great anxiousness." Half a dozen special teams that could detect biological and chemical warfare agents were also sent to six other cities.

IN TENET'S VIEW, a terrorist could wreak havoc on the United States at this point with any attack. The impact of a second large strike was almost unfathomable—with a radiological or nuclear weapon, truly unimaginable. Since neither the CIA nor the FBI were "inside the plot," as Tenet liked to say, he believed a good form of deterrence was to try to give the terrorists the idea that the U.S. was aware of things being planned. Since the terrorists didn't know what the U.S. knew and didn't know, it was a potential deterrent to find a way basically to "tell them we know." This might force them to worry and certainly would make the operational environment rougher for them.

On that morning, Monday, October 29, Tenet told Mueller that it was so serious—and the potential benefits of causing a stir so great—that a second global alert should be issued to the public.

Mueller and Attorney General John Ashcroft began preparations to make the announcement later that day.

The NSC met at 9:15 A.M. Tenet said he was going to meet with Transportation Secretary Norman Mineta and the new director of homeland security, former Pennsylvania Governor Tom Ridge. The topic: "How to change our security posture." That meant doing things differently at airports and elsewhere so potential terrorists would encounter different procedures, mix up what they might see. Tenet said he wanted to make sure they were coordinated on "how to try and disrupt and deter whatever might be coming."

Tenet summarized the threat reporting. Intelligence showed that al Qaeda was planning to use a hijacked aircraft to attack a nuclear facility—either a nuclear power plant, or worse, storage sites of nuclear weapons or other nuclear weapons facilities.

With the vivid images of the World Trade Center towers in flames not even seven weeks old, the prospect of a nuclear equivalent silenced the group.

"Dick Cheney's going to stay gone for a while," the president said. The vice president was already off at a secure location many miles away.

Referring to the intelligence, Tenet said, "It suggests to me there's a worldwide threat. We should button up our embassies and our military facilities overseas, and we should all be implementing continuity of government things." That meant each of the principals should make sure as much as possible that they were not with their deputies in the same place.

"Our coalition is holding together pretty well," Powell said. "They are not as hysterical as the press suggests. But there is a level of nervousness that's reflected on the Arab street." The day before, militants had killed 16 people in a Roman Catholic church in Pakistan.

The headlines about collateral damage from the bombing campaign were harder to stomach. Saturday's *New York Times* front page said, "U.S. PLANES BOMB A RED CROSS SITE," a mistake the U.S. had now made twice. No one was killed, but warehouses full of much needed humanitarian supplies were destroyed. Powell spoke with restraint: "To the extent we have collateral damage as a result of the U.S. operations, it inflames the situation." But then he took a direct shot at the Pentagon. "It's a problem, and we need to redouble our efforts to avoid collateral damage."

Rumsfeld felt he had already maximized efforts to avoid such damage, issuing unprecedented, even draconian orders not to shoot or drop bombs unless there was specific intelligence about the targets, preferably U.S. eyes also having verified the target.

Bush sprang to the defense. "Well, we also need to highlight the fact that the Taliban are killing people and conducting their own terror operations, so get a little bit more balance here about what the situation is." He jumped ahead to add that they needed to focus on Afghanistan after the Taliban, make sure the tribes in the south "see themselves in the post-Taliban Afghanistan," as he put it.

"We also need a public relations campaign focused around the Taliban. We need a donors' conference," he continued, meaning all the countries who were making humanitarian donations to Afghanistan, "someone who will organize it as an offset to Ramadan. We need—how to get the coalition something to hang its hat on when we continue the bombing during Ramadan. We need to have humanitarian help during Ramadan, the likes of which Afghanistan has never seen. We also need a political initiative in this time period."

"The president's calls to Crown Prince Abdullah were very helpful," Rumsfeld said, referring to the de facto leader of Saudi Arabia. Bush was continuing to make calls to Arab leaders to prepare them for his decision that bombing would not stop during Ramadan. Many of the Arab leaders had privately told the president that while they would have to criticize the decision publicly, they understood his position.

"Franks needs to push the Afghan people on the need to choose—freedom for themselves or to continue under the illegitimate Taliban regime," Rumsfeld said. He wanted the general to assist in the political task of motivating the Afghans. Rumsfeld said that 70 percent of the strikes would be in support of the opposition today. Fahim was still not moving, but he said he had received the message to focus on supporting the opposition. "We're going to resupply Dostum today, Khalili tomorrow. And we're going to try to get stuff to Karzai tomorrow. And we're still getting in our teams.

"We're dividing our air campaign 60-40 between Mazar-e Sharif and the Shamali Plains for later this week. That's the plan." Despite the suggestions from Powell and others that they mass at one point, the secretary said, "We cannot concentrate in any one place. There are just not enough targets." He liked preplanned targeting, but the truly important targets were going to be identified on the battlefield by the CIA and his Special Forces teams.

The president had a question. "How do we make sure our teams are strong enough to avoid getting run over by the Taliban?"

The CIA and Special Forces teams of several dozen men were out in some pretty rough places, and alone. They could be attacked, run over, slaughtered or kidnapped and held hostage. It was not for the meek. Suppose one of the teams met the fate of Abdul Haq?

Rumsfeld and Tenet had exfiltration plans if a team got into extremis.

"Are they robust enough to be able to defend themselves?" Bush asked.

The answer was yes and no.

"They could be hit by the enemy or by friendly fire," Rumsfeld said.

"People get bought off," Tenet reminded. "Our people are at risk. We need to look at our extraction capability. We need to make sure we can protect our people."

The biggest protection were the teams' radios that could be used to call in precision strikes on an attacking enemy.

It was getting very gloomy.

RICE CALLED HADLEY to her office and they closed the big, heavy, dark door.

Was he all right working at a potential and likely Ground Zero?

Yes, he said, but he hoped that if anything happened, it wouldn't be something that would get his family, just him. Was she comfortable?

"Yes, you know," she said, "I'm a minister's daughter. I made peace about that a long time ago."

They agreed they should talk to the NSC staff, and made arrangements to do so one night. The staff, made up mostly of foreign service and military officers who had served in dangerous parts of the world, did not want to be moved.

• • •

AT THE PRINCIPALS' meeting Monday night, without the president, there was lots of jousting about what to do. If they were going to try to take Mazar, then what were they doing bombing the Shamali Plains? Rumsfeld continued to insist that there just were not enough targets unless they went beyond the Mazar targets.

Powell worried again that it was bombing for bombing's sake, unconnected to a military objective. He had been a junior infantry officer in Vietnam and knew personally the limits of airpower. He also worried that the United States was playing superpower bully, trying to move the opposition forces, the Northern Alliance and the various warlords, around on the chessboard as if they did not have a stake in this war. At one point, he asked, "Do *they* have any ideas about what they want to do, as opposed to what *we* think they ought to do?"

The question of the political objective lingered. Who would rule Afghanistan if the Taliban were deposed? How? What was the mechanism for some kind of democracy in a country dominated by tribal factions? The experts pretty much agreed that after the Soviets had been thrown out in 1989, the mistake was that the United States walked away. How did the political objective, whatever it was, relate to the military objective? Were they married up?

"We can't afford to lose," Rice said. "The Taliban proved tougher than we thought."

Tenet said they had dropped supplies to Dostum and Attah, but in the south the only person doing much—and that wasn't a whole lot—was Karzai, who had 400 to 500 fighters.

Rumsfeld lamented that in Mazar the Taliban had at least double and perhaps triple the forces of the Northern Alliance.

Powell took the floor to argue against Americanizing the war. "I'd rule out the United States going after the Afghans, who have been there 5,000 years." It could take all the airlift capacity of the American military to move the necessary force. Unless it was possible to intercept the Taliban's communications, they would be elusive. "They will not be there when you get there," he said. "It's a glitch in our thinking. We expected too much of the opposition. I don't know that the opposition can take Mazar, much less Kabul. What we have is First World airpower matched up with a Fourth World army." It would be better to build the Northern Alliance opposition up over the winter to at least a Third World capability to use later with U.S. airpower.

Rice returned to the immediate military problem on the ground and suggested they go back and try to examine three options: 1. Go for Mazar. 2. Go for Kabul. 3. What if they could do neither?

THE NEXT EVENING, Tuesday, October 30, the president flew up to New York to throw out the ceremonial first pitch at Game 3 of the World Series between the Yankees and the Arizona Diamondbacks. At the stadium, he went to the bullpen area to warm up. It was difficult to throw in the bulletproof vest he had agreed to wear, and he wanted to keep his arm loose.

"Are you going to throw from the rubber or the base of the mound?" asked Derek Jeter, the Yankees' star shortstop. The rubber, the highest point of the mound, was used by the regular pitchers, but it was 60 feet 6 inches from home plate, a long throw.

Bush said that he was probably going to throw from the base of the mound, some six to 10 feet closer. He didn't want to throw a wild pitch.

"If you throw from the base of the mound," Jeter said, "they are going to boo you. You really need to take the rubber."

Do you think the fans would really boo me? Bush asked—the president, in the middle of a war, launched after the attack here?

"Yeah," Jeter said. "It's New York."

"All right, I'll throw from the rubber."

He went to the dugout and was about to be announced when Jeter tucked in behind him. "Don't forget, Mr. President, if you throw from the rubber and bounce it, they'll boo you."

The president emerged wearing a New York Fire Department windbreaker. He raised his arm and gave a thumbs-up to the crowd on the third base side of the field. Probably 15,000 fans threw their arms in the air imitating the motion.

He then threw a strike from the rubber, and the stadium erupted.

Watching from owner George Steinbrenner's box, Karl Rove thought, It's like being at a Nazi rally.

20

Rice and the others were on edge as the administration was being murdered in the media. Earlier in the week, a military analyst on the *NewsHour with Jim Lehrer* had leveled the unkindest cut of all, saying that Bush was practicing "the Bill Clinton approach to warfare . . . thinking small."

On Tuesday morning, two leading conservatives, Bush's normal allies, had blasted the war effort on the op-ed page of *The Washington Post*. William Kristol said, "It's a flawed plan" because of too many self-imposed constraints. Charles Krauthammer said the war was being fought with "half-measures."

On Wednesday, October 31, some war cabinet members read a news analysis by R.W. Apple Jr. of *The New York Times*.

"Could Afghanistan become another Vietnam? Is the United States facing another stalemate on the other side of the world? Premature the questions may be, three weeks after the fighting began. Unreasonable they are not."

Since Rumsfeld had just disclosed publicly that small units of U.S. military Special Forces were operating in northern Afghanistan to provide liaison to "a limited number of the various opposition elements," Apple wrote that "their role sounds suspiciously like that of the advisers sent to Vietnam in the early 1960s." He noted that the former Soviet Union, "with good tanks in great numbers, was nonetheless stalemated and eventually defeated by Afghan rebel forces."

AT HIS WEDNESDAY morning meeting with senior staff, Bush expressed his pique at the media.

"They don't get it," the president said. "How many times do you have to tell them it's going to be a different type of war? And they don't believe it. They're looking for the conventional approach. That's not what they're going to see here. I've talked about patience. It's amazing how quickly people forget what you say, at least here in Washington." The quagmire stories made little sense to him. They had a good plan. They had agreed to it. "Why would we start second-guessing it this early into the plan?"

"WE'RE LOSING THE public relations war," the president began at the NSC meeting at 9:30 A.M. "We're not getting credit for what we are doing for the Afghan people. We need a humanitarian donors' conference as we head into Ramadan. We ought to be calling on the Taliban to let trucks pass," the convoys bringing in food and other assistance. "And if they don't, that will violate the principles of Islam."

Andrew Natsios, the head of AID, had brought a map showing areas of malnutrition, famine and privation in Afghanistan. They were mostly in the north where there had been a drought of several years. In the Pashtun-dominated south, where Taliban roots were strongest, there was adequate food, the map indicated.

"It's hard," Natsios said. "We're not well positioned. We're getting good cooperation from CENTCOM." Bush had the American military delivering the goods to send the political message.

"But our footprint and ability to deliver aid into the north is limited. We've got one airport in Turkmenistan, one airport in Uzbekistan, and we do not have the kind of land bridges we need."

"Prior to the conference," Bush said, "we need to get out to the world the facts about the situation as we found it. And what we are doing to counter it."

They had a long discussion about the role of the United Nations, and the question of who might lead Afghanistan after the Taliban.

Bush then turned to several sensitive issues with his war cabinet members.

First, Cheney wanted to discuss a CIA analysis that concluded that inadequate airpower was being directed at the Taliban. "Do we need more sorties?" he asked.

They saw dramatic increases in available targets when the Special Forces teams got into Afghanistan, Rumsfeld said. But he was having truly serious trouble. The teams weren't getting in. "We still have eight teams waiting. None went in yesterday."

"What's keeping them out?" Cheney inquired. Was it an unwillingness to take risks? Was it weather? "If we get hit again will we look too timid?"

Rumsfeld said that part of the problem was weather. The Uzbeks were also causing delays. In one case, Fahim was raising objections to another team.

Most of the others in the room were dumbfounded.

"Franks needs to lay out a winter scenario," the president said.

Rumsfeld was working on it.

"The longer it takes us to get al Qaeda," Cheney said, "the greater our risk. What would it take to hit 50 caves in 48 hours?" In case anyone missed his message, he wanted to kill more people. "What could we do with more force?"

Rumsfeld said they had increased the force a number of times, but he would check about what more could be done. They had had some bad luck and foul-ups. On a recent aerial resupply effort to Fahim, half the parachutes had not opened, causing a disaster.

"This will all take time," the president reminded everyone. "We cannot have false expectations about how long it will take. We need to condition the United Nations to be patient. The key to success will be how strong we are in the good times and in the bad, and whether we can stay focused. You keep a coalition together by being clear that we are going to win. The U.S. determination will be the key. We cannot let the world whine because we are under attack today."

As if he were speaking to an uninformed public instead of his war cabinet, he said, "This is a two front war. America is under attack. We need to fight the war at home through the homeland security. We need to fight it overseas by bringing the war to the bad guys."

Bush said he had been talking to a European leader who said the way to maintain the coalition was to have lots of consultation, for the U.S. to show responsiveness, take account of the views of others and understand their reasoning.

"Well," he said, "that's very interesting. Because my belief is the best way that we hold this coalition together is to be clear on our objectives and to be clear that we are determined to achieve them. You hold a coalition together by strong leadership and that's what we intend to provide."

This was all consistent with Bush's belief that he is an agent for change—that he must state a new strategic direction or policy with bold, clear moves. And because it would be the policy of the United States, the only superpower, the rest of the world would have to move over, would adjust over time.

RICE THOUGHT BUSH was convinced that he didn't come here to leave the world the same way he found it. In private conversations with some heads of state, most recently Japanese Prime Minister Koizumi, he was outlining a broader view of his responsibility to act. "History will be the judge," he told Koizumi, "but it won't judge well somebody who doesn't act, somebody who just bides time here."

Bush also didn't want to do things that would have small impact, Rice concluded. The country could sit on its unparalleled power and dispense it in small doses, or it could make big strategic power plays that would fundamentally alter the balance of power. Bush planted himself in the visionary camp. "I will seize the opportunity to achieve big goals," he said in an interview. "There is nothing bigger than to achieve world peace."

He had come to believe that a president should not store up political capital, that a president gets more from spending it.

Rice admired what Truman and his secretaries of state had done after World War II. The Truman Doctrine, the Marshall Plan and the policy of containment were smart, effective uses of political capital.

When I later asked Bush about big strategic plays, he referred to the Civil War and the Vietnam War. "The job of the president is to unite a nation to achieve big objectives. Lincoln understood that, and he had the toughest job of all uniting a nation." Vietnam, in contrast, was divisive and ugly. Whatever capital Johnson and his advisers had was squandered. "They couldn't achieve big goals."

RUMSFELD HAD BEEN working for several weeks on a TOP SECRET paper outlining a broad strategy for Afghanistan. It was designed to make as certain as possible that they avoid a quagmire. He dictated a TOP SECRET—CLOSE HOLD memo to Wolfowitz, Myers, Vice Chairman Pace and policy undersecretary Feith, 10 numbered paragraphs on two pages in the large 13-point type that he preferred because it was easy to read.

Subject: "Ideas to be fed into the various sections of Afghan strategy paper." He wanted to make sure they addressed intelligence, humanitarian assistance, that they engaged NATO, and attempted to open the land bridge to Uzbekistan.

"Urgently," he dictated, using a rare emphasis, "bring in Special Forces units." It was still driving him crazy that they were so slow in getting men on the ground—the major promise and symbol of the new war the president and he were set on delivering.

Another point marked: "Contingency Planning. What if we suffer a setback?"

Rumsfeld had declared publicly that day that he was following the news commentary about the alleged stalemate or quagmire in Afghanistan. "I must say that I find those differences of views often helpful and interesting and informative and educational," he had said at his regular Pentagon briefing, trying to avoid a defensive tone.

To his senior staff he had referred once to the authors and television talking heads as "K Street pundits," former government officials and hangers-on who occupied the downtown corridor of K Street that housed seemingly endless consultancies and think tanks. To Rumsfeld, K Street was a low-life refuge for those who couldn't get real jobs, or didn't have the independence of spirit to leave Washington once they were through.

"Of course that's what they are saying," he had said. "They've got the attention span of gnats." The news business manufactured urgency and expectation. He was convinced that the public was more realistic, more patient.

He was doing some research to frame the historical context of one of his favorite subjects—Pearl Harbor and World War II.

THAT EVENING WAS Halloween. Vice President Cheney and his wife, Lynne, were stashed away at the undisclosed location but he had been in meetings all day. After 37 years of marriage, Lynne Cheney, who holds a Ph.D. in English literature and has been chairwoman of the National Endowment for the Humanities, still marveled at the little thing inside her husband's head that allowed him to concentrate on what was important. These days he was worried about nothing less than the future of the world.

For Halloween, they had brought their three young grandchildren with them, ages two, three and seven. They all had carved pumpkins; not her husband, of course, but she and the children. The kids dressed up in costumes, but there was no neighborhood for trick-or-treating, so she sent them around to knock on the doors of staff members in the bunker. One Secret Service agent pulled his coat up over his head and buttoned it so he looked like the Headless Agent. He then blinked the lights on and off furiously. It was the most fun she could wring out of the evening for the kids. She found it a depressing time. When her husband had been in the Ford White House, or Congress, or when he was secretary of defense, she used to say to him at night, "Tell me everything." Not anymore. She didn't really want to ask.

21

"GOOD AFTERNOON," RUMSFELD said, stepping before the news media in the Pentagon briefing room for his televised session with the news media the next day, Thursday, November 1. "I've reflected on some of the questions that were posed at the last briefing about the speed or progress and questions about the patience of the American people if something didn't happen immediately."

He then gave a history lesson, setting up the conflict between the press, which didn't understand the current war, and the public, which did. "Today is November 1st. And if you think about it, the smoke at this very moment is still rising out of the World Trade Center, or the ruins of the World Trade Center, I should say. And with those ruins still smoldering and the smoke not yet cleared, it seems to me that Americans understand well that despite the urgency in the questions that were posed at the last briefing, we're still in the very, very early stages of this conflict.

"Consider some historical perspectives." His tone edged on condescension. "After December 7th, 1941, attack on Pearl Harbor, it took four months before the United States responded to that attack with the Doolittle Raid in April of '42" on Tokyo. It was eight months before the first land attack on Guadalcanal, he noted. Japan was bombed for three and a half years before capitulating, Germany was bombed for five years, he reminded them.

He said that on October 7, when the U.S. bombing campaign began, he had stated their limited objectives, and insisted
that they did not expect the "possibility of instant victory or instant
success."

He listed the six goals designed to change the military balance
in Afghanistan over time—not this month, not necessarily this year—
very limited, very understated goals. "Now those were the goals I put
out on October 7th. That was 24 days ago—three weeks and three
days; not three months; not three years, but three weeks and three
days. And we have made measurable progress against each one
of those stated goals from October 7th.

"In the end, war is not about statistics, deadlines, short attention spans or 24-hour news cycles. It's about will, the projection of
will, the clear, unambiguous determination of the president of the
United States—and let there be no doubt about that—and the
American people to see this through to certain victory."

History was on their side. "In other American wars, enemy
commanders have come to doubt the wisdom of taking on the
strength and power of this nation and the resolve of her people. I
expect that somewhere in a cave in Afghanistan there's a terrorist leader who is at this moment considering precisely the same
thing."

There was a certain amount of hostility in the atmosphere. A
reporter asked, "Your opening statement today wasn't about prose-
cuting war. Increasingly, it seems to be about selling the war, telling
the American people why it's taking as long as it is, and to have patience. How big a part of your job is the sales effort? What sort of
time are you dedicating to that? Are you dedicating too much time
to it? And are the people that you're talking to buying?"

Speaking somewhat through clenched teeth, Rumsfeld said
that he spent less than two hours out of his average 13½-hour day
answering media questions. "As a percentage of the day, it's relatively modest."

• • •

"IT IS IMPORTANT we show results before the winter," Cheney said at the November 1 principals' meeting at 5:30 P.M. "It's important we have a sense of urgency."

Rumsfeld said it took time to set up the targets by the Special Forces teams, and he reminded them of the continuing trouble getting more teams in. There was ground fire that was dangerous for the teams.

Powell said that over the winter they would be able to train the Northern Alliance to fight a conventional war. For example, it would be possible to train some of them as forward air controllers to call in the F-15 strikes themselves.

"I have a sense of urgency," Cheney said, meaning he didn't see it in others. "There will be a low tolerance after the next hit." He envisioned a political explosion in the United States if there was another attack, and if the administration had not done everything possible.

Rice said they needed to talk to Franks and the president about urgency.

Powell said they should focus on Mazar.

It's risky to focus on one place, Rice said. "What do we need to do if we have to take Mazar in a month?"

It was okay to focus on Mazar, Cheney said. "But if we don't get them, they'll get us." They really needed to kill more of these people, he believed. Maybe they should send out "hunter-killer" teams to stalk down the terrorists in Afghanistan.

Rice promised they would address the urgency issue with the president the next day.

As long as they were only hitting military forces and targets, Powell said they would maintain support for the war effort in most of the Muslim world.

"WELL, THERE'S BUZZING in the press," Powell said at the beginning of the NSC meeting the next day, Friday, November 2.

"Buzzing" was an understatement that brought some half-chuckles around the table. "The countries in the coalition are still with us," he added somewhat confidently.

"We have 410 trucks in northern Afghanistan, they've got snowplows. We've got about another month to bring in food." When the snow started in several weeks it would be more difficult to get food into the north.

"We need a pre-Ramadan humanitarian assistance effort," the president said.

He was assured that efforts were under way, but it was difficult to get media and public attention given the threats, the global terrorist warning, anthrax, the bombing campaign.

On homeland security, Rumsfeld said, "We're going to have nine CAPs up, Wednesday through Saturday." He listed three possible targets in the U.S. that the Combat Air Patrol needed to protect: 1. Nuclear reactors. 2. Facilities for storing and making nuclear weapons. 3. High priority landmarks ranging from the White House to Wall Street to tall buildings in other cities such as Chicago to Disney amusement parks.

"For these CAP aircraft," Bush said, "we need some keep-out zones large enough so that our aircraft have time to provide defense." He wanted large chunks of airspace controlled—the so-called keep-out zones—where planes could not fly.

"Some places we can do that, some places we can't," Rumsfeld answered. Given the air traffic of thousands of planes across the entire nation it was not realistic to have sufficiently large keep-out zones that would allow the CAP enough time to always intercept an aircraft that entered the zones.

Bush asked about resupply efforts for the Northern Alliance.

"We got a lot of supplies into Dostum and Fahim," Rumsfeld replied. "Karzai and Attah got ammunition and food yesterday, and they'll get it again today." They needed a base for humanitarian assistance in the north. The president said they needed more than a single base. "We need one in Mazar and we need one in Kabul."

Franks gave his assessment of his meetings with top people in six countries. The warmth of his reception with the Saudis surprised him, he said. They understood that this was going to be a long effort. He had found some bureaucratic resistance below the highest levels in Saudi Arabia and that meant there would be some frictions, but we'll work through them, he said.

On Qatar, he said, "We've got some requests of them. They are working through our requests.

"Musharraf is calm, confident and committed. We have to recognize that what we do in Pakistan creates problems for him in his street and we have to be sensitive to that." He reported that the Pakistani leader had told him he would like the thing in Afghanistan to end soon. He said he had responded by telling Musharraf, "That will depend more on you than it does on me."

Pakistan was the linchpin of the operation.

Uzbekistan needed more work. He recommended that Rumsfeld go see Karimov.

Franks said he had an assessment team working at Tajikistan's air base.

The U.S. needed to have more and better public affairs outreach. We need to do it at home, Franks said. "We need to get our message into the media of countries overseas. We need to be visible where we need to be visible, and invisible where we need to be invisible." He seemed to be saying that it was important to have as light a footprint as possible.

"They generally understand our effort will not be short," Franks said. "It's terribly important that we show resolve.

"We're still getting into the theater assets that we need to prosecute the war the way this war has to be prosecuted." They were sending in their own Predators for aerial surveillance, but unlike the CIA's version, the U.S. military's drones were not armed with Hellfire missiles.

He was moving in Global Hawks—high-altitude, long-range unmanned surveillance planes—and JSTARS (Joint Surveillance Target Attack Radar System), which detected ground movements of tanks or other vehicles over large areas. JSTARS did for the ground what AWACS did for air surveillance. "We're at this point getting in those kinds of assets that you really are going to need when this thing begins to move up."

Franks said they had not increased the teams on the ground since the last week. "Dostum is the best we've got. He's tired, lacks medical supplies, clothing and ammunition." But resupply would take place within seven days. Overall, Franks said they needed to do a better job getting supplies to all the opposition forces. "We need to go on high burn."

Bush said he agreed.

It turned out that the Russians were willing to send weapons to the Northern Alliance. They had some distribution networks, but somebody would have to pay for the arms. It was eventually decided that the CIA would pay. They would give their former enemy about $10 million. Rice would deal with the Russian defense minister to make the final arrangements.

Franks had been compiling a list of caves and tunnels that were possible hiding places for bin Laden, al Qaeda, the Taliban. He had 150 to 160 on his list. He said 75 of these had been struck. In addition, the CINC had a list of suspected WMD sites—and he was checking them out one by one.

"Now, Mr. President," Franks said, "let me tell you the specific problems I'm working on in the next seven days." He wanted to give Bush an operational feel for the details. One problem was that forces from the United Kingdom were having trouble getting into Pakistan, and the CINC was trying to make sure that happened. "I'm trying to make sure we can get aircraft"—a particular kind of aircraft—"based in Uzbekistan. I'm trying to get cold weather supplies in, tents, clothing," some of which he had gotten from the Russians. "I've got two more Special Forces teams I need to get in this week. I need to get JSTARS up and operating in the environment. And I've got to get my relationships square with Qatar."

As usual Cheney had been mostly silent, listening carefully, his head occasionally tilted. "I think time is on our side militarily in Afghanistan," the vice president said, "but in the broader context, we need greater urgency. The longer UBL is free, the greater risk of a hit here at home."

Tenet thought that bin Laden's freedom might or might not increase the risk. If he was free, he might order another attack. But if he was captured or killed, other al Qaeda might decide to act in retaliation or desperation. He said nothing.

"They may have nukes," Cheney said, laying out the worst case scenario. "They may have CW/BW. The allies in the region are a fragile proposition for us. The strategic consequence of a radical takeover in Pakistan or Saudi would be enormous. And third, the degree of patience in the United States may dissipate if we get hit again.

"Therefore," Cheney said, addressing Franks and Rumsfeld, "we may need to think about giving you more resources, a different timeline, more forces and a higher tempo of operations." He asked Franks if he needed more guidance about taking greater risks in the theater.

"Whether we use surrogates or use a more direct U.S. role is the issue," Franks said. "And I need to present it to you. I haven't yet satisfied myself I can present it to you."

Franks and his staff and the Joint Chiefs were forcing themselves to face the possibility that a large ground force of American troops would have to be sent to Afghanistan. The number 50,000 to 55,000 was being mentioned. It was a staggering number, suggesting the kind of land war that military history dictated should be avoided in Asia, at all costs.

The president was aware of the figure under consideration. In a later interview, he recalled dealing with "the scenario where we may need to put the 55,000 troops in there."

"What's the capability of the opposition forces?" Powell asked. "Do we need to train them?" In his 35 years in the military, he had found that good training could go a long way. Neither Powell nor anyone else was prepared for Franks's answer.

"I don't place any confidence in the opposition," the commander said. On the question of whether the Alliance could be trained, he said, "I don't know." He was depressed about Fahim, who had the advantage and was not really moving. In contrast, Dostum on horseback was aggressive, a General Patton. "Dostum rides 10 to 15 miles a day in windstorms or snowstorms with guys lacking a leg. They go to blow up a Taliban outpost and take casualties knowing they had no medical assistance."

So even though he had lost confidence in the opposition forces, Franks said he would continue with the current strategy "while at the same time doing some planning to see if we need to be able to do the kind of things the vice president described."

The president had not known that Cheney was going to raise these issues, but he had found that when Cheney asked questions it was worth listening to them. He wanted Franks to take them seriously. "When can you give me some options," Bush asked Franks, "along the lines of what the vice president talks about?"

"In one week," Franks said, "to a very small group."

Bush had previously asked Franks what response would be possible if al Qaeda struck the U.S. at home again in a major way, and he wanted to order an escalation.

"And I also owe you options of what we do if we get hit again," Franks said.

After the meeting, Cheney called Libby, who had also been in attendance. "Nobody ever said these jobs were easy," the vice president said.

22

At the Saturday, November 3, secure video NSC meeting, McLaughlin reported that the CIA now had four paramilitary teams inside Afghanistan. The plan was to have the agency's Delta team, which had just joined Khalili some 100 miles west of Kabul, link up with Jawbreaker and Fahim north of Kabul and drive south to the capital.

The other two teams would drive north on Mazar, Alpha with Dostum and Bravo with Attah.

"The bad guys are looking for good news in the next few days," he told them. The threat reports were escalating again.

The news on both fronts was bad—little progress on the ground in Afghanistan and a big possibility of another attack at home. And that attack may have already started with the mailing of anthrax spores. The day before, Bush had referred to a "two front war."

Wolfowitz was standing in for Rumsfeld, who was on a quick four-day trip to Russia, Tajikistan, Uzbekistan, Pakistan and India, and he too had some disappointing news. "The weather is bad. We lost a second Predator because of icing. We've got 16 left. We're producing more."

"How about the pending invasion of Mazar?" the president

asked. "Did somebody say it was going to happen on November 5th?" That was two days away.

Yes, that was the plan. They were not sure it could be counted on.

General Myers had something positive. "We've got a third military Special Forces team in with Khalili now." That team was working with the CIA's Delta team and Khalili near Bamiyan.

"So you've got four or five left to get in, right?" the president asked.

"Right."

AT THE MONDAY, November 5, NSC meeting, Wolfowitz attempted to demonstrate that they were turning up the heat. He reported that "90 percent of our sorties now are in support of the opposition"—targets called in by the Special Forces A-teams, hitting the front lines and troop concentrations of the Taliban and al Qaeda.

"Our sortie rate is up 20 to 30 percent," he said. "We're using F-16s and F-15s out of Kuwait. It's a long haul." Kuwait, which had been liberated by the United States in the 1991 Gulf War, was willing to allow offensive strikes from its territory, but it was 1,000 miles from Afghanistan.

A Middle East leader had told General Franks the U.S. didn't need to stop fighting during Ramadan, Wolfowitz reported, and that in 37 of the last 54 years there had been fighting during Ramadan—most of it Arab against Arab.

The president, of course, had already made the decision to bomb during the Muslim holiday.

But the leader had said that they should ease up on strikes during prayer time, Wolfowitz reported. That became the formula they adopted.

"In the north," the president asked, "what is the strength of the enemy?" The intelligence reports, done by sector in the country, had been all over the lot. Though he didn't say it, Tenet knew that the best the CIA could give was really a WAG—a wild assed guess.

"Are we giving the tribals an impossible task?" Bush continued. After all, Fahim in the northeast had a numerical advantage but he was not moving. Dostum, who was overwhelmingly outnumbered, was trying to move.

Wolfowitz said that the Taliban were getting reinforcements but Franks thought that had a good news side—it would create more targets.

"I want to hear more from Don about that," Bush said.

THAT AFTERNOON THE president met with Algerian President Abdelaziz Bouteflika. Algeria is the largest country in Africa and the CIA was heavily subsidizing its intelligence service, spending millions to get their assistance in the war against al Qaeda.

The December 1999 arrest of Ahmed Ressam, a low-level Algerian terrorist operative, had not only helped break up the millennium terrorist plot but also had tipped the CIA to the existence of an Algerian al Qaeda network of black Africans. The result: a doubling of the known number of al Qaeda in the world, a significant and disturbing discovery. Tenet took it as a warning that the CIA had to look at not just Arab faces but also African faces in counterterrorist operations.

Bush promised the Algerian president that the United States would complete its mission and go home. "The biggest problem we have is an impatient press corps. They want the war over yesterday. They don't get it."

AT THE TUESDAY, November 6, noon Pentagon press briefing, Rumsfeld said that he thought it would take months to deal with the Taliban and al Qaeda.

"What has led you to come to that conclusion?" a reporter inquired.

"It is clearly an estimate," Rumsfeld replied. "I did not suggest one, two or three months; I said months rather than years. That means it could be as long as 23."

The reporters laughed.

"I've got a full range from one or two to 23. And I thought to myself when I was asked that question, I spontaneously responded to the best of my ability and said, Hmmm, I'll bet you it's months, not years. Could I be wrong? I suppose. Do I think I am? No."

More laughter.

AT THE MORNING NSC on Wednesday, November 7, Tenet reported that the CIA was still trying to get its Charlie paramilitary team in with Ismail Khan in the west.

"There seems to be progress around Mazar-e Sharif," he said, tantalizing everyone. But the full battlefield picture, as always, was troublingly unclear.

Rumsfeld said, "There are four more Special Forces teams to go in—are in the process of going in." That meant they still weren't in—nothing had changed since Saturday. "We're resupplying Dostum, Attah and Khan. We're continuing to work on the caves."

"The cave story is important," the president said. He was closely following the intelligence, including the overhead Predator video. "It highlights the problem in this war," he said, quickly adding, "But it also highlights U.S. steadfastness." Searching the cave complexes for Taliban and al Qaeda was difficult and tedious, and dangerous.

LATER THAT DAY, November 7, Tony Blair flew over on the Concorde to visit Bush. They met briefly in the Oval Office, gave a joint press conference in which they attempted to boost each other and the anti-terrorism cause, had an early dinner with aides and then went upstairs to confer alone.

Bush wanted to unburden, talk things through with a peer, another head of state. He wanted some eyeball time with his chief ally. He and Blair were in this together—both had staked their public offices, careers and reputations on the current undertaking.

The situation was not as happy as they had portrayed it publicly. Afghanistan was bogged down and questions abounded: When were they going to get the Uzbeks to agree to full basing rights? The Uzbeks were playing silly buggers with them. What about Mazar? Was Kabul in danger of a Northern Alliance takeover, leaving "Johnnie Pashtun" out in the cold? How could they detach the Pashtuns from the Taliban? What could be the inducement? More money, security, a sense that the United States and Britain were on the winning side? They needed to dress up the notion of inevitable victory.

For the first time, the Middle East situation seemed to have an impact on the two leaders' strategy for dealing with Afghanistan. For Blair, Palestinian leader Yassir Arafat still could be engaged in security and confidence-building steps with the Israelis, however small. He seemed a necessary evil. Bush increasingly viewed Arafat as just evil.

Blair flew back that night after about six hours in the United States.

"WE MIGHT TAKE Mazar in 24 to 48 hours," Tenet told skeptical colleagues at a principals' meeting on Thursday, November 8. Dostum and Attah were engaged in an envelopment of the city. "One is seven and one is 15 kilometers from the town." He said he would lean on the Pakistanis to use their tribal ties in southern Afghanistan to get the south to rise. "We don't have anything working in the south, and we have nothing to put on the table."

He had yet another piece of bad news. "The Iranians may have switched sides and gone to side with the Taliban." Iran, one of the biggest supporters of the Northern Alliance before September 11—in conjunction with the U.S., Russia and India—was now worried that the United States might gain some kind of foothold in Afghanistan. Sensitive intelligence showed that the Iranian Revolutionary Guard, the radical element that held real power, was shipping weapons to the Taliban, and that it was reaching out to al Qaeda. Some al Qaeda were using Iran as a transit point out of Afghanistan into places like Yemen.

The only upside was that it suggested the Northern Alliance was closer to victory than anyone had thought.

Rumsfeld had an idea for incentives. "We've got to tell the tribal groups in the south if they throw in and help us, we will accept their having a role in the government. The test is whether they will act now against al Qaeda and the Taliban." He was suggesting a kind of amnesty program—sign up now and your past associations will be forgotten. This was necessary because all the tribes in the south had had some ties to the Taliban. To disenfranchise them from the new government would give them no incentive to help now.

"I agree," said Powell in an unusual concurrence with Rumsfeld, "that's the right test." It was the kind of practical deal that Powell liked. Purity wouldn't work. This was practical politics.

HANK WENT TO Afghanistan to assess the front lines with some of the agency's paramilitary teams. The millions of dollars in covert money the teams were spreading around was working wonders. He calculated that thousands of Taliban had been bought off. The Northern Alliance was trying to induce defections from the Taliban themselves, but the CIA could come in and offer cash. The agency's hand would often be hidden as the negotiations began—$10,000 for this sub-commander and his dozens of fighters, $50,000 for this bigger commander and his hundreds of fighters.

In one case, $50,000 was offered to a commander to defect. Let me think about it, the commander said. So the Special Forces A-team directed a J-DAM precision bomb right outside the commander's headquarters. The next day they called the commander back. How about $40,000? He accepted.

AT THE FRIDAY, November 9, NSC meeting, General Franks reported, "We're doing 90 to 120 sorties a day; 80 or 90 percent are going to support the opposition. We're focusing on Mazar." He said they were supplying five of the 10 main tribal leaders. "We're doing cold weather gear and ammunition. We assemble the packages in Texas, they're staged in Germany. It takes two days to get them into Germany, and then we distribute them two or three days thereafter." They were starting to get a reliable logistics chain.

"By the end of the month, we're going to have it in good shape around Mazar. And we're working on Fahim Khan to get him to move."

Then Franks turned to the kind of detailed summary he had begun providing the president and the war cabinet.

"There are seven things I'm working on this week: Trying to get the U.K. into the Paks; I'm trying to get more combat aircraft into Uzbekistan; I'm trying to get my basing and staging out of Tajikistan squared away; I'm trying to get cold weather kits to the opposition; I'm working my seven Special Forces teams—I'll have another with Ismail Khan, the CIA will go in tonight, the military will be in in the next two or three days; I've got two JSTARS"—the advanced ground surveillance systems; "I'm bringing in more assets."

Turning to the immediate operations, he said, "I'm attacking leadership; I'm supporting the opposition; I'm supporting direct action by our troops against bad guys; I'm working caves and tunnels. There are 450 caves between Kandahar and Kabul and the Pak border, and that number will go to 1,000. These are areas where we believe people may be. We've damaged over a hundred.

"We've got to keep our expectations low," he concluded.

"Tommy, are you getting what you need?" the president inquired. It was a question he asked frequently.

"I'm happy," Franks said. "I'm getting what I need. The war is going great."

"We need a specific winter strategy, to arm the president and the secretary of defense with," Bush said.

"We will not stop in the winter," Rumsfeld replied. "We can continue most of what we are doing now throughout the winter."

"Let's not talk about a winter strategy," Powell said. A seasonal designation might be interpreted as a change of strategy. "Let's just talk about a strategy."

"Great," the president said. But whatever the label, it did not diminish the communication problem. "We need some points to refute the notion that the coming of winter means we've failed."

"What is the mission as to Kabul?" Card asked. "Is it a political mission? Is it a military issue?"

"No one wants the Northern Alliance in Kabul," Powell said, "not even the Northern Alliance." The Alliance realized that the southern tribes could go bonkers seeing their rivals in the capital.

Cheney, who was staying at his undisclosed location during this period, walked outside at one point and said to an aide, "It's not pretty, but it's progress."

THE CIA AND Special Forces teams were concentrated around Mazar-e Sharif, the city of 200,000 on a dusty plain 35 miles from the Uzbek border. A week earlier, a Special Forces lieutenant colonel had been infiltrated into the area with five other men to coordinate the work of the A-teams. The teams were directing devastating fire from the air at the Taliban's two rings of defensive trenches around the ancient city.

One team had split into four close air support units, spread out over 50 miles of rugged mountain terrain. The absence of fixed targets had freed up the U.S. bombers for directed attacks by the separate units, which were able to use bombs as if they were artillery. The big difference was the precision and the size of the munitions. These were 500-pound bombs. Taliban supply lines and communications had been severed in the carpet bombing. Hundreds of their vehicles and bunkers were destroyed, and thousands of Taliban were killed, captured or had fled.

One front line Taliban commander with several hundred men agreed to switch sides and let the Northern Alliance forces through, undermining the defensive perimeter.

At one point Dostum, riding a dark pony, led a cavalry charge of perhaps 600 horsemen. Attah struck simultaneously. Two BLU-82 "Daisy Cutter" bombs weighing 15,000 pounds each were dropped, leaving a 600-yard radius of devastation, killing many and rupturing the lungs and eardrums of those who were not killed.

The massive violence the U.S. could bring was finally being coordinated.

Well after lunch, Army Lieutenant Colonel Tony Crawford, an intelligence specialist and executive assistant to Rice, walked into her corner West Wing office.

"Mazar has fallen," he said. "We're getting reports that Mazar has fallen."

"What does that mean?" Rice asked skeptically. "Are they in the center of the city? What does 'Mazar has fallen' mean?"

Crawford said he would go find out what it meant.

He was back shortly to report that Dostum's troops were indeed in the center of the city. The locals were throwing off their Taliban clothing. They were celebrating, sheep were being sacrificed. Women were waving, cheering and clapping.

What does the national security adviser do in such a situation? She turned on CNN, which confirmed the reports, and called Rumsfeld to tell him the news.

"Well," he replied, "we'll see."

His view was that first reports are almost always wrong, and this sounded like one that was. Maybe it fell today, and maybe it won't have fallen tomorrow.

Rice walked down to tell the president. He had already heard. "That's good," he said, controlling his enthusiasm.

She noticed that he didn't get out a cigar to chew—a standard sign of genuine celebration.

Bush recalled eight months later, "The thing I do remember is the mating up of the such-and-such Northern Alliance guy and so-and-so and they're heading up the valley whatever it was."

But at the time Bush asked Rice, "Well, what next?"

AT 4:05 THAT afternoon the president welcomed Saudi Foreign Minister Prince Saud, a Princeton-educated economist and businessman, for a private meeting. "We have to show solidarity to get rid of the terrorists in Afghanistan," Saud told him.

"I think Osama bin Laden hates you more than he hates me," Bush said.

"It's an honor to be hated by someone like him," the prince replied. Fifteen of the 19 hijackers were Saudis. The Saudis believed that bin Laden specifically chose Saudi hijackers to cause a schism between the U.S. and themselves.

"We will not do anything to damage the U.S. economy," Saud said. The Saudis supplied about 8 percent of the oil consumed daily in the U.S. They could cut production and drive prices sky high.

On Saturday, Bush flew to New York City for a morning address to the United Nations General Assembly and called for the creation of a Palestinian state.

At the Waldorf Towers suite, the traditional lodging for presidents, Bush had his first meeting with Pakistani President Musharraf.

"You're in an extraordinarily difficult position," Bush said, "but you made the right choice."

"We are with you," the Pakistani leader said. "We will take as much time as it takes."

"I want it to end early," Bush said. He was playing to one of Musharraf's major concerns. "It's important to find the enemy and use every resource." But he added a new dimension. He had become fascinated with the ability of the National Security Agency to intercept phone calls and other communications worldwide. If they got the key phone calls, future terrorism might be stopped, certainly curtailed. Bush summarized his strategy: "Listen to every phone call and close them down and protect the innocents."

Musharraf said that despite the evidence and the concerns, he did not think bin Laden and al Qaeda had nuclear devices. He was worried that the Northern Alliance, a bunch of tribal thugs, would take over Afghanistan.

"I fully understand your concern about the Northern Alliance," Bush said.

Musharraf said his deep fear was that the United States would in the end abandon Pakistan, and that other interests would crowd out the war on terrorism.

Bush fixed his gaze. "Tell the Pakistani people that the president of the United States looked you in the eye and told you we wouldn't do that."

Musharraf brought up an article in *The New Yorker* by investigative reporter Seymour Hersh, alleging that the Pentagon, with the help of an Israeli special operations unit, had contingency plans to seize Pakistan's nuclear weapons should the country become unstable.

"Seymour Hersh is a liar," Bush replied.

After 6 P.M. that evening, Bush and Musharraf went to the Empire Room of the Waldorf-Astoria to make statements and answer a few questions from reporters.

What about the Northern Alliance taking Kabul?

"We will encourage our friends to head south, across the Shamali Plains, but not into the city of Kabul," Bush said.

MONDAY, NOVEMBER 12, at the NSC meeting, Hank described the movement on the ground with a map. "In the north, Taliban forces are now trapped in Konduz, but they are continuing to fight. We've advised the Russians. They are going to deploy forces on the Tajik border to interdict the Taliban if they seek to go into Tajikistan." Tens of thousands of Russian troops were secretly coming to assist. Bush was delighted. Putin was going to visit the United States the next day.

"In Bamiyan, there's a combined Special Forces team with Khalili," Hank said. "Khalili has occupied Bamiyan. He's moving to Wardak, and then he's going to go to Kabul. Ismail Khan has taken Herat."

The real surprise was Kabul, Hank said. Some 10,000 to 12,000 troops were moving in groups of 500 on the capital. The resistance was light. "It's a risk that the Taliban will shell Kabul from a ridge to the south."

"That's a good target for our air strikes," the president said. He realized such air strikes might be turning the tide, that the earth was starting to move.

One Pashtun commander with 4,000 fighters had joined the Northern Alliance leader Fahim to march on Kabul. "He's going to drive south. He's going to pick up some Pashtun commanders and move south of Kabul," Hank said. "Ismail Khan is prepared to go down the ring road to Kandahar.

"Here's what we've got working in the south. We've got Karzai, he's hooked up with some elders in Uruzgan Province." They were working with individual commanders with very small numbers of fighters, some larger networks, even some tribals near the Taliban stronghold of Kandahar. For the tribals closer to the Pakistani border, in Khowst and Paktia, Hank said, "We're engaging our Peshawar office to get in contact with them."

Hank said they were trying to accelerate contacts in the south now that the north had begun to move. It was important to keep the balance between north and south so that all elements would have a legitimate claim to participate in the post-Taliban government.

The deputy interior minister of the Northern Alliance said he had 500 men inside Kabul, reportedly to quell an outbreak of violence. But the hard-core fighters were in the eastern provinces near Tora Bora and the Pakistani border.

It was a stunning turn of events—the Northern Alliance and enough southern commanders were joining together to stabilize Kabul—at least in the short run.

"In Mazar, the Northern Alliance forces are now in control up to the Friendship Bridge," Rumsfeld said. That could open the land resupply route. The Uzbeks, who had closed the bridge in 1996 when the Taliban came to power in Afghanistan, had said they would not open it until the southern part of it was secure. For the first time now, friendly tribals were right up there on the southern part of the bridge.

"That will open it up to humanitarian assistance," Rumsfeld said. Potentially millions of tons of food, medical supplies, clothing and other assistance could flow into Afghanistan.

"The Northern Alliance has taken Taloqan. It is surrendered, there is not much resistance. You've got two teams, 28 people each, on the ground in four vehicles south of Kandahar. They are arresting and interdicting and disrupting and sowing confusions. We are going to send them in for a few days, and then pull them out. It's creating mayhem.

"The CINC wants the Paks to close the transit points between Afghanistan and Pakistan to seal what's going in and out."

"We need to press Musharraf to do that," the president said.

He did not conceal his astonishment at the shift of events. "It's amazing how fast the situation has changed. It is a stunner, isn't it?"

Everyone agreed. It was almost too good to be true.

They turned to the questions of getting other countries involved, pressing Britain, Jordan, France and Turkey to help.

"What are the prospects of getting one of these guys to go into Mazar?" Rumsfeld asked. "We'd like three or four countries to go in, not the U.N., not NATO, but a unified command. And the purpose would be to ensure that people behave themselves"—mainly Dostum and Attah and those folks—"to hold the airport, and maybe mount a major NATO relief effort by air. It might be some sort of coalition of the willing."

"We need a strategy that may be a model for other cities," Bush said.

"Franks is going to be working all of this out through the liaison missions," Rumsfeld said, referring to the countries that had senior officers at Franks's Tampa headquarters.

"Three additional points: Do we want to take Kabul? The CINC should be involved on questions like that, on whether towns should be taken. We need his voice and his recommendation first." Franks's ideas were suddenly more important.

He added a second point: "We need to all be on the same page. People inside are starved or killed—that's the risk if we keep out.

"Also, if we keep out, it suggests a control that we don't have." Surrounding the city and staying on the outskirts might not be sufficient.

"It's a military operation with respect to Kabul," the president said. He wanted Kabul taken. "Then we need a political structure once it's taken. And Tommy needs to decide how to secure it. Politically, we need to send a signal that the Northern Alliance will not run post-Taliban Afghanistan. Once we secure Kabul, and the commanders have to decide how to do that, Tommy Franks has to decide how to do that, it'll be governed by a broadly representative group, as will the rest of the country.

"We need to have the right distribution of decisions between the military operation and the political control," he said.

THE PRINCIPALS MET later in the day to discuss Kabul.

Tenet said that Bismullah Khan, one of Fahim's sub-commanders, would be on the outskirts of the city by tomorrow. And Fahim had called the Jawbreaker team for guidance.

Tenet and Franks believed they should stay on the outskirts of the city. "Reporting suggests that the Taliban are leaving the city," Tenet said, "and will try to move south or east. We have not been able to corroborate how much has moved out of the city or moved to the ridgeline south of the city where there is a shelling problem. There are still pockets of Arabs in the city."

"They need airpower tomorrow," Rumsfeld said. "They could be on the outskirts of the city by tomorrow night. Look, our goal is to get the al Qaeda. That's our military goal and our advice to the Northern Alliance should further those goals."

Rumsfeld was trying to offer a corrective to the political talk about the impact of taking Kabul on the governance of Afghanistan. The real question, he was saying, was how will the taking of Kabul affect the mission of pursuing al Qaeda and other bad guys. "Franks wants to apply U.S. airpower and asks them to hold short. To the extent the military flees the city, he intends to go after them."

"I'm concerned about a vacuum in Kabul," Cheney said. "Do we have the luxury of coming to the edge of the city?"

Rumsfeld replied, "We want to get a multilateral force into Kabul soon."

"We want to focus on UBL and al Qaeda," Powell said. "Not sure about the situation in the city. Until we do, we want to focus on al Qaeda and UBL and destroy the Taliban as they head south. We've got to avoid Kabul, which will suck up all our available manpower."

"What's the humanitarian situation?" Rice asked.

"We don't know," Tenet answered.

"Relief organizations must know," Powell interjected. "We'll pulse and find out."

"Will the Taliban flee the city, or will they make it hard for us?" Rice asked.

No answer was forthcoming.

"I agree we should have a multilateral force ready to go," Powell said. He was going to try to call U.N. Secretary General Kofi Annan to get him to put more energy into pulling together that multilateral force.

"Well I guess where we are is we're going to hold on the outskirts, see what happens in the city, prepare for a military administration, and then have a broader political structure that will move in," Rice said.

"We're still at war," Rumsfeld reminded them.

"Should U.S. forces go in?" Cheney asked.

"It's being considered," Rumsfeld said.

"We should consider it," Powell said. Such a presence could be stabilizing.

"It'll take a week to put together a multilateral force," Rumsfeld said. He didn't want his forces doing this alone. "If we want to go fast, we have to put in U.S. and U.K. Special Forces."

"It'll be a very infantry-intensive effort," Powell noted.

"The 10th Mountain is in Uzbekistan, right?" Cheney asked. It was an Army division but included only about 1,000 of its troops.

"Yes," Rumsfeld said, "and we also have Marines offshore."

General Myers said, "We could move to Bagram Air Base and then base things in Kabul." The air base was 30 miles north of the capital.

"Well," Rumsfeld said, "we want someone else with U.S. forces." He wanted to avoid what might smack of nation building by U.S. combat troops. "We need to move quickly," he agreed. "We use whatever Franks is comfortable with.

"So we're going to apply our airpower, we're going to allow the Northern Alliance to move toward the outskirts of the town, we'll tell them to hold short of the town." Any Taliban military that try to leave, Rumsfeld said, "We're going to hit them."

"Well," Rice said, "Franks needs to get back to us on what kind of force he wants if we've got to do Kabul."

Both what he might need initially and then later, more permanently, Rumsfeld said.

"If we're going to go to the edge of Kabul," Powell said, "we decide later on all the evidence what to do next. And then we can decide what kind of military force to put in and then what civil administration to replace it."

The principals were groping, attempting to micromanage the situation on the ground from Washington. There might be uncertainty, but that didn't mean they didn't have ideas.

On November 11, the first Special Forces A-team, Triple Nickel, shifted fire to Bagram Air Base and in a short period of time called in 25 air strikes. They counted 2,200 enemy casualties and destruction of 29 tanks and six command posts, freeing up the Alliance to move on Kabul.

THE MORNING NEWS on Monday, November 12, flashed to the White House that American Airlines Flight 587 had crashed outside New York City on Long Island after takeoff. The reaction was, "Oh, my God! It's happening again." Tunnels and bridges into New York City were shut down at once. All air traffic was banned in a designated sector around New York. American Airlines directed all aircraft into and out of New York to land.

The president called New York Mayor Rudy Giuliani. "Your character is being tested to the extreme," Bush said, promising all possible assistance.

It soon became clear that the cause of the crash was mechanical failure, not terrorism.

• • •

AT THE NSC meeting Tuesday, November 13, Tenet reported. "Bismullah Khan is outside Kabul. There's disorder within Kabul. He went in to calm it down." Pashtun leader Abdurrab Rasul Sayyaf also put 400 to 500 people in the capital. "Their intention is to withdraw once someone comes in to take over the administration of the city."

"We need to manage the publicity here," Bush said. "We need to emphasize the cowardly atrocities that Taliban performed as they left the city."

Powell reported on the efforts to put together a government.

"The key is to show movement," the president said, "that we've got a manageable process that's leading somewhere."

"The U.N. needs to get in fairly early," Powell said.

"But they need to go quickly," Bush reiterated.

Rumsfeld said, "We've got to counsel patience. This is a hard country—what we're trying to put together.

"They're moving from Mazar to Hermez. Several thousand have surrendered in Konduz. There are some bad guys in Bamiyan. Bamiyan is surrounded but not yet taken. In Kandahar, there have been attacks on the airports; we don't know by whom. Herat has fallen. Kabul there are 2,000 Northern Alliance forces as police. Our people are with them. The two Northern Alliance groups in the city are cooperating. . . . This guy Sayyaf is ready to go to Jalalabad. We don't really want him in Kabul. He'll be disruptive. We want him to move east."

"Can we use Special Forces to disrupt the Taliban retreat?" the president asked.

"Good question," Rumsfeld said. "Let me ask about that. We're moving people in to Bagram airport, to bulk up to go after al Qaeda to the east."

"The U.S. forces will not stay," the president said. "We don't do police work. We need a core of a coalition of the willing"—adopting Rumsfeld's phrase from several days earlier—"and then pass on these tasks to others. We've got a job to do with al Qaeda. We need to look at WMD targets.

"There's a fertilizer plant we are worrying about. We need to know better what we're dealing with," he added. The suspicion was that it might be a lab for weapons of mass destruction.

Next Bush focused on the missing piece in all this. "Can we use our Special Forces to disrupt convoys in the northeast where UBL seems to be moving?" he asked.

There were some nods from around the table.

"Inspect every SUV that's moving in this area," he directed. "Hunt and seek. Patrol the roads."

"The south is going to be more classic guerrilla struggle against the Taliban than holding ground," Tenet said. "It's going to be a re-supply challenge. We want to try to marry up our southern strategy today. There are tribals who are willing to hunt al Qaeda for us. We need a communication channel and a way to coordinate it."

Rice asked about Pakistan.

"Tommy says the first priority is to close the border," Rumsfeld said. "Our concept is to—"

"If he moves elsewhere," the president interrupted, "we're just going to get him there."

EPILOGUE

THE CIA PARAMILITARY teams and the Northern Alliance intercepted some Taliban and al Qaeda radio communications as American bombs started to fall on their troop concentrations. The sounds of explosions and panic could be heard. What many remembered most were the screams.

There was a television antenna on top of a small hill in Kabul that had been a favorite target of the Soviets though they had never succeeded in hitting it. The Northern Alliance had also tried and failed. An American jet streaked in and, with one bomb, the antenna was gone. Word spread through the capital: The Americans are going to win, this is over.

ON MONDAY, NOVEMBER 12, General Myers reported to the president that while three days earlier the Northern Alliance had controlled less than 15 percent of Afghanistan, it now had forces in about half. Afghanistan was cut in two, the north controlled by the Alliance. Konduz, Herat and Bamiyan had fallen.

Most significantly, Kabul had been abandoned, with thousands of Taliban and al Qaeda fleeing south to the Pakistan border and east to the Tora Bora region. Rice received reports from the Situation Room on the fall of Kabul that were first based on media coverage, not their own intelligence. When she passed them on to the president, he said, "This thing is just unraveling on them, it's just coming apart." Soon there were pictures of real liberation—women in the streets doing all the things that had been forbidden previously. Rice felt they had underestimated the pent-up desire of the Afghan people to take on the Taliban.

The NSC debate about whether or how to take Kabul, or to keep the Northern Alliance out, or whether to bomb during Ramadan had been overtaken by events. The Alliance and a variety of Pashtun tribals occupied the city. There was an uneasy equilibrium but there had not been a bloodbath.

Taliban leader Mullah Omar explained the retreat to his troops, "Defending the cities with front lines that can be targeted from the air will cause us terrible loss." The confrontation had shifted from a classical force-on-force stalemate to an extraordinary exploitation of American power. The president later recalled, "It looked like our technologies may have been too sophisticated until we were able to match them up with the conditions on the battlefield." Now the CIA paramilitary, the Special Forces and the bombers made it impossible for the Taliban and al Qaeda to hold on to territory or even assemble in large numbers.

At his November 27 briefing to the news media, Rumsfeld took the position that this outcome had been certain all along. "I think that what was taking place in the earlier phases was exactly as planned." The suggestions that things had not gone well initially were uninformed. "It looked like nothing was happening. Indeed, it looked like we were in a"—and he asked the press to join in—"all together now, quagmire."

Reporters chuckled softly.

ON DECEMBER 7, the Taliban's southern stronghold of Kandahar fell, effectively leaving the Northern Alliance, its Pashtun allies and the U.S. in charge of the country. It was front page news but there was no big celebration. Bush had promised no parades and no sur-render signing ceremony. He was right. It wasn't clear what it meant.

In all, the U.S. commitment to overthrow the Taliban had been about 110 CIA officers and 316 Special Forces personnel, plus massive airpower.

Powell was to help set up a new government in Afghanistan in conjunction with the United Nations. He appointed James F. Dobbins, a 59-year-old veteran diplomat and former assistant secretary of state, to head the negotiations with the Afghanistan opposition groups to find a leader.

Dobbins knew the division of labor for the region was split comically among three State Department bureaus. The South Asia bureau was in charge of Afghanistan, Pakistan and India; the European bureau had Uzebekistan and the other "Stans"; the Near Eastern bureau had Iran.

He made the rounds at the CIA, where several officials mentioned Hamid Karzai, the moderate Pashtun, as a leader who had broad appeal. Karzai had been a junior minister with the Taliban and he had defected years ago and joined the opposition. General Franks also recommended him.

Dobbins joined a conference in Bonn, Germany, brokered by the U.N., where factions of the Afghan opposition were trying to see if they could agree on a leader. The new head of the Pakistani intelligence service said Karzai was a possible, and the Russian representative told Dobbins, "Yes, he's been to Moscow, we know him well, we think he's a good person."

The U.S. Defense Department representatives in Bonn opposed consulting the Iranians, but Powell told Dobbins to go ahead and do so.

"Oh yeah," Iranian Deputy Foreign Minister Mohammad Javad Zarif told Dobbins at the mention of Karzai. "He lived in Iran for a while and we think well of him."

In Bonn, the Afghans negotiated at all-night sessions, so Dobbins met Zarif at breakfast as they slept. "You know, yesterday I read in the press that your foreign minister was making a statement about how Iran opposed a peacekeeping force," Dobbins said one morning. "Why is he saying that when you here keep telling us you favor a peacekeeping force?"

"Well," Zarif replied, "you can just consider it a gesture of solidarity with Don Rumsfeld."

Dobbins was amused that even Zarif knew that Rumsfeld was opposed to peacekeeping forces.

"You know, Jim," Zarif added, "both you and I are well beyond our instructions at this point, aren't we?"

Dobbins was nation-building. He found Karzai had good communication skills, empathy and an ability to forge personal relationships rapidly. The Alliance and the Pashtuns chose Karzai as their new leader and he took the oath of office in Kabul on December 22. Regime change had been accomplished 102 days after the terrorist attacks in the United States.

IN DECEMBER, A battle began in Tora Bora in the White Mountains, elevation about 15,000 feet, where many al Qaeda and Taliban had fled—supposedly including bin Laden. Three Special Operations men and two from the CIA infiltrated right into the guts of Tora Bora and for about four days called in air strikes using their laser designators. At one point the five directed a B-52 strike some 1,500 yards from their position.

Pakistani forces were posted on their side of the border to interdict the fleeing terrorists and they captured several hundred. The Afghan tribals were supposed to do the same on their side, but Hank concluded they had done a sorry job. Also, there had been poor coordination with the Pakistanis and there had been no Plan B. From the available intelligence, Hank believed that around December 16, bin Laden walked or rode by mule into Pakistan with a core group of about a dozen outriders, probably at Parachinar, a finger of Pakistani territory about 20 miles wide that juts into Afghanistan.

The president's personal scorecard of al Qaeda leaders captured or killed was showing thin results. Bush had put a big "X" through the photo of Muhammad Atef, who had served as bin Laden's military chief and top planner of the September 11 attacks. Atef had been confirmed dead in the heavy bombing the previous month.

Initial reports that bin Laden's top associate, Dr. Zawahiri, had been killed prompted Bush to go to his Oval Office drawer, take out his scorecard and put an "X" though his picture. But the CIA soon determined that the killing could not be confirmed, and Bush dutifully erased the "X." In all, 16 of the 22 top leaders were still at large, including bin Laden.

TENET WAS EXTREMELY proud of what the agency had accomplished. The money it had been able to distribute without the kind of traditional cost controls had mobilized the tribals. In some cases, performance standards had been set: Move from point A to point B and you get several hundred thousand dollars. A stack of money on the table was still the universal language. His paramilitary and case officers in and around Afghanistan had made it possible—a giant return on years of investment in human intelligence.

CIA or CIA-supported teams were covertly breaking into places around the globe to gain detailed information on the whereabouts of suspected terrorists. Hundreds and eventually thousands of suspects were rounded up, taken into custody, and interrogated by cooperating foreign intelligence services and police.

Cofer Black had been right, people would have to die. On November 25, Johnny "Mike" Spann, a paramilitary officer with the CIA Alpha team that took Mazar, was killed when 600 Taliban and al Qaeda revolted at a prison fortress outside the city. Spann was the first U.S. combat fatality in the war. Contrary to CIA tradition, Tenet released information about Spann. It was front page news in nearly every newspaper.

Spann had served 10 years as a Marine before joining the CIA. The request that he be buried at Arlington Cemetery was turned down. They were running out of room. John McLaughlin called Andy Card and told him, "We are going to present him with the Intelligence Star, which is the equivalent of the Silver Star, and that typically is the hurdle you have to cross to get into Arlington." Card took it to the president, who approved.

Later a 79th star was added to the marble wall at the entrance to CIA headquarters where agency officers who gave their lives in the line of duty are honored.

The CIA calculated that they had spent only $70 million in direct cash outlays on the ground in Afghanistan, and some of that had been to pay for field hospitals. The president considered it one of the biggest "bargains" of all time. At headquarters they had created a so-called Magic Map that electronically located their dozens of paid assets and sources inside Afghanistan so they could be warned to move away from planned bombing. The assets were directed away on more than 100 occasions, and not a single one was killed in the first phase of the war.

In the end, Tenet believed they would find state sponsorship of the September 11 attacks. It was all part of the granularity of terrorism. Not specific authority, direction or control, but elements—a little money, training, equipment, communications, hiding places. His focus initially was on Iran. He believed that eventually they might find Iranian tracks in September 11. The Revolutionary Guard has a sophisticated network, and they had both motivation and capability. They are opportunists. Iran's long-term political agenda in the Middle East is served exactly by the sort of instability that bin Laden was trying to create.

Al Qaeda bought services wherever it could find them. So the classic model of direct support and control of terrorism no longer applied. Tenet had everything but proof that there was state sponsorship.

For years, the CIA had thought Syria was responsible for the bombing of Pan Am Flight 103 over Lockerbie, Scotland, in 1988. It had taken close to a decade to establish that it was Libya. Anyone who had not been through one of these complicated terrorist investigations had better hold on to his hat, Tenet believed. The CIA would develop leads and go places that did not at first seem possible.

Over the course of his 8 A.M. intelligence briefings, Tenet presented all this to Bush. Yes, there would be Iranian mood music in this, and likely in the end, in the same, convoluted, indirect way, Iraqi mood music. "You should discount nothing," he told the president.

"We'll follow it where it takes us," Bush said.

Tenet believed he had learned a personal lesson about the price of doubt and inaction. Bush had been the least prepared of all of them for the terrorist attacks. As he sat with the president 15 to 30 minutes nearly every morning Tenet saw what was driving him. He was going to act. There are always a hundred reasons not to act, not to move. The fearful wouldn't act. Those not afraid would work their way through all the problems that surfaced. Problems overwhelmed some people, and they would come up with 50 reasons why they were insoluble. Not Bush. Suddenly the CIA had a new ethos—no penalty for taking risks or making mistakes. Bush had given it to them.

Tenet himself had been too fearful and hesitant prior to September 11, too afraid to push the envelope. He had been yelling and screaming about the bin Laden threat for years. In a memo as early as 1998, he had declared "war" against bin Laden but he had not come out straight to Clinton or Bush and proposed, "Let's kill him." Clinton had responded with additional funding, enabling the CIA to reestablish a covert presence in Afghanistan, but no lethal authority. Bush, though quick to respond after September 11, did not pursue the bin Laden threat aggressively enough in his first eight months in office.

• • •

ON JANUARY 9, 2002, *Washington Post* reporter Dan Balz and I went to Rumsfeld's office to interview him for a newspaper series we were doing on the first 10 days after the September 11 attacks. Characteristically, Rumsfeld wanted to deal in broad strategic concepts, not specifics, and he had jotted down 12 of them on a piece of paper—everything from the necessity to preempt terrorists to the opportunity to rearrange the world.

We wanted to deal with specific moments, and Balz asked him about the day after the attacks when Rumsfeld had raised the question, Is there a need to address Iraq as well as bin Laden?

"What the hell did they do!" Rumsfeld exploded. "Give you every goddamn classif—... take that off the ..."

I urged him not to worry.

"I didn't say that," Rumsfeld declared and then tried to pretend that someone else had shouted. He pointed to Larry DiRita, his civilian special assistant. "Larry, stop yelling over my shoulder, will you please?"

I said that perhaps we could put an 18½-second gap in our tape.

"Now you're talking," Rumsfeld said.

The 19-page transcript that the Defense Department later released of the interview deleted his explosion and the "hell" and "goddamn."

A COUPLE OF months later on March 19, 2002, I was at the Pentagon for interviews when I ran into Rumsfeld just inside the front entrance. He was walking fast, jacket on, his tie slightly loose. He had a large, heavy bandage across the back of his neck where a tumor had been removed. (His spokesperson, Torie Clarke, had drafted a short press release saying that he had had a "fatty tumor" removed. Rumsfeld struck out the word "fatty.")

I stopped him to ask a question. In his early days as defense secretary, Rumsfeld had clearly anticipated that the United States was going to be surprised by some attack, perhaps something along the lines of September 11—the totally unexpected. How did you figure that out? I inquired.

He replied that when he had headed the Ballistic Missile Commission he had examined what intelligence the U.S. agencies had about three significant "events" or weapons developments in key countries. What he discovered was that U.S. intelligence had learned about the events from five to 13 years after they occurred. "We were surprised," he said, "but we didn't know about the surprise for years!" He became very intense about this, launching off in a verbal high-dive about his concept that the "unknown unknowns" were the real killers, the times when U.S. intelligence didn't even know what they didn't know.

I could see the trifocal lenses in his glasses we were so close. We were standing just inside the entrance as a parade of uniformed military men and women and civilians walked by.

"Known threats are not the worry," he said. On one occasion he had asked about the number of warnings before the USS *Cole* had been attacked in Yemen in 2000. The answer had been in the thousands.

"Can you believe that!" Rumsfeld said. The sea of warnings becomes meaningless. No one really paid attention and if people acted on each threat, he said, the U.S. would be chased out of places like Yemen.

How was the war going? I asked.

"There is the war you see and the war you don't see," he said. This was accompanied by appropriate hand motions—the war up here, above and seen, and the war down there, covert, unseen.

"They'll hit us again," Rumsfeld said in a matter-of-fact tone. "We have them off balance." He then jabbed three of his fingers into the center of my chest, tipping me back and slightly off balance.

Nice wrestling move, I thought, but then I shifted forward, taking the bait. I said that it was not enough because I had regained my balance rather quickly.

Rumsfeld gave one of his big, healthy, happy, full-faced smiles that overpower his face. He had made his point. We talked for a few more minutes. He asked for my address and a fax number so he could send me some material on his work on the defense commissions and walked off preppy and peppy. A man at war? It didn't seem that way. He was very comfortable, exuding self-confidence. I didn't know if he was too confident.

IN THE SPRING, after having had the run of Afghanistan for nearly five months, the U.S. military discovered huge amounts of munitions that the Taliban and al Qaeda had hidden in caves. In one they found 2 million rounds of ammunition; in others mortars, rockets, even some tanks. It was a whole underground support system. It was quite embarrassing to discover it so late in the game.

"Are you going to destroy all of this?" Bush asked Rumsfeld.

"No," he replied, "we're saving it to arm the new Afghan army."

Rice joked that it was going to be called Rumsfeld's Cavalry.

Rumsfeld wondered why they couldn't just let the Afghan warlords create an army. Powell and the State Department argued that Karzai was their guy and they needed a strong central government so Afghanistan did not, yet again, become a great power game in which all interested parties would try to carve out territory or spheres of influence.

Rumsfeld had become something of a media star because of his daily televised briefings. On Wednesday, May 1, 2002, he and General Pace, the JCS vice chairman, had been answering questions for half an hour when a reporter asked what Rumsfeld had achieved. He bristled.

"We fashioned a new defense strategy," he said. "It is a strategy that is more appropriate for the 21st century than what we had, we believe. We are convinced, we are unanimously convinced—the senior civilian and military leadership."

He listed new constructs, planning guidance, plans, the selection of maybe a dozen new four star officers. "We have been involved in the global war on terrorism," he said. He had to contend with department procedures which can take two years. "The freight train comes down the track and it's filled way over there, and until it runs to the end, you can't see what's inside of it. And every time you try to reach in, it's like putting your hand in a gear box, because this depends on that, and this depended on that, and each piece depended on something else. And you think you're making a wise decision if you grab in the middle of it, but in fact, if all the layers that led to those things are not readdressed back up, you end up with a situation that is kind of ad hoc; it is—it's a perfectly responsible, isolated decision, but if you make a series of them, they end up random; they don't end up with coherence. And so all this appetite to kill this, or do that, or start this, my attitude is, look, we'll do it the best we can. And as I look back, I say to myself, 'Not bad.' "

A reporter tried another question.

"Oh, no, no. I love that ending. I—(laughter). If you think I'm going to mess that one up, you're wrong! No, sir! I'm out of here!"

ONE OF POWELL'S greatest difficulties was that he was more or less supposed to pretend in public that the sharp differences in the war cabinet did not exist. The president would not tolerate public discord. Powell was also held in check by his own code—a soldier obeys.

Bush might order, Go get the guns! Get my horses!—all the Texas, Alamo macho that made Powell uncomfortable. But he believed and hoped that the president knew better, that he would see the go-it-alone approach did not stand further analysis. Hopefully, the Afghan war had provided the template for that understanding.

The ghosts in the machine were Rumsfeld and Cheney in Powell's view. Too often they went for the guns and the horses.

• • •

IN THE SPRING of 2002 the Israeli-Palestinian conflict became so violent that it threatened to overwhelm the war on terrorism. Palestinian suicide attacks escalated. On March 27, a suicide bomber killed 29 and injured 140 at a Passover seder. Israeli Prime Minister Sharon launched a small war, dubbed Operation Defense Shield, into Palestinian-controlled areas and cities in the West Bank.

There was a growing chorus from abroad that the U.S. had to get involved. At an NSC meeting, Bush said he wanted to send Powell to see if he could calm things down, get some peace process restarted. Powell was reluctant. He said he didn't have much to offer, too little leverage with either side. The U.S. couldn't be more desirous of peace than the parties themselves, Israel and the Palestinian Authority.

Even Rumsfeld argued that Powell should not be used just to try to stop the bleeding. The secretary of state should not just be expended, thrown into a diplomatic firefight with no positive agenda or script. Failure would be a serious blow to his prestige and to the U.S.

We are in trouble, the president told Powell. "You're going to have to spend some political capital. You have plenty. I need you to do it."

"Yes, sir."

As they were walking out of the Situation Room, Bush turned to Powell. "I know how hard this is going to be but you have enough standing in the region and with the parties and just in your own situation that you can afford it."

Powell understood this to mean, You can lose three layers of skin, you've got underlayers.

The president was going to give a speech outlining a policy to get negotiations restarted. Arafat would have to denounce terrorism unequivocally and Sharon would have to begin to withdraw.

Do you understand what you're saying to the Israelis? Powell asked him. You're going to have to look Sharon in the eye and say get out.

He said he understood.

On April 4, Bush delivered a Rose Garden speech calling on the Palestinians to end the terror. "I ask Israel to halt incursions into Palestinian-controlled areas and begin the withdrawal from those cities it has recently occupied." Powell would be going to the region the next week to seek support.

Two days later in Crawford with Tony Blair, Bush said, "My words to Israel are the same today as they were a couple of days ago: Withdraw without delay." He later backtracked. His heart seemed to be with the Israelis.

In the Middle East, Powell was getting rudder orders from the White House—go left, go right, correct your course so many degrees.

First, Cheney and Rumsfeld sent word through Rice that Powell should not meet with Arafat. "Aw, Arafat, he's a spent force, leave him alone," Rumsfeld said.

Powell knew it was ridiculous to try to negotiate without meeting with both parties. But everyone in Washington was worrying about Israel and there was mounting pressure from both Republicans and Democrats to back Sharon.

Powell had to worry about some 300 million irate Arabs who were starting to burn cars in embassy parking lots. There were demonstrations in places where there had never been before, such as Bahrain, a bastion of pro-Americanism. Arafat and Sharon were two bad guys, Powell thought, but he couldn't ignore one. He went ahead. The first meeting with Arafat was merely okay, but a second was much worse.

After 10 days, having made little progress, Powell was preparing a departure statement that proposed an international conference and security negotiations.

Rice called Armitage at the State Department to ask him to tell Powell to scale back his statement, make less of a commitment about future negotiations. There were real concerns that Powell was going too far.

In Washington, Armitage was almost chained to his desk so he could talk to Powell between his meetings. It was midnight, 7 A.M. in Jerusalem, when Armitage explained Rice's concerns.

Powell went nuts. Everybody wanted to grade papers! he said. No one wanted to step up, face reality! They wanted to be pro-Israel and leave him holding the Palestinian bag by himself. They had sent him out on a nearly impossible mission.

"I'm holding back the fucking gates here," Armitage reported. "They're eating cheese on you"—an old military expression for gnawing on someone and enjoying it. People in the Defense Department and the vice president's office were trying to do him in, Armitage said. He had heard from reliable media contacts that a barrage was being unloaded on Powell. He was leaning too much to Arafat, the White House was going to trim his sails, he was going to fail. Armitage said he couldn't verify who was leaking this, but he had names of senior people in Defense and in Cheney's office.

"That's unbelievable," Powell said. "I just heard the same thing." He had had cocktails with some reporters traveling with him and they reported that their sources in Cheney's office were declaring he had gone too far, was off the reservation, and about to be reined in.

"People are really putting your shit in the street," Armitage said.

Rice reached Powell and said all the others thought it was best he say nothing more, that he say he was going back to Washington to consult with the president.

Powell, who had been engaged in a grueling shuttle, erupted. Was he just supposed to say, thank you very much for your hospitality, good-bye!

Rice said she was worried that he was committing the president and the administration more deeply than they all wanted.

Guess what? Powell countered. They were already in. They couldn't launch an initiative with a high-profile presidential speech like that and not expect to propose some plan or follow-up. But he agreed to trim back some on his statement.

Rice called Armitage again. She sounded nervous. She had to do a television show on this. What was Powell doing? What's he going to say?

He'll be fine, Armitage promised. We know the general outline. I just don't have the words because he wrote it himself.

Powell was up until about 3 A.M. writing his remarks, knowing that he was out at the end of a long stick.

On April 17, he made his departure statement in Jerusalem. It was 20 paragraphs of Powell at his diplomatic best—smooth, upbeat, even eloquent. He was able to dress it up and point toward a negotiated future, while avoiding mention of his failure to get a cease-fire.

It didn't make much of a splash. He hadn't solved the Middle East problem; there was no breakthrough. But it settled some things down for the moment, and the president later thanked him.

THE PRESIDENT DESPERATELY wanted a signed treaty with the Russians to reduce strategic nuclear weapons. He wanted it to be simple and sweeping. The agreement would be a sign of the new relationship with the Russians and demonstrate that they were no longer the primary enemy. Bush would also show he had delivered Putin.

Rumsfeld flooded the principals with close to a dozen classified memos—often pejoratively called "Rummygrams" or "Snowflakes"—voicing objections to a written nuclear reduction agreement with the Russians. Powell watched in some wonderment as Rumsfeld delivered a series of requests: that the treaty not be legally binding, that it not specify numbers of nuclear weapons, that it have a clause that would allow the U.S. to withdraw at a moment's notice, that it provide flexibility, that it require verification, and that smaller tactical nuclear weapons be included.

If the Russians were now our friends, a new ally, Rumsfeld argued, why did we need a treaty? What difference would a piece of paper make?

The answer was that the president wanted a piece of paper. Rumsfeld lost on all counts. On May 24, 2002, Bush and Putin signed the "U.S.-Russian Treaty on Strategic Offensive Reductions" in Moscow. It was two pages long. Both countries agreed to reduce their strategic nuclear warheads to between 1,700 to 2,200 by the year 2012. The treaty promised friendship, partnership, trust, openness and predictability.

WHEN IT CAME to fighting terrorism, the president also wanted world leaders to equate their national interests with American interests. Some would go along with him when their interests and goals coincided roughly with his, but go their own way when they did not. Bush didn't like that when it happened and at times he took it personally.

Earlier in the year, Bush was meeting with President Ali Abdallah Salih of Yemen when it became clear to him that Yemen was not with him to the extent he thought necessary. Salih was dodging. Yemen was the soft underbelly of al Qaeda action, as terrorists slipped in and out of Saudi Arabia across their shared 700-mile border. Some CIA analysis suggested that Yemen might be the place where al Qaeda would reconstitute itself.

Yemen had given the CIA permission to fly its Predator aerial drone to track al Qaeda in a highly secret operation. But Salih was boxing up the operation, placing restrictions on it. This was the kind of divergence of interest that infuriated Bush. It suggested to him that Yemen was really against him.

And it wasn't only Yemen. Bush wasn't getting everyone to buy into his anti-terrorist vision 100 percent. No one was going to be as committed as he. After his trip to Europe and Russia in late May 2002 the president called the NSC together.

"We've lost our edge," he said. "I want us to remember that

we have got to be on the cutting edge." There was some slacking off in his own circle, and he was not going to have it. He required a mental attitude of total focus and obsession.

Yet the circumstances had changed. The edgy duality of life in the weeks and months after the attacks had subsided. Bush could pressure and talk, but life in the United States had increasingly returned to normal.

THE IRAQ ISSUE heated up substantially. It was going to be the next real—and perhaps the greatest—test of Bush's leadership and the role of the United States in the world.

Iraq carried lots of baggage. When Rice first signed up to be Bush's foreign policy adviser before the 2000 presidential campaign, she had raised the issue with him. Bush told her he disagreed with those who thought that his father had ended the war against Saddam in 1991 too quickly. At the time, Bush senior, Secretary of Defense Cheney and Chairman of the Joint Chiefs of Staff Powell had all agreed to end the war after achieving the stated goal of the U.N. resolution: evicting Saddam's armies from Kuwait. The U.S. would not drive to Baghdad to oust Saddam. Chasing down the retreating Iraqi army might look like a massacre. Half of Saddam's army was destroyed. He had suffered one of the most humiliating military defeats in modern history. Surely he was finished. The CIA and various Arab leaders predicted that he would soon be deposed, that some Iraqi Army colonel or general would put a bullet in him or lead a coup.

Saddam survived and Bush's father was defeated for reelection in 1992 by Clinton. In 1998 when Saddam shut down U.N. inspections of facilities suspected of making weapons of mass destruction, Clinton ordered Operation Desert Fox. Some 650 bomber and missile sorties were launched at Iraq over a three-day period, but Saddam would still not allow the U.N. inspectors back in.

Still Bush defended his father and his advisers. "They did the right thing at the time," he told Rice. His father was limited by the U.N. resolution authorizing the use of force only to get Saddam out of Kuwait. She agreed and noted that often in history leaders had blundered by letting a short-term tactical success change their strategic goals. Going to Baghdad to force Saddam from power might have been an entirely different matter. Because something seemed militarily easy was not a reason to do it, she said.

After Bush's initial decision not to attack Iraq immediately following the September 11 terrorist attacks, the issue had continued to percolate in the war cabinet—actively for Cheney and Rumsfeld, passively for Powell, who was not spoiling for another war.

When the president delivered his first State of the Union address on January 29, 2002, the big headline was his declaration that Iraq, Iran and North Korea were "an axis of evil." But he had said that the real peril and potential catastrophe was the growing availability of weapons of mass destruction to terrorists or these regimes.

Bush had considered raising this danger in his speech to Congress nine days after the terrorist attacks but he postponed, thinking such candor might be too much for the public at that time.

"I will not wait on events," he said in the State of the Union address, hinting that he would act preemptively—a strategy that he later articulated more directly.

AS ONE OF the first steps against Saddam, the president soon signed a new intelligence order significantly expanding the CIA covert operation to oust Saddam. He allocated $100 million to $200 million in new covert money—vastly more than the $70 million the CIA spent in Afghanistan. He increased support to the Iraqi opposition, stepped up intelligence gathering inside Iraq and prepared for possible deployment of CIA paramilitary teams and U.S. Special Forces similar to those used in Afghanistan.

Iraq is not Afghanistan, Tenet warned the president. The Iraqi opposition was much weaker, and Saddam ran a police state. He was hard to locate, and he used decoy look-alikes. Without companion military action and other pressure, Tenet told the president, the CIA had only a 10 to 20 percent chance of succeeding.

Bush, nonetheless, concluded that a larger covert operation would help prepare for a military strike by vastly increasing the flow of intelligence and contacts that might be needed later.

In April, the president began publicly declaring a policy of regime change in Iraq. In June he formally declared that he would launch preemptive attacks against countries believed to be a serious threat to the United States.

POWELL STILL HAD not squared his relationship with the president. During the first half of 2002, Armitage had received reliable reports that Rumsfeld was requesting and having periodic private meetings with Bush. Powell was not particularly worried, because he could usually find out what had transpired through Rice, though she had had some difficulties initially finding out herself.

"It seems to me that you ought to be requesting some time with the president," Armitage suggested to Powell. Face time was critical, and it was a relationship that Powell had not mastered.

Powell said he recalled his time as national security adviser for Reagan when everyone was always trying to see the president. He didn't want to intrude. If Bush wanted to see him, any time or any place, he was, of course, available. He saw Bush all the time at meetings, and he was able to convey his views.

"You've got to start doing it," Armitage said. He was the fucking secretary of state. It wouldn't be an imposition. Better relations would help in all the battles, would help the department across the board.

In the late spring of 2002—some 16 months into the Bush presidency—Powell started requesting private time with Bush. He did it through Rice, who sat in on the meetings which took place about once a week for about 20 to 30 minutes. It seemed to help, but it was like his experience in the Middle East, no big breakthroughs.

During the summer, Powell was over at the White House one day with time to kill before a meeting with Rice. The president spotted him and invited him into the Oval Office. They talked alone for about 30 minutes. They shot the breeze and relaxed. The conversation was about everything and nothing.

"I think we're really making some headway in the relationship," Powell reported to Armitage afterward. The chasm seemed to be closing. "I know we really connected."

IN EARLY AUGUST, Powell made the diplomatic rounds in Indonesia and the Philippines and, as always, kept in touch with what was happening at home. Iraq was continuing to bubble. Brent Scowcroft, the mild-mannered national security adviser to Bush's father during the Gulf War, had declared on a Sunday morning talk show on August 4 that an attack on Iraq could turn the Middle East into a "cauldron and thus destroy the war on terrorism."

Blunt talk, but Powell basically agreed. He had not made clear his own analysis and conclusions to the president and realized he needed to do so. On the long flight back, from nearly halfway around the world, he jotted down some notes. Virtually all the Iraq discussions in the NSC had been about war plans—how to attack, when, with what force levels, military strike scenario this and military strike scenario that. It was clear to him now that the context was being lost, the attitudes and views of the rest of the world which he knew and lived with. His notes filled three or four pages.

During the Gulf War, when he had been chairman of the Joint Chiefs of Staff, Powell had played the role of reluctant warrior, arguing to the first President Bush, perhaps too mildly, that containing Iraq might work, that war might not be necessary. But as the principal military adviser, he hadn't pressed his arguments that forcefully because they were less military than political. Now as secretary of state, his account was politics—the politics of the world. He decided he had to come down very hard, state his convictions and conclusions so there would be no doubt as to where he stood. The president had been hearing plenty from Cheney and Rumsfeld, a kind of A-team inside the war cabinet. Powell wanted to present the B-team, the alternative view that he believed had not been aired. He owed the president more than PowerPoint briefings.

In Washington, he told Rice that he wanted to see the president. Bush invited the two to the residence on the evening of Monday, August 5. The meeting expanded into dinner and then moved to the president's office in the residence.

Powell told Bush that as he was getting his head around the Iraq question, he needed to think about the broader issues, all the consequences of war.

With his notes by his side, a double-spaced outline on looseleaf paper, Powell said the president had to consider what a military operation against Iraq would do in the Arab world. Cauldron was the right word. He dealt with the leaders and foreign ministers in these countries as secretary of state. The entire region could be destabilized—friendly regimes in Saudi Arabia, Egypt and Jordan could be put in jeopardy or overthrown. Anger and frustration at America abounded. War could change everything in the Middle East.

It would suck the oxygen out of just about everything else the United States was doing, not only in the war on terrorism, but all other diplomatic, defense and intelligence relationships, Powell said. The economic implications could be staggering, potentially driving the supply and price of oil in directions that were as yet unimagined. All this in a time of an international economic slump. The cost of occupying Iraq after a victory would be expensive. The economic impact on the region, the world and the United States domestically had to be considered.

Following victory, and they would surely prevail Powell believed, the day-after implications were giant. What of the image of an American general running an Arab country for some length of time? he asked. A General MacArthur in Baghdad? This would be a big event within Iraq, the region and the world. How long would it be? No one could know. How would success be defined?

"It's nice to say we can do it unilaterally," Powell told the president bluntly, "except you can't." A successful military plan would require access to bases and facilities in the region, overflight rights. They would need allies. This would not be the Gulf War, a nice two-hour trip from a fully cooperative Saudi Arabia over to Kuwait City—the target of liberation just some 40 miles away. Now the geography would be formidable. Baghdad was a couple of hundred miles across Mesopotamia.

The Middle East crisis was still ever-present. That was the issue that the Arab and Muslim world wanted addressed. A war on Iraq would open Israel to attack by Saddam, who had launched Scud missiles at it during the Gulf War.

Saddam was crazy, a menace, a real threat, unpredictable, but he had been largely contained and deterred since the Gulf War. A new war could unleash precisely what they wanted to prevent— Saddam on a rampage, a last desperate stand, perhaps using his weapons of mass destruction.

On the intelligence side, as the president knew, the problem was also immense, Powell said. They had not been able to find bin Laden, Mullah Omar and other al Qaeda and Taliban leaders in Afghanistan. They didn't know where Saddam was. Saddam had all kinds of tricks and deceptions. He had an entire state at his disposal to hide in. They did not need another possibly fruitless manhunt.

Powell's presentation was an outpouring of both analysis and emotion that encompassed his entire experience—35 years in the military, former national security adviser and now chief diplomat. The president seemed intrigued as he listened and asked questions but did not push back that much.

And Powell realized that his arguments begged the question of well, what do you do? He knew that Bush liked, in fact insisted on, solutions, and he wanted to take his views all the way down the trail. "You can still make a pitch for a coalition or U.N. action to do what needs to be done," he said. International support had to be garnered. The U.N. was only one way. But some way had to be found to recruit allies. A war with Iraq could be much more complicated and bloody than the war in Afghanistan, which was Exhibit A demonstrating the necessity of a coalition.

The president said he preferred to have an international coalition, and he loved building one for the war in Afghanistan.

Powell responded that he believed the pitch could still be made to the international community to build support.

What did he think the incentives and motives might be of some of the critical players such as the Russians or the French, the president asked. What would they do?

As a matter of diplomacy, Powell said he thought the president and the administration could bring most countries along.

The secretary felt the discussion became tense several times as he pressed, but in the end he believed that he had left nothing unsaid.

The president thanked him. It had been two hours—nothing of Clintonesque, late-night-at-the-dorm proportions, but extraordinary for this president and Powell. And Powell felt he had stripped his argument down to the essentials. The private meeting with just Bush and Rice had meant that there was not a lot of static coming in from other quarters—Cheney and Rumsfeld.

Rice thought the headline was, "Powell Makes Case for Coalition as Only Way to Assure Success."

"That was terrific," Rice said the next day in a phone call to Powell, "and we need to do more of those."

The tip-off about the potential importance of the evening was when Card called Powell the next day and asked him to come over and give him the same presentation, notes and all.

The dinner was a home run, Powell felt.

BUSH LEFT FOR his Crawford vacation the next afternoon, as Iraq continued to play to a packed house in the news media. There was little other news, and speculation about Iraq filled the void. Every living former national security adviser or former secretary of state who could lift pen to paper was on the street with his or her views.

On Wednesday, August 14, the principals met in Washington without the president.

Powell said they needed to think about getting a coalition for action against Iraq, some kind of international cover at least. The Brits were with us, he noted, but their support was fragile in the absence of some international coalition or cover. They needed something. Most of Europe was the same way, he reported, as was all of Arabia, especially the U.S. friends in the Gulf who would be most essential for war. And Turkey, which shared a 100-mile border with Iraq.

The first opportunity the president would have after his vacation to address formally the subject of Iraq was a scheduled speech to the United Nations General Assembly on September 12, Powell pointed out. There had been some talk about making the speech about American values or talking about the Middle East. But Iraq was topic A. "I can't imagine him going there and not speaking about this," Powell said.

Rice agreed. In the atmosphere of continuing media discussion, not to talk about Iraq might suggest that the administration was not serious about Saddam's threat, or that it was operating in total secrecy. And Bush liked to explain to the public at least the general outlines of where his policy was heading.

They discussed how they would face an endless process of debate and compromise and delay once they started down the U.N. road—words not action.

"I think the speech at the U.N. ought to be about Iraq," Cheney agreed. But the U.N. ought to be made the issue. It should be challenged and criticized. "Go tell them it's not about us. It's about you. You are not important." The U.N. was not enforcing more than a decade of resolutions ordering Saddam to destroy his weapons of mass destruction and allow weapons inspectors inside

Iraq. The U.N. was running the risk of becoming irrelevant and would be the loser if it did not do what was necessary.

Rice agreed. The U.N. had become too much like the post–World War I League of Nations—a debating society with no teeth.

They all agreed that the president should not go to the U.N. to ask for a declaration of war. That was quickly off the table. They all agreed that a speech about Iraq made sense. Given the importance of the issue, it had to be addressed. But there was no agreement about what the president should say.

Two days later, Friday, August 16, the NSC met, with the president attending by secure video from Crawford. The sole purpose of the meeting was for Powell to make his pitch about going to the U.N. to seek support or a coalition in some form. Unilateral war would be tough, close to impossible, Powell said. At least they ought to try to reach out and ask other countries to join them.

The president went around the table asking for comments, and there was general support for giving the U.N. a shot—even from Cheney and Rumsfeld.

Fine, Bush finally said. He approved of the approach—a speech to the U.N. about Iraq. And it couldn't be too shrill, he cautioned them, or put too high a standard so that it would be obvious to all that they weren't serious. He wanted to give the U.N. a chance.

Powell walked out feeling they had a deal, and he went off for a vacation in the Hamptons on Long Island, New York.

IT WAS FOUR days later when I went to Crawford, Texas, for my final interview with President Bush on August 20, 2002. A number of his closest aides had suggested I interview him in Crawford, the place he feels most comfortable. It was 11 months after the terrorist attacks. He and Laura Bush had built a beautiful, small, one-story home in a secluded corner of their 1,600-acre ranch. Their home overlooks a man-made lake. It was his vacation, and the president was dressed in jeans, a short-sleeved shirt and heavy, working cowboy boots. He seemed relaxed and focused.

Most of my questions dealt with the war in Afghanistan and the broader war on terrorism. His answers are fully reflected in this book. But he made a number of points worth contemplating now.

I asked the president whether he and the country had done enough for the war on terror. The possibility of another major attack still loomed. But the absence of an attack reenforced the sense of normalcy. Washington and New York City 2002 could not have been further from London 1940 or America after December 7, 1941. He had not put the country on a war footing, demanded sacrifices from large numbers of citizens, or taken what for him would be the unthinkable and draconian step of raising taxes or repealing his 2001 tax cut. Was it not possible that he had undermobilized given the threat and the devastation of September 11?

"If we get hit soon again," I asked him, "big, spectacular—people are going to look back and say, we did a lot but we didn't do enough?"

"The answer to your question is, Where do you mobilize? We're mobilizing in the sense that we're spending," Bush said. He mentioned big budget increases for the FBI, CIA, firefighters and others, the first responders to terrorist attacks.

I said that someone had mentioned to me that there were only about 11,000 FBI agents but nearly 180,000 United States Marines. Could not some of those Marines, some of whom are excellent intelligence officers and security experts, be assigned to airports and other vulnerable, potential targets? He was spending most of his time on the issues of the war and homeland security. Rice was spending probably 80 percent of hers. Where was the rest of the government?

"It's an interesting question," he replied. "The answer is, if they hit us hard, the answer is no"—that he did not do enough. "If they don't hit us hard, the answer is, we did it right."

I said that I had talked with Karl Rove who said that ultimately the war would be measured by the outcome. "Everything will be measured by results," Rove had said. "The victor is always right. History ascribes to the victor qualities that may or may not actually have been there. And similarly to the defeated."

Bush agreed but he said the problem was that the war had turned into a kind of international manhunt. The terrorists had to be chased one by one. It was not just to satisfy what he called "a public blood lust." At the same time, he knew the importance of getting bin Laden—"decapitating" the al Qaeda leadership.

He was of the view that there was no convincing evidence of whether bin Laden was alive or dead. He wondered about the absence of communication from him, not a single taped message. "All I know is that he is a megalomaniac," Bush said. "Is he that disciplined that he can be quiet for now nine months?"

"Why have they not struck again?" I asked.

"Maybe we're pretty good at what we're doing," Bush said. But maybe not. The investigators had established that the September 11 attacks had been at least two years in the planning. Perhaps, he suggested, he had underestimated the other side, that they spent more time on their long-range efforts, that what might happen right now had been in the works much longer.

The president raised a more chilling prospect. It was the gravest worry of the FBI, that members of al Qaeda, "cold, calculating killers" he called them, had buried themselves into American society, hanging out in garden apartments or anywhere else, waiting for their prearranged moment to strike. "Maybe there's a planning cycle of four years," he said.

I WANTED TO attempt to understand the president's overall approach or philosophy to foreign affairs and war policy. The Taliban had been deposed, but possibly bin Laden and certainly many in his al Qaeda network had escaped. Other terrorist attacks were expected. The United States now had some 7,000 troops on the ground in Afghanistan, which was still a dangerous, unstable place. Karzai was in continual jeopardy even with American Special Forces acting as his bodyguards.

The theoretical pronouncements Bush had made about not nation building have been discarded almost wholesale in the face of the need to keep Afghanistan together. He was at times acting like the Afghan budget director and bill collector.

"If I have asked once, I have asked 20 times, I want to see the cash flow projections of the Afghan government," Bush said. "Who owes money? I wrote a letter the other day dunning these people over in Europe for money." He learned it only costs $500 a year to pay a trained Afghan soldier. "I said it makes no sense to train people for a military and then not pay them."

Until that day in Crawford, I had not heard the sweeping aspirations Bush has for his presidency and the United States. Most presidents have high hopes. Some have grandiose visions of what they will achieve, and he was firmly in that camp.

"I will seize the opportunity to achieve big goals," Bush told me as we sat in a large room in his home with the breeze comfortably blowing through the screens. "There is nothing bigger than to achieve world peace."

Action was not just for strategic purposes or defensive purposes, he said. "You see, it's like Iraq," he said. "Condi didn't want me to talk about it." He and Rice, who was sitting with us during the interview, laughed. "But wait a minute," he continued. "Just as an aside, and we'll see whether this bears out. Clearly, there will be a strategic implication to a regime change in Iraq, if we go forward. But there's something beneath that, as far as I'm concerned, and that is, there is immense suffering."

Bush glanced at Rice. "Or North Korea," he quickly added. "Let me talk about North Korea." But he seemed to mean Iraq also. Iraq, North Korea and Iran were the "axis of evil" he had identified in his State of the Union speech.

The president sat forward in his chair. I thought he might jump up he became so emotional as he spoke about the North Korean leader.

"I loathe Kim Jong Il!" Bush shouted, waving his finger in the air. "I've got a visceral reaction to this guy, because he is starving his people. And I have seen intelligence of these prison camps—they're huge—that he uses to break up families, and to torture people. I am appalled at the . . ."

I asked if he had seen the overhead satellite photography of the prison camps provided by the U.S. intelligence agencies?

"Yes, it appalls me." He wondered how the civilized world could stand by and coddle the North Korean president as he starves his people. "It is visceral. Maybe it's my religion, maybe it's my—but I feel passionate about this." He said he also realized that the North Koreans had massive military might poised to overrun the U.S. ally South Korea.

"I'm not foolish," the president continued. "They tell me, we don't need to move too fast, because the financial burdens on people will be so immense if we try to—if this guy were to topple. Who would take care of—I just don't buy that. Either you believe in freedom, and want to—and worry about the human condition, or you don't."

In case I didn't get the message, he added, "And I feel that way about the people of Iraq, by the way." He said that Saddam was starving his people in the outlying Shiite areas. "There is a human condition that we must worry about.

"As we think through Iraq, we may or may not attack. I have no idea, yet. But it will be for the objective of making the world more peaceful."

In Afghanistan, he said, "I wanted us to be viewed as the liberator."

I asked him specifically about the time in late October 2001 when he had told his war cabinet that a coalition was held together not by consultations as much as by strong American leadership that would force the rest of the world to adjust.

"Well," the president said, "you can't talk your way to a solution to a problem. And the United States is in a unique position right now. We are the leader. And a leader must combine the ability to listen to others, along with action.

"I believe in results. If I said it once, I said, I know the world is watching carefully, would be impressed and will be impressed with results achieved. It's like earning capital in many ways. It is a way for us to earn capital in a coalition that can be fragile. And the reason it will be fragile is that there is resentment toward us.

"I mean, you know, if you want to hear resentment, just listen to the word unilateralism. I mean, that's resentment. If somebody wants to try to say something ugly about us, 'Bush is a unilateralist, America is unilateral.' You know, which I find amusing. But I'm also—I've been to meetings where there's a kind of 'we must not act until we're all in agreement.' "

Bush said he didn't think agreement was the issue, and I was surprised at the sweep of his next statement.

"Well, we're never going to get people all in agreement about force and use of force," he declared, suggesting that an international coalition or the United Nations were probably not viable ways to deal with dangerous, rogue states. "But action—confident action that will yield positive results provides kind of a slipstream into which reluctant nations and leaders can get behind and show themselves that there has been—you know, something positive has happened toward peace."

Bush said a president deals with lots of tactical, day-to-day battles on budgets and congressional resolutions, but he sees his job and responsibilities as much larger. His father had with some regularity derided the notion of a "vision" or "the vision thing" as unhelpful. So I was also surprised when the younger Bush said, "The job is—the vision thing matters. That's another lesson I learned."

His vision clearly includes an ambitious reordering of the world through preemptive and, if necessary, unilateral action to reduce suffering and bring peace.

During the interview, the president spoke a dozen times about his "instincts" or his "instinctive" reactions, including his statement, "I'm not a textbook player, I'm a gut player." It's pretty clear that Bush's role as politician, president and commander in chief is driven by a secular faith in his instincts—his natural and spontaneous conclusions and judgments. His instincts are almost his second religion.

When I specifically asked about Powell's contributions, the president offered a tepid response. "Powell is a diplomat," Bush responded. "And you've got to have a diplomat. I kind of picture myself as a pretty good diplomat, but nobody else does. You know, particularly, I wouldn't call me a diplomat. But, nevertheless, he is a diplomatic person who has got war experience."

Did Powell want private meetings? I asked.

"He doesn't pick up the phone and say, I need to come and see you," Bush said. He confirmed that he did have private meetings with Powell which Rice also attended. "Let me think about Powell. I got one. He was very good with Musharraf. He single-handedly got Musharraf on board. He was very good about that. He saw the notion of the need to put a coalition together."

"I'LL GIVE YOU a tour," the president proposed after two hours and 25 minutes. We walked outside, and he climbed behind the wheel of his pickup truck and motioned me toward the passenger side. Rice and a female Secret Service agent squeezed into the cramped passenger back seat. Barney, his Scottie dog, parked himself between us in the front and was soon in his master's lap.

We wound slightly down from the flatlands into a small valley, where surprising rock formations probably 60 to 100 feet high could be seen in the distance. The president took each turn in the gravel road slowly, savoring the expanse. He provided a commentary on the trees and land, the deep forest areas and open plains. He noted downed trees that would need to be chopped up or patches of forest that seemed thriving, or where he himself had cleared cedars, a nonnative tree that takes precious water and light from nearby oaks and other hardwoods.

He seemed to have a particular destination in mind as he tucked the truck into a hidden corner of trees and stopped. We got out, having come perhaps two miles across his property. Rice said she was not going to get out because she did not have the right shoes. The Secret Service agent did not follow, so the president and I walked alone toward a wooden bridge about 20 yards away.

As we crossed it, a giant limestone rock formation maybe 40 yards across loomed above us, nearly white in color, shaped like a half-moon, with a steep overhang. It looked as if a mammoth seashell had grown out of the Texas canyon. A tiny natural waterfall tumbled from the center of the overhang. The rock looked ancient, as old as the Roman catacombs. The air had a sweet, pungent smell that I could not identify. Bush started tossing rocks at the overhang, and I briefly joined in.

As we walked back, Bush again brought up Iraq. His blueprint or model for decision making in any war against Iraq, he told me, could be found in the story I was attempting to tell—the first months of the war in Afghanistan and the largely invisible CIA covert war against terrorism worldwide.

"You have the story," he said. Look hard at what you've got, he seemed to be saying. It was all there if it was pieced together—what he had learned, how he had settled into the presidency, his focus on large goals, how he made decisions, why he provoked his war cabinet and pressured people for action.

I was straining to understand the meaning of this. At first, this remark and what he had said before seemed to suggest he was leaning toward an attack on Iraq. Earlier in the interview, however, he had said, "I'm the kind of person that wants to make sure that all risk is assessed. But a president is constantly analyzing, making decisions based upon risk, particularly in war—risk taken relative to what can be achieved." What he wanted to achieve seemed clear: He wanted Saddam out.

Before he got back in his truck, Bush added another piece to the Iraq puzzle. He had not yet seen a successful plan for Iraq, he said. He had to be careful and patient.

"A president," he added, "likes to have a military plan that will be successful."

"CHENEY SAYS PERIL of a Nuclear Iraq Justifies Attack," Powell read in *The New York Times* from his vacation the morning of August 27. It was the lead story. The vice president had given a hard-line speech the day before, declaring that weapons inspections were basically futile. "A return of inspectors would provide no assurance whatsoever of his compliance with U.N. resolutions," Cheney had said. "On the contrary, there is a great danger that it would provide false comfort that Saddam was somehow 'back in his box.' " He gave voice to his deep concerns about weapons of mass destruction that the war cabinet had heard many times. In the hands of a "murderous dictator" these weapons are "as grave a threat as can be imagined. The risks of inaction are far greater than the risk of action." Cheney's speech was widely interpreted as administration policy. The tone was harsh and unforgiving. It mentioned consultations with allies but did not invite other countries to join a coalition.

Powell was astonished. It seemed like a preemptive attack on what he thought had been agreed to 10 days earlier—to give the U.N. a chance. In addition, the swipe at weapons inspections was contrary to Bush's year-long assertions that the next step should be to let the weapons inspectors back into Iraq. That was what everyone—the U.N. and the United States—had been fighting with Saddam about since 1998 when he had kicked the inspectors out.

The day after Cheney's speech, Rumsfeld met with 3,000 Marines at Camp Pendleton in California. "I don't know how many countries will participate in the event the president does decide that the risks of not acting are greater than the risks of acting,"

Rumsfeld said. Powell could decode this: Cheney had asserted that the risks were in not acting, and Rumsfeld had said he didn't know how many countries would join if the president agreed with Cheney. Rumsfeld also said that doing the right thing "at the onset may seem lonesome"—a new term for acting alone, in other words unilateralism.

To make matters worse the BBC began releasing excerpts of an earlier interview that Powell had done in which he had said it would be "useful" to restart the weapons inspections. "The president has been clear that he believes weapons inspectors should return," Powell had said. "Iraq has been in violation of many U.N. resolutions for most of the last 11 or so years. And so, as a first step, let's see what the inspectors find. Send them back in."

News stories appeared saying that Powell contradicted Cheney, or appeared to do so. Suddenly, Powell realized that the public impression of the administration's policy toward inspectors in Iraq was the opposite of what he knew it to be. Some editorial writers accused Powell of being disloyal. He counted seven editorials calling for his resignation or implying he should quit. From his perspective all hell was breaking loose. How could I be disloyal, he wondered, when I'm giving the president's stated position?

When Powell returned from his vacation, he asked for another private meeting with the president. Rice joined them over lunch on September 2, Labor Day, as Powell reviewed the confusion of August. Was it not the president's position that the weapons inspectors should go back into Iraq?

Bush said it was, though he was skeptical that it would work. He reaffirmed that he was committed to going to the U.N. to ask for support on Iraq. In a practical sense that meant asking for a new resolution. Powell was satisfied as he left for South Africa to attend a conference.

On Friday evening, September 6, Powell was back and joined the principals at Camp David without the president.

Cheney argued that to ask for a new resolution would put them back in the soup of the United Nations process—hopeless, endless and irresolute. All the president should say is that Saddam is bad, has willfully violated, ignored and stomped on the U.N. resolutions of the past, and the United States reserves its right to act unilaterally.

But that isn't asking for U.N. support, Powell replied. The U.N. would not just roll over, declare Saddam evil and authorize the U.S. to strike militarily. The U.N. would not buy that. The idea was not saleable, Powell said. The president had already decided to give the U.N. a chance and the only way to do that was to ask for a resolution.

Cheney was beyond hell-bent for action against Saddam. It was as if nothing else existed.

Powell attempted to summarize the consequences of unilateral action. He would have to close American embassies around the world if they went alone.

That was not the issue, Cheney said. Saddam and the blatant threat was the issue.

Maybe it would not turn out as the vice president thought, Powell said. War could trigger all kinds of unanticipated and unintended consequences.

Not the issue, Cheney said.

The conversation exploded into a tough debate, dancing on the edge of civility but not departing from the formal propriety that Cheney and Powell generally showed each other.

The next morning the principals had an NSC meeting with the president. They did a rerun of the arguments and Bush seemed comfortable asking the U.N. for a resolution.

During the speech-drafting process, Cheney and Rumsfeld continued to press. Asking for a new resolution would snag them in a morass of U.N. debate and hesitation, opening the door for Saddam to negotiate with the U.N. He would say the words of offering to comply but then, as always, stiff everyone.

So the request for a resolution came out of the speech. Meetings on the drafting continued for days. The speech assailed the

U.N. for not enforcing the weapons inspections in Iraq, specifically for the four years since Saddam had kicked them out.

"You can't say all of this," Powell argued, "without asking them to do something. There's no action in this speech.

"It says, here's what he's done wrong, here's what he has to do to fix himself, and then it stops?" Powell asked in some wonderment. "You've got to ask for something."

So the principals then had a fight about what to ask for. What should the "ask" look like?

They finally agreed that Bush should ask the U.N. to act.

Powell accepted that, since the only way the U.N. really acted was through resolutions. So that was the implied action. Calling for a new resolution would have really nailed it, but the call to "act" was sufficient for Powell.

Tony Blair told Bush privately that he had to go the U.N. resolution route. David Manning, the British national security adviser, told Rice the same.

TWO DAYS BEFORE the president was to go to the U.N., Powell reviewed Draft #21 of the speech text the White House had sent him with EYES ONLY and URGENT stamped all over it. On page eight, Bush promised to work with the U.N. "to meet our common challenge." There was no call for the U.N. to act.

At a principals' committee meeting without the president just before Bush left for New York City, Cheney voiced his opposition to having the president ask specifically for new resolutions. It was a matter of tactics and of presidential credibility, the vice president argued. Suppose the president asked and the Security Council refused? Saddam was a master bluffer. He'd cheat and retreat, find a way to delay what was required. What was necessary was getting Saddam out of power. If he attacked the United States or anyone with the weapons of mass destruction available to him—especially on a large scale—the world would never forgive them for inaction and giving in to the impulse to engage in semantic debates in U.N. resolutions.

Rumsfeld said they needed to stand on principle, but he then posed a series of rhetorical questions, and did not come down hard about the language.

Cheney and Powell went at each other in a blistering argument. It was Powell's internationalism versus Cheney's unilateralism.

"I don't know if we got it or not," Powell told Armitage later.

The night before the speech, Bush spoke with Powell and Rice. He had decided he was going to ask for new resolutions. At first he thought he would authorize Powell and Rice to say after his speech that the United States would work with the U.N. on them. But he had concluded he might as well say it himself in the speech. He liked the policy headline to come directly from him. He ordered that a sentence be inserted near the top of page eight, saying he would work with the U.N. Security Council for the necessary "resolutions." It was added to the next and final draft, #24.

"He's going to have it in there," Powell reported to Armitage.

At the podium in the famous General Assembly hall, Bush reached the portion of the speech where he was to say he would seek resolutions. But the change hadn't made it into the copy that was put into the TelePrompTer. So Bush read the old line, "My nation will work with the U.N. Security Council *to meet our common challenge.*"

Powell was reading along with Draft #24, penciling in any ad-libs that the president made. His heart almost stopped. The sentence about resolutions was gone! He hadn't said it! It was the punch line!

But as Bush read the old sentence, he realized that the part about resolutions was missing. With only mild awkwardness he ad-libbed it, adding two sentences later, "We will work with the U.N. Security Council for the necessary resolutions."

Powell breathed again.

The president's speech was generally a big hit. It was widely praised for its toughness, its willingness to seek international support for his Iraq policy, and its effective challenge to the U.N. to enforce its own resolutions. It was a big boost for Powell who stayed behind in New York to rally support for the policy, especially from Russia and France, who as permanent members of the Security Council could veto any resolution.

The next day Iraq announced that it would admit new weapons inspectors. Few believed it was sincere. See, the vice president argued, the U.S. and the U.N. were being toyed with, played for fools.

BUSH BELIEVED A preemption strategy might be the only alternative if he were serious about not waiting for events. The realities at the beginning of the 21st century were two: the possibility of another massive, surprise terrorist attack similar to September 11, and the proliferation of weapons of mass destruction—biological, chemical or nuclear. Should the two converge in the hands of terrorists or a rogue state, the United States could be attacked and tens of thousands, even hundreds of thousands of people could be killed.

In addition, the president and his team had found that protecting and sealing the U.S. homeland was basically impossible. Even with heightened security and the national terrorist alerts, the country was only marginally safer. The United States had absorbed Pearl Harbor and gone on to win World War II. For the moment the country had absorbed September 11 and gone on to win the first phase of the war in Afghanistan. What would happen if there was a nuclear attack, killing tens or hundreds of thousands? A free country could become a police state. What would the citizens or history think of a president who had not acted in absolutely the most aggressive way? When did a defense require an active offense?

Bush's troubleshooter, Condi Rice, felt the administration had little choice with Saddam. "The overwhelming, unmitigated disaster and nightmare is that you have this aggressive tyrant in a couple of years armed with a nuclear weapon, with his history and desire and willingness to use weapons of mass destruction," she said in an interview. "Are you prepared to let this nightmare stand?" Some intelligence experts said it would be four to six years before he had a nuclear weapon. "I've been in this business a long time and people always underestimate the time, they rarely overestimate the time. If we're wrong and we had four or five or six years before he posed a nuclear threat, then we just went early. If anyone willing to wait is wrong, then we wake up in two or three years, and Saddam has a nuclear weapon and is brandishing it in the most volatile region in the world. So which of those chances do you want to take?

"The lesson of September 11: Take care of threats early."

But the president proceeded as if he were willing to give the U.N. a chance and his public rhetoric softened. Instead of speaking only about regime change, he said his policy was to get Iraq to give up its weapons of mass destruction. "A military option is not the first choice," Bush told reporters on October 1, "but disarming this man is."

In a speech to the nation Monday, October 7, the one-year anniversary of the commencement of the military strikes in Afghanistan, the president said that Saddam posed an immediate threat to the U.S. As Congress debated whether to pass its own resolution authorizing the use of force against Saddam, Bush said war was avoidable and not imminent. "I hope this will not require military action," he said.

This was all a victory for Powell, but perhaps only momentarily so. The scaled-down rhetoric did mean that the president could say no to Cheney and Rumsfeld, but it did not mean a lessening of Bush's fierce determination. As always, it was an ongoing struggle for the president's heart and mind as he attempted to balance his unilateralist impulses with some international realities.

• • •

SOME DEMOCRATS AND important Republicans wanted a public debate about what to do about Saddam and Iraq. A few offered strong public criticism of the apparent rush to war, most prominently former Vice President Al Gore and Senator Ted Kennedy. The worry about Saddam was real, they argued, but he had not directly attacked the United States or another nation. The evidence about Saddam as an imminent threat was not convincing, they said. They also said that a military strike under the new untested policy of preemption could destabilize other countries in the Middle East, trigger more terrorism from Saddam or others, leave Israel more vulnerable to attack and overturn an American tradition of generally not striking first.

By early October the U.N. had not yet agreed on new resolutions. But on October 10 and 11 the House and the Senate overwhelmingly voted to grant the president full authority to attack Iraq unilaterally. The vote in the House was 296 to 133, and in the Senate 77 to 23. The Congress gave Bush the full go-ahead to use the military "as he determines to be necessary and appropriate" to defend against the threat of Iraq.

But it was not clear what might happen in the end with Iraq, whether Bush was headed for triumph or disaster or something in between.

Whatever his course, he will have available a CIA and military that are both more capable and more hungry for action than is generally recognized.

ON FEBRUARY 5, 2002, about 25 men representing three different Special Forces units and three CIA paramilitary teams gathered outside Gardez, Afghanistan, in the east, about 40 miles from the Pakistani border. It was very cold, and they were bundled in camping or outdoor clothing. No one was in uniform. Many had beards. The men stood or kneeled on this desolate site in front of a helicopter. An American flag was standing in the background. There was a pile of rocks arranged as a tombstone over a buried piece of the demolished World Trade Center. Someone snapped a picture of them.

One of the men read a prayer. Then he said, "We consecrate this spot as an everlasting memorial to the brave Americans who died on September 11, so that all who would seek to do her harm will know that America will not stand by and watch terror prevail.

"We will export death and violence to the four corners of the earth in defense of our great nation."

AFTERWORD

THE LONG DIPLOMACY—THE SHORT WAR

THE SIX MONTHS between the president's September 12, 2002, speech to the United Nations General Assembly calling for a new resolution on weapons inspections and the beginning of the war in Iraq on March 19, 2003, might be considered the long diplomacy. It was an international roller-coaster ride, marked by abruptly rising then severely falling expectations that a military conflict could be averted.

On November 8—after seven weeks of wrangling over language and ultimate purposes—the U.N. Security Council passed Resolution 1441 by a unanimous vote of 15 to 0. It called on Saddam's regime to declare and disarm itself of all weapons of mass destruction and threatened undefined "serious consequences" if it did not comply. The unanimous vote, which included Russia, France and Syria, was widely viewed as a major diplomatic success for Powell. He was elated, and many considered it one of the best examples of pure diplomacy. The world seemed united against Saddam, who was once again isolated without identifiable friends among the nations of the world.

Saddam, who had recently secured an absolute 100 percent majority of votes in a ballot referendum on his rule—up from 99.96

percent seven years previously—agreed to accept the resolution and maintained he would cooperate with the weapons inspectors.

With substantial media fanfare, U.N. weapons inspectors, led by Swedish attorney Hans Blix, arrived in Baghdad and on November 27 began inspecting sites suspected of housing prohibited weapons and missiles. Camera crews were kept some distance away and the inspectors remained tight-lipped about what they were finding. Just a few days later, Bush publicly expressed skepticism that Saddam would comply with inspections and his remarks were taken as a renewed threat of military action.

On December 7, Iraq submitted a written declaration of its weapons programs to the United Nations. The 12,000-page document stated that Iraq had no weapons of mass destruction, though Blix said the report had a "lack of supporting evidence" to back that claim. Powell said the report "totally fails" to meet U.N. demands for full disclosure and was "another material breach" of existing resolutions. In Blix's first report in person to the U.N. Security Council on December 19, he said Iraq's actions so far were "not enough to create confidence."

The inspections process continued, with Bush and other U.S. officials continuing to voice doubts and warnings about Iraq's compliance. "Time is running out," Bush said on January 14, 2003. But some, including Powell, were still hopeful that diplomatic pressure and the threat of force would make Saddam do something to avert a war.

Antiwar protests and public skepticism of the United States's intentions increased at home and to an even greater extent abroad. Millions marched in European, Arab and Asian capitals. Several weekend demonstrations in Washington drew crowds in the tens of thousands. France carved out a role for itself as the leading antiwar power, behind the public personas of President Jacques Chirac and Dominique de Villepin, the foreign minister. In late January, de Villepin angrily said "nothing justifies envisaging military action," a comment that sent Powell into a fury.

By effectively taking the threat of war off the table, Powell was convinced the French had practically removed pressure on Saddam, who would no doubt miscalculate that the absence of unanimity meant he would not be attacked.

The unified front of Resolution 1441 fast became a memory. Blix's reports to the Security Council seemed carefully designed to steer a middle course. Since he failed either to condemn or praise Iraq's efforts, his reports did nothing to budge the emerging blocs within the Security Council. The United States and Britain were ready to declare Saddam in "further material breach" of more than a dozen U.N. resolutions calling on him to disarm. This rhetoric seemed to be a prelude to war. France and Russia —each of which had veto power over any resolution—were leading the cause for a longer inspection timetable and opposed military action without firm authority from the United Nations.

A clear and compelling case for removing Saddam still eluded the administration. Blix and the other international inspectors had found no "smoking gun" of illegal chemical, biological or nuclear weapons, and the statements coming from Bush and his advisers lacked fresh evidence and sounded recycled. President Bush spent the second half of his State of the Union address on January 28 laying out a case against Saddam, alleging that he had weapons of mass destruction and connections to al Qaeda terrorists. "It would take one vial, one canister, one crate slipped into this country to bring a day of horror like none we have ever known," Bush said.

But the main push for the U.S. position came a week later on February 5 at the U.N., where Powell presented new allegations, including intercepted conversations and satellite photography, of Iraq's secret weapons programs and cover-ups. The 90-minute audiovisual report lacked a "smoking gun" but seemed to strengthen support for the war with the American public.

The American troop buildup in the Persian Gulf proceeded quite openly. Britain, Spain, Australia and a handful of other countries publicly backed a military campaign to oust Saddam, and several Arab countries quietly agreed to offer overt or covert assistance. In order to shore up domestic support in Britain for Prime Minister Tony Blair, Bush's closest ally, the U.S. agreed to support a second

U.N. Security Council resolution which more clearly authorized military action. At a prime-time news conference on March 6, Bush said all member nations of the Security Council would be asked to "show their cards" the following week and vote on the resolution.

Four days later, with the United States having trouble even securing a majority of votes for passage, France and Russia announced they would veto any second resolution, thereby assuring its defeat. Bush, Blair and Spanish Prime Minister Jose Maria Aznar agreed to hold a one-day summit in the Azores on March 16 to discuss how to proceed.

When the representatives of the three nations appeared on Monday morning, March 17, at the United Nations to announce they would let the second resolution die without a vote, war seemed imminent. That night, President Bush went on national television and set a 48-hour ultimatum for Saddam and his two sons to leave Iraq. Bush again spelled out Iraq's alleged weapons violations and terrorist connections. "The United Nations Security Council has not lived up to its responsibilities," he said, "so we will rise to ours."

Two days later at about 1 P.M. Washington time, the war began with what military planners called S day when hundreds of Special Operations Forces, the commandos in the military services, entered Iraq to protect oil fields in the west and south while attempting to stop any Iraqi missile launches, especially into Israel.

Several hours later that Wednesday, the CIA presented Bush with evidence from human sources that Saddam would be spending the night in a bunker at Dora Farms outside Baghdad. Bush deemed it sufficiently reliable to provide an opportunity to kill Saddam, and he ordered a strike.

Though many intelligence reports indicated that Saddam had been killed or injured, there was no certainty.

At 10:15 that night, Bush delivered a nationally televised address from the Oval Office to announce the war had begun. "Now that conflict has come, the only way to limit its duration is to apply decisive force," the president said. "We will defend our freedom, we will bring freedom to others and we will prevail."

The major military action lasted three weeks, and on April 9 resistance collapsed in Baghdad. Together Marines and a group of Iraqi citizens more than symbolically toppled a statue of Saddam— who was either dead, injured or in hiding. Whatever the case, he was no longer in power. Regime change had been achieved. Bush and his team then had to embark on what many felt would be a more difficult and longer task than the war itself. As Bush had said, the goal was the creation of democracy in Iraq, or as Central Command General Tommy Franks listed in his announced war aims, "to help the Iraqi people create conditions for a transition to a representative self-government."

The American combat deaths in the short war were less than the 148 deaths in the 1991 Gulf War. Bush acknowledged that the U.S. military presence in Iraq could continue for two years.

Bob Woodward
April, 2003
Washington, D.C.

ACKNOWLEDGMENTS

Simon & Schuster and *The Washington Post* backed this project with the same enthusiasm, trust and flexibility they have shown me over the last three decades. They are family for me.

Alice Mayhew, vice president and editorial director at Simon & Schuster, guided this project with her usual determination, focus and genius. No one can get a book edited and published better or faster. Originally conceived as the story of President George W. Bush's first year in office, with a focus on his domestic agenda and tax cut, the book took a massive redirection, as did much else in this country, after the terrorist attacks last September 11.

Leonard Downie Jr., executive editor of *The Washington Post*, and Steve Coll, its managing editor, again gave me the freedom to pursue this independent account while the record was still available and fresh. They are extraordinary editors who practice journalism in the best traditions of the great Benjamin C. Bradlee.

Don Graham, the *Post*'s chief executive officer, and the late Katharine Graham, who died shortly before September 11, 2001, represent a special breed, the very best owners and bosses.

Dan Balz, the national political reporter at the *Post*, collaborated with me on the eight-part series "Ten Days in September," about the beginning of the crisis that was published in the *Post* from January 27 to February 3, 2002. Dan is one of a handful of truly wonderful journalists working in America—astute, quick, careful and fair-minded. He taught me a lot, and working with him was one of the best experiences of all my time at the *Post*. With the permission of the *Post*, I have used some of the material published in that series. A special thanks to one of the finest, most talented editors in the business, Bill Hamilton, who edited the series.

One of the other recent pleasant professional experiences for me at the *Post* was working with a group of exceptional national reporters on the September 11 coverage—Thomas E. Ricks, Dan Eggen, Walter Pincus, Susan Schmidt, Amy Goldstein, Barton Gellman and Karen DeYoung. Our coverage won the 2002 Pulitzer Prize for National Reporting.

I owe more than thanks to a group of editors at the *Post* who supervised me, prodded me, helped me think through the information and rewrote my copy. These are the men and women in the trenches you don't hear about that often. Reporters don't get to first base or even to bat without them. I am thinking especially of Jeff Leen, Lenny Bernstein and Matt Vita. They are the unsung heroes of journalism. Special thanks to Liz Spayd and Michael Abramowitz, who run the national staff, for all their help, assistance and graciousness.

Dana Priest of the *Post* national staff has done the finest and most exhaustive reporting on the U.S. Special Forces operations in Afghanistan. I have relied on it, independently confirmed her original work, and I give her special thanks.

Mike Allen, White House correspondent for the *Post*, is one of the most gifted and diligent reporters. Selfless and a gentleman wise beyond his years, Mike assisted me many times, in many ways, most recently on my visit to Crawford, Texas. He is a true friend. I thank his colleague Dana Milbank, the *Post*'s other gifted regular White House correspondent. Others who helped me whom I wish to thank include Vernon Loeb, Bradley Graham, Alan Sipress and Glenn Kessler.

In my view, *The Washington Post* foreign staff did the best job covering the war in Afghanistan on the ground; I have relied on the news accounts and analysis of a dozen of our foreign correspondents, especially Susan Glasser, Peter Baker, Molly Moore and John Ward Anderson.

Olwen Price transcribed many interviews expertly, often under immense time pressure. I deeply appreciate her efforts. The great Joe Elbert and his even greater photo staff at the *Post* provided many of the pictures in this book. Many thanks to Michael Keegan and Richard Furno.

At Simon & Schuster, Carolyn K. Reidy, the president, and David Rosenthal, the publisher, moved this book from manuscript to bookstore shelves in near record time. How is still a mystery to me. I also thank Roger Labrie, the associate editor; Elisa Rivlin, the general counsel; Victoria Meyer, the director of publicity; Aileen Boyle, the associate director of publicity; Jackie Seow, the art director and jacket designer; Jennifer Love, the managing editor; Paul Dippolito, the designer; John Wahler, the production manager; and Mara Lurie, the production editor. Special thanks to Jonathan Jao, assistant to Alice Mayhew, for many assists.

I give special thanks to Fred Chase, who traveled from Texas to Washington to copyedit the manuscript. He lent us his keen eye, sharp ear and wise head.

I was aided by the reporting and analysis of the war on terror in *The New York Times,* whose coverage set the standard for comprehensiveness and clarity, teaching all of us in journalism a great deal. *Newsweek, Time* and *U.S. News & World Report* provided new information and some extraordinary coverage as did the *Los Angeles Times, The Wall Street Journal, The New Yorker* and the Associated Press.

Robert B. Barnett, my agent, attorney and friend, provided wise advice and guidance as always. Since he also represents former President Clinton, Bob did not see the book until it was printed.

Jeff Himmelman, a former research assistant, spent several days reading the manuscript, improving it with suggestions large and small. He also assisted Dan Balz and myself on the "Ten Days in September" series. Josh Kobrin was of immense help to Mark Malseed and myself.

Thanks again to Rosa Criollo, Norma Gianelloni and Jackie Crowe.

My daughters, Tali and Diana, make life truly interesting.

Elsa Walsh, my wife and best friend, gave of herself again well beyond what anyone might reasonably expect. She is patient and wise, partner and keeper of most of what is good in our lives.

INDEX

PHOTOGRAPHY CREDITS

Associated Press: 24
Larry Downing (Reuters): 18
Eric Draper (The White House): 1, 2, 8, 9, 10, 12, 14, 25, 26
Tina Hager (The White House): 7
Rich Lipski *(The Washington Post):* 19
Ray Lustig *(The Washington Post):* 11, 22, 23
Pablo Martinez Monsivais (Associated Press): 5
James A. Parcell *(The Washington Post):* 6
Robert A. Reeder *(The Washington Post):* 16, 17
Joe Skipper (Reuters): 20
Dayna Smith *(The Washington Post):* 15
The Washington Post: 13
The White House: 3, 4
Heesoon Yim (Associated Press): 21

ABOUT THE AUTHOR

Bob Woodward, an assistant managing editor of *The Washington Post*, has been a newspaper reporter and editor for more than 30 years. He has authored or coauthored eight No. 1 national nonfiction best-sellers. They include four books on the presidency—*All the President's Men* (1974), *The Final Days* (1976), *The Agenda* (1994) and *Shadow* (1999)—and books on the Supreme Court *(The Brethren,* 1979), the Hollywood drug culture *(Wired,* 1984), the CIA *(Veil,* 1987) and the Pentagon *(The Commanders,* 1991). He is also author of national best-sellers on the presidential campaign *(The Choice,* 1996) and Federal Reserve Chairman Alan Greenspan *(Maestro,* 2000). He has two daughters, Tali and Diana, and lives in Washington, D.C., with his wife, Elsa Walsh, a writer for *The New Yorker.*